ELECTION 2012

እግዚአብሔር ይባርክ

Dereje Teessewra

1/25/14

ELECTION 2012

Perfecting the Science of
Presidential Campaigning

DEREJE B. TESSEMA

Gashe Publishing | Rockville, MD

HOW this HAPPENED – ELECTION 2012

Perfecting the Science of Presidential Campaigning

Published in the USA by
Gashe Publishing
PO.BOX 1362
Rockville, MD 20842

ISBN - 13: 978-0-9819518-1-2
       13: 978-0-9879518-2-9

Book Cover Design: Book Masters (www.bookmasters.com)
Book Interior Design: Scribe Freelance | www.scribefreelance.com
Line Editor: Mel Dawson

OTHER BOOKS BY THE AUTHOR

HOW THIS HAPPENED: *Analysis of how Barack Obama used his Emotional Intelligence and Transformational Leadership Skills to win his "Campaign Project"*

THE RELATIONSHIP BETWEEN EMOTIONAL INTELLIGENCE AND TRANSFORMATIONAL LEADERSHIP IN PROJECT MANAGEMENT: *A quantitative study*

To Bezakulu
The source of my Inspiration

Contents

PART THREE:
After the Fact: Analysis

O N MY WAY TO NEW ORLEANS I had a couple of hours layover at Charlotte Airport. To rest my legs from the morning's 26.2 mile DC Rock and Roll Marathon race and use the waiting time productively, I sat at one of the sport bars and continued writing the chapter I started on the plane. Next to me were a woman and a middle aged man discussing different topics while also waiting for their flights. After a while the lady left and the man turned towards me and asked what I was writing. I told him that I was compiling information from various sources for an event. He persisted further saying, "… must be a serious event that took your attention all this time." "Yes," I replied, "it is a serious event – the 2012 U.S. Presidential Election. Many dedicated journalists, political analysts, poll experts, news network reporters and scholars have eloquently covered the topic in great detail through various media and I'm collecting information from these sources acknowledging their contribution, compiling and analyzing the different pieces of information so that others could use it as a single source of information on "What Happened" in 2012. I could see his curiosity and he asked me what made me want to write about this? I replied, "American politics has always fascinated me, especially after living on three continents and seeing the price people pay to be allowed to cast their votes. This is considered to be everyone's right. The openness of the American system to invite anyone to take part in the political process by embracing diversity and encouraging people to live their dreams, is amazing. I'm 46 and I have voted only three times in my life - all of them here in the U.S. Not only have I voted and made my voice heard, but in two of the three elections, I had the opportunity to actively participate in the campaign. When I left my country of origin, free elections were a dream and while studying in Germany I was not eligible to vote." He was quiet for a moment and after a few minutes he said, "this Obama thing … I can't stand it and I think it's because of my white southern boy mentality of resistance to

...or I do not know..." His comment caught me off guard but I assumed he did not mind sharing his views openly as we might never see each other again. His interest and openness to discussion caused me to close my laptop and start listening to his story.

He told me that he lives in Savanna, Georgia and was on his way back from a business trip in California. I asked him, "what about Obama?" He responded, "The whole thing ... redistribution, Obama care, entitlements ... You see, I was the first from my family to go to college and I had to work hard to save money and become a businessman. Because of his tax policy, many businesses have been shipped overseas and no one wants to invest in the U.S."I said, "but we read reports that savings from businesses jumped a record high during his first term because no one wanted to invest." He replied, "you bet, yes. And not only that, the insurance, tax, as well as fear of what is going on in Washington also play a role in businesses hoarding their money. I used to be a day trader and mortgage speculator. We made good money in mid - 2000 and lost some." I had learned that people usually keep their political views to themselves and don't ask questions unless they are close to each other, but this gentleman's open view encouraged me to ask a couple more questions. I asked him how he felt about Wall Street writing its own rules and selling those time-bomb financial products. What about the billions of dollars spent monthly on the two wars? How about the 800,000 job losses per month that had been happening at the beginning of his administration and what about the steps taken to stop the bleeding? How about the health care reform?

He looked at me smiling and said, "do not be naïve - We took a bold step to elect him as the first African-American president in this country's history but did you expect him to change things in a society that is based on entitlement, and mentality guarded by the power elite for over two hundred years? Remember Obama's changes were interpreted as altering the status quo, that "maintain the inequalities" between the working class, the middle class and a few elites. I bet this idea will continue to be resisted at all cost." Paying his bill and packing his belongings he whispered to me, "I'm now in the medical supplies business and I liked his idea of preventive care. I like his idea of eliminating the preexisting conditions. I was disappointed by the bank executives who sunk their troubled companies and left with millions of dollars in bonuses. I'm also happy that the Iraq war is done and Afghanistan's is winding down." He wished me good luck and left. I was surprised that he acknowledged the fact that progress had been made but was not sure why he didn't mention them at the beginning of our conversation.

Yes, he was not comfortable with the changes and told me how hard they would be to implement. He is not alone and there are millions supporting his view that it is an open assault on entrepreneurship and creativity. On the other hand equal numbers of people gave approval to what the president was doing, re-electing him for a second term. In the last four years the country was and still is at the edge – an expression from chaos theory where unpredictable behaviors happen including terror (not knowing how many more terror groups and lone wolf terrorists there might be to interrupt our daily lives), natural disaster, economic collapse, high unemployment, social inequality, and injustice unhappiness and lack of trust between politicians. The edge is the meeting point between order and chaos, between the known and unknown. Being at the edge in the past has helped this country become more resilient, striving for creativity and a better life. This was demonstrated during the great depression. However it can also add an element of fear when seeing the light in the tunnel is less certain. In this state, Americans wanted to have a leader who can maneuver the country out of turbulence and into stability. The question is, where is the common ground that America is used to finding between the left and right? Recent history and trends show that when we are attacked by terrorists or when natural disaster hits part of the country, we rally behind the elected officials for a while but then our support drains away and we go back to our 'camps' blaming others for the problem. It is obvious that the two parties in power have fundamental differences in their ideology and that should create healthy competition, inclusion and reflection on our differences. However, lately the Democratic and Republican parties and members of the country's governing bodies have been drifting further and further apart in ideology and tolerance. Their viewpoints are so polarized that it is hard to believe that they have the country's wellbeing at heart.

Elected officials in Congress are pushing their parties to opposite ends of the political spectrum resulting in the elimination of the common ground necessary to solve issues, seemingly bent on going into the history books with a low record of working together. Recent opinion polls show the lowest approval rate for Congress in a hundred years resulting from too much partisan fighting and too little cooperation in order to help the American people. According to a National Journal analysis which tracks the voting records of Senate and House members based on an ideological scale ranging from the most liberal to the most conservative, the 2010 Congress was the most polarized in the three decades since Journal records began. Political opinions and emotions are two faces of the same coin. They are deeply intertwined and whichever side we support we have our fair share of disappointment and joy. Our emotions were tested during the 2012 elections - from being interested and excited which made us hopeful and enthusiastic, to being worried, anxious, nervous, scared and frustrated. It also made us determined, at times powerless and distressed, other times left out and neglected. These emotions push us from two different angles. Depending on the level and intensity of our engagement, the reaction to the event may vary and I assumed that the person I had that brief, intense discussion with showed me the level and intensity of emotion involved in this election and the deep belief and value each one of us has.

When I compiled the material for this book, I realized how deeply divided the country is along ideology, race and income, generally resulting in two different responses to the same question. Part of the answer I hope to get from my writing exercise is an ideal solution to the current problems resulting from the refusal to engage in compromise. Many believe solutions would be forthcoming by adding a third party which would attract independent voters to force the two parties to come closer and talk, while others suggest allowing the Super PACs to rule the country through their influence. An interesting alternative solution provided by Congressman Tim Ryan (D-Ohio) in his speech at the Mind Body Week conference in April 2013 (a Congressman and Mindfulness conference? Yes, he also wrote a book entitled, *A Mindful Nation: how a simple practice can help us reduce stress improve performance and recapture the American sprit*), said that he established a *Quiet Time Caucus* in the House, which like any other caucus helps elected officials to sit quietly (politicians and quietness?) and be mindful, pray, contemplate and pause before making important decisions that affect the country. He and a few other members meet every week for half an hour before voting or the first day of the week to sit and quietly practice mindfulness. It is possible that his solution could be the first step to bringing these two groups of extreme and polarized folks together, helping them to reflect on their responsibilities - responsibilities which voters have bestowed on them and which are much bigger than themselves or the interest groups trying to influence them in Washington. As Blaise Pascal, the French mathematician and philosopher, said, *All of humanity's problems stem from man's inability to sit quietly in a room alone.*

In this election, we have seen that the answer to the same question had different responses or opinions from different groups. Perhaps by 2043, as the outlines of the new American diverse mosaic become less defined flowing into one another so that no single ethnic group has the majority to decide, issues will be treated as objectively and not by how one race or group reacts to it. Until then, Americans expect their elected officials to put their own interests aside and work to resolve the "countries pressing problems" - immigration, gun control, education, environment, energy and foreign policy. Change will always be faced with resistance but regardless of that and the challenges it stimulates, it has to start somewhere. That was how this country became independent from the British, how slavery was abolished and how many of the forward looking transformations took place. On the other hand, even though news media and our political personalities attract more negative attention, the 2012 election also reflected many instances showing that we are greater than our problems. The portrayed division is only at the ego level. A good example to the world, especially to nations with human rights and democracy issues, is that when all is said and done, the fight is not about personalities but about the ideas proposed by the presidential candidates Barack Obama and Mitt Romney. The ideas, paths and views they believed in to take the country through the next four years was what it came down to. Some argue that the U.S. is a constitutional state and exports democracy to the world. However here in the U.S. a constitution written a couple hundred years ago is still the law of the land from which everything is derived. Another impressive thing about elections in the Western world is that politicians fight hard to the end but as soon as the results come in, the person who lost the election concedes with grace and wishes success to the winner, pledging to support him - an unthinkable thing in many parts of the world.

Four years ago I wrote a book entitled *How this Happened: Analysis of How Barack Obama used his Emotional Intelligence and Transformational Leadership Skills to Win the Election Project* (http://www.howthishappened.com), analyzing how the president won the election with the intention of making it palatable to a wide audience, including the many millions who avidly followed the 2008 presidential election as well as professionals and scholars who may be interested in looking at how the president ran a successful campaign. The focal points were from the perspective of three theoretical frameworks – emotional intelligence, transformational leadership and project management. At the end of the book, I raised a number of questions on how the first term could play out and of the campaign for reelection. A lot has happened since then and we have now seen the events that have shaped Obama's first term presidency – Bin Laden and Gaddafi are gone, troops are coming back home, the EuroZone is in turmoil, China continues to lend us more money to save the economy, unemployment is still high, the Tea party in its six month anniversary had a home run in the 2010 mid-term elections, the Occupy Wall Street movement with the slogan, "We are the 99%" was born and died, General Motors, once on the brink of collapse, regained its leadership in the auto industry, the country's credit rating was downgraded from outstanding (AAA) to excellent (AA+), the BP accident polluted our beautiful southern seashore, hydraulic fracturing (fracking) brings oil revenue in the mid-west, the Supreme Court blessed the birth of Super PACs, saved Obama Care, and welcomed the first Latino judge to the exclusive nine, Dodd-Frank kept Wall Street honest, the sale of hand guns exceeded historic levels, Don't ask, don't tell was repealed, the first sitting president in history endorsed gay marriage, only one in ten Americans approved the job Congress was doing - the lowest approval rating in four decades and Planned Parenthood still exists. What made the 2012 election special was the number of issues raised that had different values to different groups of voters. Certainly these issues were the center point of the election and decided the winner. Some of the issues were civil liberties, civil rights, economy and job creation, education, election reform and voting rights, environment and energy, foreign policy, health care, homeland security, immigration, retirement security, science and technology, small businesses, and veteran's issues.

This book covers a broad range of topics including what happened at the 2012 presidential campaign, as well as a summary and an analysis of the events that took place in the three years leading to the beginning of the campaign, which had an influence on the outcome. It builds in sequence from the events that shaped the Obama presidency to issues which surfaced during the election, reactions from key stakeholders – voters, candidates, and media, steps taken by the campaign to address the issues and lessons learned from the $6 billion election.

Part one – Perfecting the Science of Presidential Campaigning – devotes three   Chapters on how organizational development and leadership of the campaign affected the outcome, the ground game and strategy to plan and execute tasks that had a considerable impact on the outcome, and analysis of the new paradigm in data management and analytics, forecasting and voter persuasion.

Part two – Chapters 4 through 10 include discussions on the variables that influenced the election. These include the economy, the auto bailout, financial regulations, health care, national security, the relationship between Obama and the Supreme Court, social, energy and environmental politics.

Part three – Looking beyond the 2012 election, these four chapters summarize the reaction to the election by the media, the opposing party, governing under gridlock, the debate on whether there is a need for a third party as well as the emerging image reflecting the diverse mosaic making up the American population and the trend in the changing voter composition. Hopefully you will find the book both educational and a central place to connect the dots.

DEREJE B. TESSEMA,
July, 2013

Part One

Perfecting the Science of Presidential Campaigning

"The Obama organization ran a great campaign. In my world, the definition of the better campaign is the one that wins" *Stuart Stevens, Chief Strategist for the Romney Presidential Campaign*

How was it better than the Romney campaign? Here is the raw data: the number of donors increased from 3.95 million in 2008 to 4.4 million raising $715 million from individual contributions. Online fundraising rose from $500 million in 2008 to $690 million, online voter registration jumped by 50%, over 813 field offices were used to mobilize voters, 10,000 neighborhood teams were created, 1,793,881 voters were registered, 2.2 million volunteers including approximately 1.25 million more young people have participated than in 2008, over 150 million calls were made and doors knocked on, of which over 25 million of the calls and doors knocked on were made in the last four days of the election. The result – Obama won all states except North Carolina, enabling him to win both electoral (334) and popular (62,611,250 or 50.6%) votes to retain the presidency.

In an economy struggling with high unemployment rates, a sharply divided country, where voters were said to be disengaged from the political system, where the approval rate for the incumbent president was hovering below 50%, and where the media had written off the president from re-election hopes, what made Obama's campaign become the most successful enterprise in the history of presidential elections? Part one of this book discusses what *"perfecting the science of presidential campaigning"* means, by providing a detailed analysis of how the campaign used excellent organizational development and leadership techniques, carefully planned and executed groundwork strategies, as well as used a metric driven decision support system, to win what some referred to as an improbable journey.

Chapter 1

Organizational Development
and Leadership at its Best

"I went around the country for literally a month of my life interviewing these companies and just talking about organizational growth, emerging technologies, marketing..."Jim Messina, Obama's campaign manager

ORGANIZATIONAL DEVELOPMENT – THE CAMPAIGN AS A LEARNING ORGANIZATION

In December 2010 when the president asked Jim Messina to run his re-election campaign, Messina, according to the Bloomberg BusinessWeek reporter, replied *"that he's flattered, but he'll only take the job on one condition": "you have to understand, this will be nothing like the last campaign".* The president replied *"I thought that last one went pretty well".* Messina responded, *"It did but everything is different now".*

When he made the statement, Messina understood the dynamic on the growth and use of technology, as well as the power of data analytics to change the election dramatically between 2008 and 2012. Facebook's user numbers jumped from a couple of hundred of millions to almost a billion. Twitter had exploded, the use of mobile technology and apps surprised the industry and technology in general began to be an asset for doing successful business.

After Jim Messina accepted the job to become the re-election campaign manager, he quit his job as White House deputy chief of staff and headed to the West Coast for what Joshua Green called, *"the highest-wattage crash course in executive management ever undertaken"* by CEOs and senior executives of successful companies. Later, in one of his interviews Messina said, "I went around the country for literally a month of my life interviewing these companies and just talking about organizational growth, emerging technologies and marketing". Since modern presidential campaigns are bounded by expectations to produce much in a short period of time like most companies in the private sector, lessons from those executives who built their firms and made them profitable in a short period of time, were the starting point for Messina and the campaign. The end result of that successful trip was that Steve Jobs of Apple, Steven Spielberg of DreamWorks, Eric Schmidt of Google, Marc Benioff of Salesforce, and other senior executives from Facebook, Zynga, Microsoft and many others, helped design the blueprint of the Obama 2012 campaign to function like a business enterprise that relies on metrics and periodic evaluations.

As the 2012 election witnessed a paradigm shift in campaign organizational settings from hierarchically structured and Newtonian linear relationship to networked, dynamic and complex business enterprises, the campaign leaders were forced to venture out on an exploration of a broader range of organizational development and leadership styles more suited to address challenges. Some of these challenges were diversity of the population, the emergency of new technology and the use of better and faster data management systems. In his April 2011 video message, Messina described his vision thus, "*the campaign has to be metrics driven. We are going to measure every single thing in this campaign*".

The first action he took to implement his vision was to keep the headquarters of the campaign in Chicago outside of the political environment, hire experts with no or little political background to create a totally different business enterprise, and outline those metrics where the success and failure of the campaign would be measured against. Some of the key metrics were related to amount of money raised to support the campaign, the establishment of groundwork in key swing states at an early stage, redesigning campaign ads to target specific groups of voters and the resulting effect, attracting more volunteers to power up the campaign, maximizing the use of technology to reach out to more voters, and using various analytical tools to parse the data and find the psychological reception points, behaviors, patterns and trends of voters to design customized messages.

The sixth floor of 1 Prudential Plaza, Obama's campaign headquarters in Chicago, was not only a "War Room" to oversee the entire activities but also a "Research and Development lab" to address these challenges and run a successful campaign. The leadership of the campaign was aware of the fact that for an organization to be successful, it had to adopt what Peter Senge outlined as the "five learning disciplines". These are:

- Personal Mastery – initiation to expand personal capacity that would create the result desired, as well as an organizational environment which encourages all its members to develop themselves toward the goal and purposes they choose
- Mental Models –help to reflect and clarify the improving members' internal pictures of the purpose of the campaign, seeing how they shape their actions and decisions.
- Shared Vision – help to build a sense of commitment in a group, by developing shared images of the future the campaign seeks to create as well as the principles and guiding practices the campaign hope to accomplish.
- Team Learning – help to transform conversational and collective thinking skills, so that groups of people can reliably develop intelligence and abilities greater than the sum of individual members' talents.
- Systems Thinking – a way of thinking about, and a language for describing and understanding the forces and interrelationships that shape the behavior of systems. This approach would help the campaign to become more agile and flexible to changes in voter's perception and external situations the campaign had no control over.

Even though the campaign was officially launched in April 2011 in the first two years after the 2008 election, the Obama campaign office was working behind the scenes preparing the groundwork including a "lessons learned document" to find out what went wrong and what worked during the last election that could be used as a starting point for the re-election project. In April 4, 2011, when the campaign filed paperwork to the Federal Election Commission, there were only 42 people on the payroll. The explosion of resources started in summer of 2011 after the first 60 field offices were opened. While the Republicans battled in the primaries, the Obama team had already established their field offices and started operating in many states. In July 2012, over 650 people were working in the campaign office and by October 2012 – the peak time of the election – over 4,000 people were on the payroll, working in all 813 field offices around the country and heavily concentrated in the battleground states.

The author built the following depiction (Figure 1) of the campaign's organizational hierarchy based on information gathered from various sources including the campaign's main office (Obama for America). It should not be considered complete, but rather is meant to provide a visual representation of what we learn from various sources. The author has neither confirmation nor approval of this structure from the campaign office. In the chart, the leadership team is divided into four categories.

The first team is made up of the presidents' inner circle, a small dedicated and close-knit group who have been with the president since his political career began, including David Axelrod, Rahm Emmanuel, Valerie Jarrett and others, the Democratic National Committee members, National Co-chairs, and senior advisors. This team set the tone for the election and worked on the big picture.

The second team – the leadership team "LT" – consisted of a handful of qualified and tested experts, many of whom had worked in the previous campaign in different capacities and were now tasked with helping Jim Messina plan and execute his job. This leadership team included Jen Dillon O'Malley and Stephanie Cutter (campaign deputy managers), Jeremiah Bird (national field director), Marlon Marshall (deputy national field director), Rufus Gifford (national finance director), Sara El-Amine (national training director), Buffy Wicks (project vote director), Katherine Archuleta (political director), Yohannes Abraham (deputy national political director), Betsy Hoover (digital organizing director), Rachel Haltom-Irwin (national GOTV director), David Simas (director of opinion research), Teddy Goff (national digital director), Mitch Stewart (battleground state director), James Kvaal (policy director), Mark Beatty (deputy battleground state director), and Jeffrey Gabriel (dashboard program manager). This team represented the 19 departments outlined by the campaign.

Below the leadership team, we see a layer consisting of the technical lead team which managed the hundreds of youth and professionals engaged in various functions. This is the team that Eric Schmidt of Google is said to have advised Jim Messina to create, and it consisted of *"innovators, people who can get stuff done quickly,"* rather than those with political backgrounds. It included Harper Reed, chief technology officer who told Messina right after he got hired, "show me what you want on a white board. I'll build it for you", and who later delivered the surprise of the campaign – the key infrastructure that supported the campaign's digital experimental lab. It also included, Joe Rospars, chief digital strategist who was the 2008 digital director and came back to advise the campaign, Marie Ewald, deputy digital director who helped the campaign raise millions through online fundraising, Dan Wagner, chief analytics officer who directed the development of tools that analyzed various data sources, to find relationships, patterns, trends among voters, Dan Ryan, director of front end development who built the magic instrument – Dashboard – the campaign's online get-out-the-vote (GOTV) platform, Dave Sebag, director of digital products who directed the development of the campaign's critical Facebook sharing tool which enabled Obama's supporters to persuade friends and family to vote and help the campaign, Amelia Showalter, digital analytics director who helped design the various fundraising email subject lines enticing supporters to open them, and Kyle Rush, the web developer who managed the one-click donation program that attracted over 1.5 million people.

The last part of the organization consisted of the campaign's field offices created using the "snowflake model" … (referred to as the "T-Model"), where one paid field staffer recruited five unpaid neighborhood team leaders who in turn recruited networks of 20 volunteers. Each outward-extending network resembled a snowflake and got support primarily from its State Operations department and other related groups.

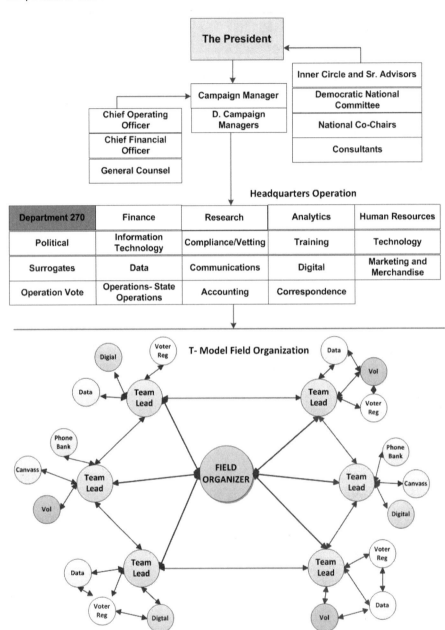

Figure 1: Hypothetical Organizational Chart for the Campaign

Throughout the campaign season the 4,000 employees of the campaign, many consultants and millions of volunteers got support, guidance and coordination from over 19 different departments which were organized like a Fortune 100 company. For better understanding of the functions, a brief summary of each department that was listed in the Obama for America web page is presented below:

270: Department 270 whose name was derived from the 270 electoral votes needed to retain the Presidency, directed the campaign's state strategy and programs. Most importantly, the department oversaw the grassroots programs in the states and coordinated the President's ground game.

Accounting: This department was responsible for paying, tracking and reconciling funds and financial disbursements, as well as keeping accounting records, receipts of contributions and other miscellaneous revenue.

Analytics: Analytics used data that the campaign collected, as well as information from outside sources to help departments such as 270, Digital, Fundraising, Media and Project Vote make strategic decisions about their operations, allowing them to better allocate resources.

Communications: Communications managed the campaign's external communications and media relations. This department monitored the media coverage of its officials and surrogates in both the national and regional press. It also managed and distributed all press releases, advisories and other forms of communication on behalf of the campaign.

Compliance/Vetting: In addition to making sure the campaign accepted financial support only from sources allowed by the federal election commission (FEC), the vetting team reviewed all contributions to make sure that funds from lobbyists were not accepted. In addition to vetting, the department ensured the campaign was in compliance with the various requirements placed on federal committees by the FEC.

Correspondence: The correspondence department was responsible for responding to the needs, comments and questions of constituents.

Correspondence addressed concerns received, tracked comments coming in and ensured that information was flowing to the appropriate departments. It also proactively reached out to various constituencies on behalf of other departments to make sure that every voice was heard, recognized, responded to and respected.

Data: Team Data was focused on turning information into action. The team worked with virtually every department on the campaign to manage campaign databases and online tools, create reports, audit and clean up source data, and provide training and support to the various States.

Digital: The Digital Team was responsible for online fundraising, email, text messaging, video, social media, and design. It worked to integrate online and offline organizing and used web-based tools to connect supporters to the campaign.

Finance: The finance department oversaw the fundraising operations that fueled Obama for America activities in all 50 states.

Human Resources: The Human Resources (HR) department was responsible for development, implementation and evaluation of ongoing HR policies, programs, functions and activities with an emphasis on the benefits and payroll areas, and ensuring that the organization was in full compliance with applicable laws and regulations. Its role was to create an environment of respect, empowerment, inclusion and winning from the very first day that a new staffer steps into the doorway.

IT: The Information Technology department supported the systems and personal technology that people required to run basic office applications, use cell or landline phones, exchange emails or simply surf the internet.

Marketing & Merchandise: The Marketing & Merchandise Department oversaw all grassroots fundraising for the campaign. This included direct mail, personal grassroots fundraising and telemarketing operations. It was also responsible for all of the campaign merchandise as it related to fundraising, including development, production, marketing and sales – online and offline. In addition, it worked in close coordination with the digital team in all grassroots fundraising efforts.

Operation Vote: Operation Vote was the department that drove campaign efforts for core constituencies and the nexus between the field and paid media activities for these constituencies.

Operations - State Operations State Operations ensured that the grassroots field programs and state staff had the resources they needed to operate effectively, and developed systems and processes to facilitate their work. It provided day-to-day support in hiring and bringing on board new staff members, opening offices, managing budgets, planning and executing events and logistics. In addition, the State Operations team served as a liaison for state staff to other campaign departments, such as Human Resources, Technology, Compliance and Accounting.

Political: The political team helped the campaign's efforts by ensuring that key national and state stakeholders were engaged and working in synergy with the re-election operation. The department worked closely with elected officials, party leaders, labor and union leaders around the country.

Research: The Research Department gathered information, provided content and answered questions about the President and his administration's record and accomplishments, to staff at HQ and in the field, supporters and key allies. It also monitored attacks and smears, correcting the record when opponents and critics attempted to distort it.

Surrogates: The surrogate team engaged with people outside of the campaign (from business leaders to politicians to musicians and actors), to get them involved in re-electing the president. The team connected with all departments both in HQ and across the country to make sure surrogates were well prepared to help the campaign raise funds, amplify messages and grow grassroots support.

Tech: The technology team built systems and applications to support campaign. Members included software developers, user experience designers, product managers and infrastructure management. The department liaised with every other team to make their systems work more smoothly and effectively, and to design new software to accomplish campaign objectives.

Training: The Training Department developed the programs and resources the campaign staff and volunteers used, to teach others how to grow the campaign in their communities. It recognized patterns of challenges that staff and volunteers faced in the field and created initiatives and programs to address those challenges. The training department also produced many of the written materials that field staff used on a daily basis, such as how-to-guides, PowerPoint presentations, one-pagers of best practices, staff management and coaching resources and volunteer leadership manuals.

CLOSE AND UNIQUE CULTURE OF THE CAMPAIGN

Considering the campaign as an organization, culture plays a major role in how knowledge is created, disseminated and preserved, and also influences the way people in campaign offices interact with each other, accomplish their tasks, implement policies and procedures and ultimately win the election. Organizational culture is defined as "*a pattern of shared basic assumptions that was learned by a group as it solved its problems of external adaption and internal integration that has worked well enough to be considered valid and, therefore, to be taught to new members as the correct way to perceive, think and feel in relation to those problems*". In a campaign, there are two sets of dynamics that drive the process for knowledge creation – converting tacit knowledge into explicit knowledge from veteran politicians and campaign consultants, and moving that knowledge from the individual level to the group, organizational and inter-organizational level, in order to make informed decisions during the campaign trail. When organizations are not aware of their culture, the progress toward success will have numerous problems such as organizational conflict, lack of institutional cohesion and performance reduction.

The ideas and advice the campaign received from Silicon Valley executives, introduced a market culture similar to that experienced by those businesses including the creation of various positions and job descriptions such as chief technology officer, chief information officer, chief scientist, digital director and others. This new culture merged with the clan and adhocracy cultures demonstrated during the 2008 election to create a new "Obama 2012 hybrid culture" that was based on several constructs. In the clan culture type, the organization emphasizes internal focus and flexibility where teamwork, openness and participation are the center point. In this culture organizational leaders encourage the development of a human work environment that facilitates employees' participation, commitment and loyalty.

In the adhocracy culture type, the core assumption is that change fosters the creation or generation of new resources, as well as adaptability, flexibility and creativity. This culture is mostly found in organizations where specialized or temporary teams are required for tasks that are highly technical and have high levels of uncertainty and ambiguity, as well as emphasizing individual risk taking and anticipating the future. In the market culture, on the other hand, achievement is focused on competitiveness and aggressiveness, resulting in high productivity and shareholder value in the short and immediate term. Clear goals and contingent rewards motivate employees to perform and meet stakeholder expectations aggressively.

Key values of Obama's hybrid campaign culture included accountability, adaptability, collaboration, commitment, diversity, professionalism, recognition and rewards, empowerment, courtesy and respect and innovations. The 5Fs of work culture were demonstrated by the team while operating under intense pressure: *fast* where the organization believes in speedy action to respond to any allegation, or demands, *friendly* where the campaign practices strong people orientation and emotional intelligence, *flexible* where they believed in the spirit of innovations to respond to issues, *fun* where people at headquarters and field offices had fun despite the stress they were faced with, and *focused* where headquarters remained strongly focused to squeeze each and every vote in the battleground state, to make a difference. Another culture the Obama team inherited from West Coast tech companies was the unique dress code and work environment. The culture has changed from the traditional campaign office structure of closed rooms to an open collaborative unit. The layout was designed with input from Facebook executives, and planned not only to create a collaborative and open space spread on one floor like a business organization, but also with the use of various relaxing tools including gym balls for sitting. Andrew Romano from Newsweek who visited the office in early 2012 wrote a piece on the new culture the campaign embraced saying:

> "In a dark, distant corner of the office, a team of more than a dozen developers sat on big, bouncy yoga balls, tapping away on the customized black keyboards they brought from home. Many of them had unusual facial hair, or unusual piercings, or both which may be why I heard someone refer to them as "those guys who look like they're occupying the office. Nonetheless, the developers were very much welcome at One Prudential Plaza. For months now, they have been figuring out how to rewrite the campaign's code – created when the iPhone was a novelty, when Twitter barely existed, and when Facebook was one tenth its current size.

INTELLIGENCE AND LEADERSHIP IN PRESIDENTIAL CAMPAIGN TRAILS

In this election all forms of intelligence - Intelligence Quotient (IQ), emotional intelligence (EQ) and spiritual intelligence (SQ) were at work by the candidates and their campaign staff to convince voters, donors and the media. Gardner broadly defines intelligence as "the ability to solve problems or to create products that are valued within one or more cultural setting". Others defined it as a mental activity directed toward purposive adaptation to, selection and shaping of, real-world environments relevant to one's life. The two candidates of course, probably have higher Intelligence Quotients as IQ only measures general intellectual abilities determined by intelligence tests. In the last few decades however, the rule of the game has changed and a successful person is judged not only by how smart he (or she) is, or by his training, expertise and the wealth he might have. Instead, one is increasingly judged by how well he handles himself and others.

This measurement has little to do with what we were told was important in schools or colleges – that it is enough to have intellectual ability and technical know-how to do the job. It focuses rather on personal qualities, such as self awareness, self regulation, emotional self assessments, social responsibility, assertiveness, self actualization, empathy, motivation, impulse control and reality testing. In the new paradigm, these qualities are considered to be a person's emotional intelligence (EQ). Peter Salovy and John D. Mayer defined emotional intelligence as *"the ability to monitor one's own and other's feelings and emotions, to discriminate among them and to use this information to guide one's thinking and action"*. In this election we have seen times where campaigns have hit rock bottom or rode high due to several unplanned and unanticipated issues that popped up, like the Supreme Court's decision on Health Care, the Benghazi attack, the October unemployment rate, Hurricane Sandy and others, and voters have witnessed how the emotional reactions to these events helped or hurt the candidates.

LEADING CHANGE IN THE SOCIAL MOVEMENT VS. LEADING TO ADDRESS SPECIAL GROUP'S INTEREST

The election was a choice between leading change in social movements and leading to address special groups' interests, or between the transformational and transactional leadership qualities demonstrated by the two candidates. Social movement emerges as a result of the efforts of purposeful actors – individuals, organizations – to assert new public values, form new relationships rooted in those values and mobilize the political, economic and cultural powers to translate these values into action. Since there was a strong difference in view between the two protagonists, the end game plan was not only to win the election, but also to change the course in which the country is heading. Transformational leadership as described by Bass and Avolio, is leadership that elevates the desire of followers for achievement and self-development, while also promoting the development of groups and organizations, it is leadership that, instead of responding to the immediate self-interest of followers with a carrot or a stick, arouses in the individual a heightened awareness to key issues, as well as to the group and organization, while increasing the confidence of followers, gradually moving them from concerns for existence, to concerns for achievement, growth and development. On the other hand, transactional leadership is an agreement or contract to achieve specific work objectives, discover individuals' capabilities and specify the compensation and rewards that can be expected upon successful completion of the task.

James Burns, presidential biographer and leadership scholar said, "transforming leaders define public values that embrace the supreme and enduring principles of a people. These values are the shaping ideas behind constitutions and laws, and their interpretations." Since this election was defined by many issues, the public wanted to know the direction the elected leaders would take the country, or according to Aristotle's definition their ethos – trustworthiness or credibility of their character, logos – the logic used to support their plan and vision, and pathos – their emotional persuasive appeal when they went to the voting booth. During times when people have so little faith in one another and so little confidence in the willingness of others to do what is right, the country needs a strong voice to dispel disillusionment, and it takes someone of great courage to face this time and give the country hope and direction. When voters went to the polls during this election, they had in mind the person they thought would demonstrate the kind of leadership they wanted in the next four years. Having seen the outcome of the elections, we can safely say that most voters were looking for a transformational leader that displayed the following seven characteristics.

Agent of change: a leader who creates adaptive, entrepreneurial, innovative and flexible organizations. His personal and professional image makes it possible for him to successfully lead people in such an environment, i.e., to stimulate changes and to realize them successfully.

Courage: a leader who is ready and able to assume an appropriate attitude, to take a risk and face the status quo in the organization. His intellectual abilities allow him to face reality even though it may not be pleasant.

Openness and faith in one's followers: In his relationship with his followers, he is open and sincere, ready to foster confidence when required. So, although he possesses great power, he is sensitive with regard to his followers' needs and does his best to empower them whenever possible.

Led by values: a person who formulates a set of essential values which are to be emulated and exhibits behavior which is in accordance with these values.

Lifelong learning: a leader who tries to draw lessons from his own experience for future situations. In that sense he is ready when necessary to make radical changes in his own attitudes, approach, behavior, etc.

Ability to face complex, ambiguous, and uncertain situations: a leader who is ready to face any situation in which he finds himself. Considering the levels of complexity and uncertainty of contemporary conditions and atypical situations which confront the country almost daily, a leader's ability and ingenuity in successfully handling such conditions is of extreme importance.

Visionary abilities: A leader who is an effective visionary. He must be able to imagine a future state and successfully articulate that state in ongoing and enthusiastic communication with followers in order to achieve such a state.

Chapter 2

The Ground Game

"If we just run the same campaign as 2008, we stand a good chance of losing … We've got to run a new campaign." *Jim Messina's, April 2011 video message*

The marvel of this election was how the Obama team quietly planned the ground game years before the 2012 general election. The campaign initiated many field offices used for 2008, expanded the organizational network in battleground states to a historic level and kept those offices dormant until the president launched his re-election campaign in April 2011. The other critical step they took at an early stage occurred when many previous campaign staff were packing up for Washington to work in the new Administration and the Democratic National Committee. Jeremy Bird who had run operations in Ohio, travelled to Chicago to form a small group of experts including Dan Wagner the data analysis guru, to start working on a 'lessons learned' document later called *Postmortem*, which analyzed how the president won over McCain.

They started the analysis by interviewing field experts who ran operations in swing states including Ohio, Pennsylvania, and Colorado. The task included many phone interviews with organizers and volunteers, collecting data from the various electoral groups to find out what worked and could be used again for the 2012 election, as well as what did not work. Like any 'lessons learned' document, this one became the foundation for building the campaign 2012 project. Few of the learned recommendations obtained from the previous election included how to improve the data operation by consolidating several databases developed and used by each department, the advantage of having in-house data analysis teams compared to relying on the third party firms, how to rally voters by embedded campaign staffers in places like barbershops and beauty salons making those areas hubs for organizing African-American and Hispanic neighborhoods, and more.

Planning for the election program starts by setting the vision and mission, identifying milestones, mobilizing resources (money, manpower), mapping the various paths to get to the 270 electoral college votes, managing expectations of key stakeholders (voters, donors, volunteers, and media) , establishing a risk management plan, organizing the political ads, and monitoring the execution of the plan. One could say the process performed by the campaign was exemplified as "project and program management at its best".

To properly plan and execute all these activities, time was of the essence and one big advantage the campaign had compared to Romney, was time. Obama had one full year to set up the organization's field offices, acquire resources, consolidate the existing database and design new analytical models and tools. In 2011, the campaign spent $126 million ... three times more than the Romney campaign ... to establish the groundwork in many of the nine battleground states and to hire field directors and other key resources. In his April 25 video address, Jim Messina set five key goals to be performed in order for the campaign to be successful: (a) expand the election, (b) build something new, (c) grow the grassroots in the States, (d) measure the progress and (e) work for every vote. The campaign then set the following several strategies to accomplish the goal – "Having the president win the second term". This chapter is dedicated to expanding each strategy and provides detailed analysis.

- Raise enough money - $1 billion to support the campaign.
- Establish groundwork in swing states at early stage.
- Redesign the campaign ads targeting specific groups in the swing states.
- Attract more volunteers to power up the campaign.
- Capture the audience's attention for negative campaign.
- Maximize the use of technology.
- Recruit the best and brightest campaign staff.

- Build a forecasting or predictive profile for voters based on their, sex, age, ethnic affiliation, neighborhood composition, past voting record and their reaction toward change in the media.

STRATEGY #1: HOW TO RAISE $1 BILLION TO SUPPORT THE CAMPAIGN

In the 2008 presidential election the combined television advertisement cost of the two campaigns was $2.5 billion, and everyone in the Obama campaign including Messina knew that in order to have a successful campaign, enough money had to be raised. They also realized when considering the sluggish economy and high unemployment rate, that raising money would be difficult. The campaign therefore had to develop a variety of fundraising strategies to attract more donors. Unlike the Romney campaign and its super PAC allies who continued to raise money using traditional methods, the Obama team decided to use various technology and analytic tools to identify and reach out to millions of potential donors across the country.

One of the campaign's first steps was revising the 2008 donors' database. After reviewing donor profiles, the team found out that other than the name, address and amount contributed, the information held was insufficient with regards to other variables, important to keep these donors active. Although the 2008 campaign was credited with being technologically advanced, the initial review of how things were at the beginning of the 2012 campaign showed weak links. There were separate, disconnected databases from 2008, as well as a lack of analytic tools required to extract the variables necessary to build an informative picture of typical voters, their preferences and other key indicators. Once the new digital lab under Messina connected the databases, the analytic team began to find patterns in behaviors, preferences and other important indicators that could be used to persuade donors to contribute, and the fundraising team developed several ways to reach out to voters based on this information.

When the election was over, it was believed over a billion dollars had been raised –a record in the history of presidential elections. The tables below provide detailed information of the contributions that came in and spending by the candidates, parties and Super PACs. Over 57% of the Obama contributions were under $200, 33% of them were contributions between $200 - $2,499 and 11% reached the maximum $2,500 allowed for individual donation. Conversely, only 24% of the Romney's donors contributed under $200, 37% gave between $200 – $2,499, and 39% of them contributed the full $2,500.

SOURCES OF FUNDS	BARACK OBAMA	MITT ROMNEY
Individual Contributions	**$715.1M**	**$443.4M**
Small Individual Contributions	$233.1M	$80.0 M
Large Individual Contributions	$490.0M	$366.0M
Party Committee	$255.1M	$371.4M
Primary Super PAC	$78.8M	$ 153.8M
Candidate self-financing	$5,000	$52, 500
Federal Funds	$0	$0
Other	$522, 529	$1,643,99

Table 1: Contribution to the Candidates. Adapted from OpenSecrets.org http://www.opensecrets.org/pres12/index.php. Retrieved on January 11, 2013

DESCRIPTION	OBAMA	ROMNEY
Candidate Spending	$684.0 M	$433.3M
National Party Spending	$286.0 M	$379.0 M
Outside Spending	$134.0 M	$412.3M
Total Spending	**$1.103B**	**$1. 225B**

Table 2: Spending related to presidential race by campaigns and parties. Adapted from http://www.opensecrets.org/pres12/index.php. Retrieved on January 11, 2013

The campaign used several ways of fundraising, mostly supported by online methods. Some of these include mass email with different headings, one-click donation, text donation, celebrity dinners, and the Obama fashion line. A summary of each strategy used by the campaign to raise the money is listed below.

DIGITAL FUNDRAISING = $504 M

Digital fundraising covers a consolidated approach of using cutting edge technologies including sending different emails to a group of supporters with different titles asking them to donate, use of social media sites like Facebook and Twitter, mobile apps, and the official Obama for America website. Over 80 percent of the donations for the campaign came through digital fundraising and the amount was higher by $100 million compared to the $403 million raised in 2008.

EMAILS WITH DIFFERENT HEADINGS

Over 800 customized emails designed to look and feel personal were sent by Obama, Michelle, the vice president, surrogates, high profile celebrities and many campaign staffers to millions of supporters keeping them informed of what was going on and asking them to donate. The titles of a few of the hundred emails he received during the campaign are summarized below.

"Pick up the phone right now, Go vote – and forward this, Two simple words, The last time I'll ask you this, We're almost there, How this ends, Don't brush this off, This is dangerous, Some bad news, Hey, High five, We send a lot of emails – here is why, Real quick, Do me a favor, Reporting back to you, Listen up, I'll be blunt, This is big, big news, This is in your hands, A little bittersweet, You're amazing, I hope you do something about it, Good morning, The First Lady Knocked it out of the park, Seriously, thank you, If the President loses, You won't get many more of these emails, This is critical, the end. Warning: *I will be outspent,* This picture is cute, No-one should have the power to buy an election, We could lose if this continues, Excuse me, Your seat on Barack's bus, An emotional moment in the Oval Office, Hell no, My father, We got beat, Barack and I wanted to meet you next week, The Defeat of Barack Hussein

Obama, Marriage, Billion with a "B", Much better odds, I tried, Me again, and If the general election were today".

TRACKING EMAIL TITLES AS "HOLLYWOOD BOX OFFICE SALES"
Even though at times the emails were said to be overwhelming, the campaign's email messaging, fundraising and optimization strategy worked. Most of the $690M raised came from these carefully designed email appeals. They had been explored by a group of twenty writers working with Toby Fallsgraff, the campaign's email director and piloted under the leadership of Amelia Showalter, director of digital analytics. Multiple email drafts prepared with different subject lines were sent to small groups to see how much money they would generate. The data then was analyzed and the best designed, winner of the pilot project title contest, was used for the broader supporter pool.

Even for the pilot studies, the team used various analytic tools including Bayesian conditional probability to identify how much an email with a certain title would raise as compared to a different title. This resulted in the team realizing that using ordinary titles like the ones that users see in their inbox from friends and family members, attracted more attention than the formal campaign style emails. According to a Bloomberg BusinessWeek report, Obama's June email *"I will be outspent"*, outperformed 17 other tiles and raised more than $2.6 million. Like the Hollywood box office report, the campaign was able to identify the amount of money raised by email using predicted analytic techniques. The top 20 titles studied in the lab which raised the most money were: Some Scary numbers ($1.9M), If you believe in what we're doing ($0.91M), Last call: Join Michelle and me ($0.9M), Would love to meet you ($0.75M), Do this for Michelle ($0.71M), Change ($0.71M),The most popular Obama ($0.66M), Michelle time ($0.6M), Deadline: Join Michelle and me ($0.6M), Thankful every day ($0.55M), and The one thing the polls got right ($0.4M).

ONE-CLICK DONATION - "STREAMLINING THE CHECKOUT PROCESS" - $115 MILLION
While analyzing the internet traffic on the main site, the Obama team noticed that a quarter of the clicks on its fundraising e-mails were from mobile devices, but only a small number of donations were collected. To

solve this problem, the team developed a mobile app for both iPhones and Android phones that could be downloaded from an apps store. The One Click Quick Donate Program was scheduled to limit the interaction time between donors and the system, by storing essential information including credit card numbers. Since implementing this program, subscribers donated four times more than the average contributors.

TEXT DONATION –

As the first presidential campaign to accept small dollar donations via text messages, the Obama team launched the *"GIVE to 62262"* messages to millions of supporters. According to Jim Messina, "accepting small donations by text message will help us engage with even more grassroots supporters who want to play a role by donating whatever they can afford to the campaign, and get the president elected in November." The brilliant idea behind this step was not only to collect small donations, but also to collect the phone numbers of those who donate as a source for disseminating the campaign's messages. Even though both campaigns used text donations, the Obama campaign benefited more since Obama had a larger grassroots network and more of the donations to the campaign came from smaller donors. The additional advantage of this effort was that it activated millions of small donors not only empowering them by making them a recognized part of the campaign, but also creating the possibility of reaching out to and bringing in more people into the political process.

OBAMA FASHION LINE – THE RUNWAY TO WIN COLLECTION = $40 MILLION +

When Anna Wintour, the Editor-in-Chief of Vogue and the campaign came up with the idea to create the "Obama fashion line – the Runway to Win Collection", Fox News mocked it saying "Obama is selling yoga pants and soy candles", and GOP members at the Republican National Convention called it "Ritzy". Who thought that Rachel Zoe, Tracy L Cox, Nanette Lepore, Yigal Azrouel, Ricky Martin, Stefani Greenfield, Chanel Iman, Phil Fung, Aurel Stender, and 20 other designers would collaborate to create the Obama fashion line, producing items from Thakoon Panichgul scarves to yoga pants. The team held runway fashion shows in New York and Chicago, featuring celebrities like Scarlett

Johansson and others. The idea was to raise money not only from selling $15 T-shirts, but also from merchandize that cost up to $95. As a result, this project raised over $40 million for the campaign.

DINNER WITH OBAMAS AND CELEBRITIES = $20 MILLION +

As an attempt to bank on celebrities for fundraising, the Obama campaign designed several events that centered on celebrities from both the west and east coasts, including George Clooney, Julia Roberts, Reese Witherspoon, Spike Lee, Will Smith, Oprah Winfrey, Ellen DeGeneres, Cher, Sarah Jessica Parker and Matthew Broderick, Mariah Carey and Alicia Keys, Jessica Alba, Jeremy Renner, Cee - Lo Green, Dave Matthews, the Foo Fighters, and Jon Bon Jovi. Emails were sent to millions of contributors who, entered their names in a raffle that would allow them to join the Obamas or some of these celebrities, for dinner. Two events were planned - one in the west coast with George Clooney and one in the east coast with Sarah Jessica Parker.

Clooney's Fundraising Event- the president attended a fundraising event at George Clooney's home to raise a record of $15 million in one day. Even though it was announced that a donation of $3 or more would be eligible to enter a raffle to win tickets to dine with George Clooney and the president, the campaign targeted women between 40-48 years old who were interested in dining with Clooney. Over ten thousand donors contributed an average of $23 in hopes of winning a ticket, raising almost $10 million.

Sara Jessica Parker's Fundraising Event- Similar to the George Clooney event, in early summer of 2012, the President and First Lady attended a fundraising event at the home of actors Sarah Jessica Parker and Matthew Broderick. This was estimated to have raised about $2 million from an attendance by 50 people who paid $40,000 each, and a few who won raffle tickets out of thousands of ticket holders. Another event in Manhattan featuring dinner for 250 people was organized by Mariah Carey and Alicia Keys raising $2.5 million.

STRATEGY #2 – ESTABLISHING THE GROUNDWORK IN SWING STATES

One of the critical success factors for the Obama campaign was how they started to reach out to the battleground states as early as one year before the official campaign was launched, analyzing the different combinations or optional paths to get to the required 270 electoral votes. Towards the end of the run up to the election, while the Romney team scrambled to move resources from one state to another, the Obama team was playing their various cards - paths which had been planned and organized months ahead. At the beginning of the election Jim Messina, the campaign manager, sent out a brochure entitled "*2012 Road Map to Victory*" to the campaign's supporters, in which he outlined the work ahead including the opportunities and challenges as follows:

"This year, there are key states that will help determine the winner in the 2012 Presidential election. How effective we are in capturing these states will be decided by a confluence of opportunities and challenges."

OPPORTUNITIES:
- *Young People*: More than eight million new voters have come of age since the last Presidential election.
- *New registrants*: After the 2010 midterm elections, Democrats still have a significant registration advantage over Republicans in key battleground states. And Republican registration of new voters in these states is down from four years ago.
- *Republican opponents*: To win his Party's nomination and appeal to the Tea Party wing of the Republican Party, the republican candidate has adopted positions far outside what mainstream America could accept.
- *Strong Grassroots Campaign*: Built over four years, the on-the-ground community based volunteer operatives will help to create the greatest number of possible pathways to 270 electoral votes.
- *Embracing New Technologies*: Utilizing new technologies that are farther-reaching and more innovative to connect with as many people as possible. The campaign will focus on continuing to expand their web presence and use social networking media (Facebook, Twitter) to establish an ongoing two-way conversation with voters and supporters.

KEY CHALLENGES:

- *Republican Super-PACs*: Groups on the other side were promising to throw hundreds of millions of dollars into this election - we're seeing it now among the Republican candidates. That's how far they'll go to defeat the President and roll back the clock on all the progress we've made.
- *Election Law*: Last year, 24 states including Florida, Texas and Wisconsin, passed laws that imposed burdensome requirements on the right of Americans to vote.
- *The Electoral landscape will be more challenging:* The country and the electorate have changed since 2008. We will have to work hard to mobilize different coalitions from battleground states to battleground states.
- Independent Voters: Roughly 30% of voters in 2008 and 2010 identified themselves as "independents". We must work to first identify voters who are open to the President's message and then talk about how they benefit from the President's policies."

The signature of the Obama campaign was its ability to maximize positive events and turn around challenges to opportunities. The very first step the campaign took, was to examine and design various paths to victory using the "Electoral College" map calculation. According to Messina, the campaign mapped out over 40 pathways to victory and narrowed them down to five.Using John Kerry's electoral map of 2004 as a baseline, the campaign developed these five paths – West, South, Midwest, Florida (later updated by the campaign) and Expansion. A summary of each path is outlined below.

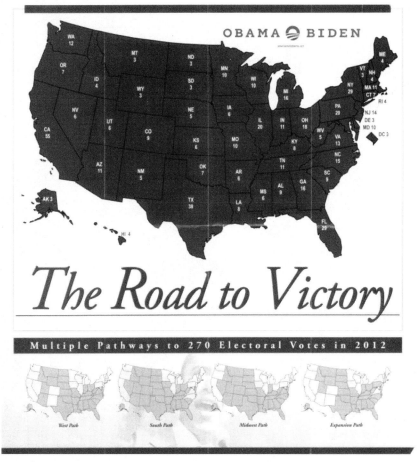

Figure 2: The Road to Victory: Multiple Pathways to 270 Electoral Votes in 2012. Adapted from Obama for America

BASELINE — KERRY'S 2004 STATES - 246 ELECTORAL COLLEGE VOTES

John Kerry won 19 states - California, Connecticut, Delaware, Hawaii, Illinois, Maine, Maryland, Massachusetts, Missouri, Minnesota, New Hampshire, New Jersey, New York, Oregon, Pennsylvania, Rhode Island, Vermont, Washington, Wisconsin and the District of Columbia. The campaign used these states as the baseline to work from in designing the above mentioned four paths.

Baseline
Start with Kerry States

292

Figure 3: Obama's campaign 2012 Baseline Electoral College Map. Adapted from *"2012 Road Map to Victory"* (Obama for America)

The West Path: Colorado, New Mexico, Nevada, and add to Iowa = 272

The campaign realized that in 2008, Colorado, New Mexico and Nevada helped the president get elected and they wanted to keep those States in their column. They were labeled as battleground States and a lot of resources and mobilization efforts were directed from the appropriate team led by Mitch Stewart, Battleground States Director. Millions of dollars were spent in these areas for ground programs including voter registration, persuasion and turnout. According to the campaign office, 48 hours leading into the election over 14,000 in Colorado, and close to 2800 in Nevada GOTV (Get Out To Vote) individual shifts participated. In Colorado, alone over 13 million doors were knocked on and phone calls were made during the campaign's lifetime. The result was as planned. Obama kept all three states in his column cashing in 20

Electoral College Votes (Colorado 51.2%, Nevada 52.3%, New Mexico 52.9%).

Florida Path

Due the high number of electoral vote and the composition of voters, there was a massive field operation in all Florida 102 offices. Over 360,000 new voters were registered and close to 22 million phone calls were made and doors knocked. The result Obama won Florida by a thin margin collecting all Electoral College votes.

South Path: North Carolina and Virginia- the new south

One of the reasons for hosting the Democratic National Convention in North Carolina was to create opportunities for the state and energize voters because polls showed that the state was leaning towards the Republicans months before the election. The campaign assembled a strong network of neighborhood teams throughout the region and spent millions of dollars on online, TV and other advertisements. The national database supported by the Dashboard, a newly designed interfacing tool, helped many volunteers living in other states make phone calls and contact potential voters in the State. The analytic team at headquarters used various data triangulation methods to identify potential voters and supporters, and prepared hundreds of customized messages to individuals in North Carolina and Virginia. One of the micro-targeting strategies, narrowcasting was also used in different parts of the region. Narrowcasting is a technique of buying media market to specific areas targeting specific households. 100 field offices were opened, 53 in North Carolina, and 47 in Virginia. This was more than the Romney campaign which only opened 72 field offices. In the last two days of the election there were 112,142 GOTV individual shifts working around the clock to call and knock on doors in these two States. The result was close to what the campaign planned: retained one State that Obama had won in 2008 (Virginia), and lost North Carolina.

Table 3 shows a summary of data comparing the number of field offices, Obama's new voter registration, phone calls and results.

SOUTH PATH	NO. OF FIELD OFFICES		NO. OF DOOR KNOCKS AND PHONE CALLS (OBAMA ONLY)	NEW VOTER REGISTRA-TION (OBAMA ONLY)	RESULTS	
	Obama	Romney			Obama	Romney
Virginia	47	29	14 Million	140,000	50.8%	47.8%
North Carolina	53	24	17 Million	340,000	48.4%	50.6%
Florida	102	48	22 Million	>360,000	50.0%	49.1%

Table 3: South Path: Number of field offices, Obama's new voter registration, phone calls and Election results.

Midwest Path: **The Firewall** - Ohio 18, and Iowa 6 Electoral Votes at stake

It was understood that whoever won Ohio would have a simpler path clinching the presidency. *"The state of Ohio is a critical part of the Midwest pathway strategy. So far our campaign has spent more time on the ground in Ohio than in any other state in the country. We must build a strong grassroots organization to win this November". To do that, we must immediately make a considerable investment of resources – time and money – in the state while also continuing our operations in the other key Midwest states."* This was Jim Messina's message to supporters around the country acknowledging that the "buck stops in Ohio". In the Midwest path, Ohio and Iowa, two critical States needed to win the presidency, were also the center of attention for the campaign. The intensity of campaigning here could be seen in the next section as evidenced by the number of field offices opened, campaign events scheduled, phone calls and door knocks made and survey of potential voters conducted.

Only in Ohio
TV Ads

From Clarksburg, Ohio with a population of 455 to Cleveland, one of the largest cities in the state with over 450,000 people, Ohioans were in the months leading to the election, bombarded with radio, TV and online messages ending with *"I'm Barack Obama and I approved this message"* and *"I'm Mitt Romney and I approved this message."* From April 2011 to October 26, 2012, over 181,000 ads were aired in Ohio with a price tag of $114 million, and over 58,000 of them were aired only in September. The Obama campaign aired over 85,000 ads and the Romney campaign over 34,000 ads. Most of them were repeated several times a day. Bloomberg calculated that the Obama *"Fact Check"* ad was aired 2,600 times, whereas the Romney ad, *"Where did all the money go"* was aired 2,700 times. The 2012 presidential election set a record for the number of TV ads aired.

According to Wesleyan Media Project, as of October 29, the two candidates, their party committees and supporting interest groups sponsored 1,015,615 ads, a 39.1% increase over 2008 and a 41% increase over 2004. The media also reported that the Obama campaign outspent Romney's 2.6:1 on ads in the general election period, but Republican outside groups (Super PACs) cut the difference by airing hundreds of thousands on local broadcast and national cable. In Ohio on only one TV channel, eleven ads were aired within 20 minutes demonstrating how Ohio was inundated with ads from both sides. Reuters described the ad-bombardment as follows:

"It is 6:10 P.M on a Thursday in October, just days before the U.S elections. Before the clock hits 6:29 p.m., 11 political ads will have aired on local NBC channel in Columbus, Ohio. One tells voters that Democratic President Barack Obama has not proposed a legitimate economic plan for the country. Another suggests that policies of Republican candidate Mitt Romney would undermine the future of America's children. Yet another says Romney would effectively deny many women crucial cancer screenings by proposing cuts to Planned Parenthood.

The very next ad calls Obama an extremist on abortion, who supports leaving babies "out to die"

In the final stretch of the campaign, an ad by Romney on Jeep and Chrysler sparked controversy in Ohio and is believed to be the turning point for the Obama campaign. The ad stated: *"Who will do more for the auto industry? Not Barack Obama. The truth: Mitt Romney has a plan to help the auto industry. He's supported by Lee Iacocca and The Detroit News. Obama took GM and Chrysler into bankruptcy and sold Chrysler to Italians who are going to build Jeeps in China. Mitt Romney will fight for every American job."* A few hours after this ad, the Obama campaign responded with the following: *"When the auto industry faced collapse, Mitt Romney turned his back. Even the conservative Detroit News criticized Romney for his "wrong-headedness on the bailout". And now after Romney's false claim of Jeep outsourcing to China, Chrysler itself has refuted Romney's lie. The truth? Jeep is adding jobs in Ohio. Mitt Romney on Ohio jobs? Wrong then – dishonest now".* The Obama campaign spent millions of dollars in Ohio to portray Romney as a job killer who opposed Obama's decision to bail out the auto industry.

Early voting was an advantage for the Obama campaign and in Ohio a good number of voters cast their votes early giving the campaign an encouragement and assurance that their hard work had paid off.

Get Out To Vote effort: On November 5, 17, 566 and on Election Day, 32, 854 Get Out To Vote individual shifts were making phone calls, knocking on doors and convincing voters to head to the polling places. A total of 17 million door knocks and phone calls were made in Ohio alone, registering over 140,000 new voters.

Voters Survey and Forecasting: One of the critical sources of information was survey and polling data collected from the nine battleground states. In Ohio, the campaign conducted thousands of calls to voters every week and since each voter profile had a unique identifier with hundreds of variables associated with it, response from the latest poll could easily be analyzed to see the shift in opinion due to events in the campaign or ads aired. According to Time Magazine, "the Obama analytics team had polling data from about 29,000 people in Ohio alone – a whopping sample that composed nearly half of 1% of all voters there

– allowing for deep dives into exactly where each demographic and regional group was trending at any given moment". This massive data analysis gave the campaign a pulse check tool to identify voters that were persuaded one way or another during the debates, subsequent TV and radio ads, as well as any activities that surfaced nationally including the unemployment rate, Hurricane Sandy, and so on.

MID-WEST PATH - THE FIREWALL	NO. OF FIELD OFFICES		NO. OF DOOR KNOCKSAND PHONE CALLS (OBAMA ONLY)	NEW VOTER REGISTRA-TION (OBAMA ONLY)	RESULTS	
	Obama	Romney			Obama	Romney
Ohio	122	40	17 Million	140,000	50.1%	48.2%
Iowa	66	13	6.5 Million		52.8%	46.1%
Wisconsin	68	24			52.8%	46.1%

Table 4: Mid-West Path: Number of field offices, new voter registration, phone calls and Election results

The Expansion Path: Give Arizona a shot

As their fifth possible path, the Obama campaign planned to change Arizona from red to blue. Jim Messina and his team were gathering information on the ground in both Arizona and Texas, to see if it would be feasible to open field offices and mobilize resources. In his early message to supporters, Messina mentioned that "The Kerry baseline States provide President Obama with a solid foundation of support across the country, but we must be prepared for every possibility. With that in mind, we are working hard to get our message out in a number of States that weren't part of our pathway plan in 2008. One of those States is Arizona. Today, there are hundreds of thousands of eligible but unregistered voters in the State – and a recent poll shows president Obama with a slight lead over his likely Republican opponents. Arizona offers a great electoral opportunity." In the beginning the campaign realized that it would be better to keep the 2008 map by mobilizing critical resources in the nine battleground States. The campaign had only one field office in Arizona and four in Texas. At the end of the campaign, the Obama team opened and operated in over 575 field offices in these marginal areas- Ohio having the most with 122, followed by Florida with 102. In comparison, the Romney campaign operated a total of 213 field offices in the same areas. Of what was planned, the Obama team lost only North Carolina even though the team there had 53 offices to mobilize resources.

The $120 million investment made by the campaign in 2011 had raised eyebrows in the media. The Obama campaign's high "burn rate", meaning spending more money than the amount raised was translated by many as a sign of an inefficient and troubled campaign. However, for the successful completion of any project, it is important to conduct advanced groundwork as well as go through the all-encompassing process of extensive project initiation, planning, execution, monitoring and controlling. The Return on Investment (ROI) on the early spending on the campaign resources was therefore very high.

STRATEGY #3 ATTRACT MORE VOLUNTEERS TO POWER UP THE CAMPAIGN
"Having all of the metrics in the world won't do you any good if you don't have that dedicated army of volunteers to carry out the plan on the ground".
— James Messina, Campaign Manager.

Between April 2011 and November 2012, 2.2 million volunteers participated in the largest grassroots campaign in history. These volunteers worked in 813 field offices organized in the 10,000 neighborhood teams and helped to register 1.8 million voters. They made over 150 million door knocks and phone calls which translates into one out of every 2.5 people in the entire country being contacted by the campaign. This was surprising news because for the most part of the election, the campaign had been counted out by media forecasting that "his supporters wouldn't turn out, we will never see the kind of voter participation we saw in 2008", and even asking questions like "Is Obama toast?" or "Can Obama win?" However, as Messina in his email to supporters once said, "the best campaign team and volunteers in the history of politics" turned the impossible to unbelievable.

Five hundred thirty one days before the election (May 2011), Mitch Stewart, the battleground state director outlined the field organization and mobilization strategy, to empower millions of grassroots groups using a T-model organizational development as follows:

> *"What we've learned is that organization building takes a long time, relationship building takes a long time. The other thing that we all know that September and October, we will see a sea of volunteers coming to our offices and we know we have to have infrastructure in place to properly channel that energy. Now what we learned is the best way to do is what we call a T-model, where we empower local volunteers to take a leadership role within our campaign, make decisions for our campaign in their neighborhoods or in their community based of off both work done leading up to the election, but also because of the experiences. But we have a lot of work to do."*

Three programs were implemented to help recruit volunteers-summer organizers program, one – on – one conversation with voters and supporters and grassroots planning sessions.

Summer Organizers Program: Eight weeks summer organizers program started on the first week of June and ended on the first week of August 2011, to train and inspire a new generation of grassroots supporters. Record numbers of volunteers applied to the program and those who were accepted made a two month commitment to organize their communities, register voters, go door to door to help the campaign to establish the groundwork. Stewart called this team "the heart and soul of this campaign".

One-On –One Program: At the beginning of the campaign the team promised to reach out to every single person who donated or volunteered to the 2008 campaign, and ask them to get involved once more in the 2012 election. A year before the election, the campaign announced that it had contacted one million voters and supporters and that they did it, not using mass email or telemarketing calls, but rather by using one on one conversation in person if possible, otherwise on the phone. This responsibility was first given to volunteers who had been active in the 2007 and 2008 campaign, but hadn't been very active in the last two years. In early November 2012, the campaign released a memo announcing that it had conducted over 150 million conversations with voters and supporters through various means. Figure 3 below shows the one – on – one conversation model.

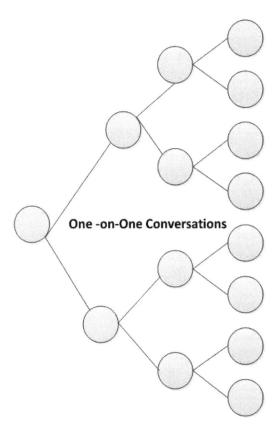

Figure 4: One-on-one Conversation model. Adapted from Obama for America

Grassroots Planning Sessions: These sessions were planned for the campaign to allow volunteers to sit down with other volunteers and map out what the campaign would look like. During the course of the election, hundreds of grassroots planning sessions were conducted. One staffer described this effort thus, "These grassroots planning sessions are so crucial to the future of the campaign that we're thinking about them as part of our organizational DNA. They're an opportunity for staff, volunteers and supporters to come together, online and offline and help plan what the campaign will look like in our communities, how we'll organize our neighborhoods most effectively and how we'll reach out to new supporters in the weeks and months ahead".

After the election one volunteer from California posted her experience as a grassroots supporter on the campaign website in this way:

"When our field office opened, my husband, 12-year-old daughter and I were there almost every day. My daughter and I even took a leadership role -- she was our tally captain! This is the kind of experience that changes your life. My children not only have a better understanding of the political system, but also have a first hand experience of how community engagement can make a difference. On Election Night, they felt that difference. They were so excited for the President because they had a sense of ownership -- they had personally helped him achieve the win. On Election Night, I truly believed we were all winners." -- Kerry, California

I was one of the volunteers who worked in a number of field offices in Virginia. Even though I live in Maryland, like most Marylanders who crossed the Potomac River to volunteer in Northern Virginia, I made phone calls and knocked on doors in the weeks leading to November 6. On Election Day, I worked at the Alexandria office and the environment there made me feel good. I saw the enthusiasm of the volunteers ... teens through seniors, men and women of different races and faiths, all working together making last-ditch phone calls and transporting voters to the polling stations. When every space in the two storey office was completely occupied, people were sitting in the corridors and kitchen going through the list of voters, some of whom had been contacted by the campaign more than five times. One of my phone calls was to an 88 year old lady, who was released hours before from the hospital where she was admitted after a heart attack. She said "I would like one of you to come and pick me up to cast my vote. I'm glad I survived to see this day again". From the campus dormitories to campaign offices, from individual living rooms to group rented spaces, volunteers throughout the country mobilized the campaigns by knocking on doors, making phone calls until the last minutes before the polls closed. Right after the election, Jeremiah Bird, the National Field director sent the following thank you email to all volunteers

"Team,

This victory is a testament to you. Take pride in your hard work over the past 18 months ... the countless calls you made, the doors you knocked, the people you inspired to support our president. I know it wasn't always easy. But through your perseverance, you proved that a strong, grassroots organization could overcome powerful interests on the other side. You built this organization from the ground up. You helped this country stay the course. Enjoy this victory for now and rest up. There will be more work to come. Stay tuned." *Jeremiah Bird, National Field Director Nov 8, 2012*

On November 13, the campaign organized the last conference call and invited the president to personally thank thousands of his supporters who fought the hard battle by knocking doors, making phone calls and transporting voters to the polling stations. Before the president spoke, Mitch Stewart, the battleground state director gave a stunning summary of activities performed by volunteers in the battle ground states. The ground operation and organization led by the veteran campaign gurus was beyond anything anyone would have imagined. Nationally over 140 million voters were contacted either through door knocks or phone calls and on Election Day alone the number was over 10 million. The following table shows the intensive activities performed by volunteers on November 5th and Election Day.

BATTLEGROUND STATES	48 HOURS BEFORE ELECTION	
	GOTV Individual Shifts Nov 5	GOTV Individual Shifts – Election day
Colorado	5213	8869
Florida	16191	26055
Iowa	10609	11021
North Carolina	8256	11793
New Hampshire	2969	4602
Nevada	1213	1621
Ohio	17566	32854
Virginia	19887	29960
Wisconsin	15238	11574
Total	**131985**	**180932**

Table 5: Summary of activities performed in the nine battleground states on November 5th and Election Day

STRATEGY #4 CAPTURE AUDIENCE'S ATTENTION USING CAREFULLY CRAFTED ADS AGAINST THE OPPONENT

Capturing audience's attention with positive ads for the president and painting Romney negatively was the strategy used by the Obama campaign in the early stages of the race. Steven Spielberg from DreamWorks advised Jim Messina on how to capture an audience's attention, and insisted that Messina sat down with the DreamWorks marketing team to envision ways to develop a storyline that will help the campaign. The question in Chicago in early spring 2012 was not whether to launch negative ads or not, but rather which one would attract voter and media attention more. The choice was between "flip-flopper" – referring to the well-known centrist governor of a liberal state who changed his position 360 degrees to convince conservatives and win the Republican party nomination – or his Bain Capital experience as the guardian of the privileged, and punisher of the middle class workers. The

Bain Capital and its implication to the middle class was found to be more appropriate by the campaign. While the Romney campaigners prepared for big assaults in September and October, the Obama teams jammed all TV stations, cable networks and online media, painting Romney as the man who liked to fire people, was disconnected from average American life as a privileged businessman who not only outsourced his companies, but also his money in banks outside the US. Nearly twenty percent of the campaign's total budget is believed to have been spent on a summer television blitz attack on Romney, and thirty million dollars on positive ads underlying Obama's accomplishments. The Romney Economics (http://www.barackobama.com/romney/economics/) a web page developed by the Obama campaign showing Romney's Massachusetts record, his economic policies, his Bain Capital life, how as Governor he outsourced jobs to India, his Swiss bank account, his tax heavens in Bermuda and the Cayman Islands, is believed to be one of Spielberg's and the DreamWorks marketing guru's ideas.

The campaign gathered together former GTS Steel workers whose company was purchased by Bain and then closed, to confirm that Romney was indeed a "Job killer". Romney's statement "... *take a risk, get the education, borrow money if you have to from your parents...*" was another spotlight used to run a contrasting image between ordinary folks who are struggling to make ends meet and Romney, who is believed to have over $195 million of personal wealth. Some of the other leading stories that made the majority of TV ads were: Romney is turning Medicare program into a voucher system, the 47% of Americans who pay no income tax, writing off half the nation, Let Detroit Go Bankrupt and self deportation. Obama himself used several of Romney's comments in his campaign rallies. One of these was in reference to the 47% statement: "'we've always said that change takes more than one term, even one president and it certainly takes more than one party. It can't happen if you write off half of the nation before you even took office."

The history from several presidential campaigns reveals that running an early negative one worked for a number of incumbents, including Richard Nixon against George McGovern in 1972, Bill Clinton against Bob Dole in 1996 and George W. Bush against John Kerry in 2004. As a result of the early attack by the Obama campaign, Romney's approval rate at the beginning of the general election reached the lowest point in the last seven elections.

STRATEGY #5 MAXIMIZE THE USE OF TECHNOLOGY TO REACH OUT MORE VOTERS
When Messina was on the executive management tour to many technology companies, Steve Jobs the late Apple CEO, is said to have given him key strategies, including the use of mobile technology and new channels to reach out to many voters. This was to be done by using a programming application that could access the newly emerging channels including Facebook, Tumblr, Twitter, YouTube and Google in addition to the traditional Web and email. According to Jobs, four years in technology evolution is like a lifetime. 2012 was different to 2008, a light years difference in technological innovation and usage. During the first election, Twitter was a professional adventure - now it is one of the fastest news media in the world. The president had 116,000 followers in 2008, and now over 16 million. Facebook was used by less than 40 million Americans then but in 2012 it was four times larger having increased to 160 million U.S. users. Smart phones (iPhone and Android) were scarcely used then, but in this election most people have one and use it to its maximum capacity, from making online purchases, to game playing and for email and text communications. This advancement of technology created an opportunity as well as challenges to capture the attention of many young voters, donors and volunteers. As a result, the Obama team used several technologies to build systems for registering voters, organizing volunteers, collecting and analyzing available personal data including voting patterns, political contributions and consumer preferences, as well as what people read and share and how they respond to e-mails, ads, tweets and other solicitations. Some of the key technological innovations used by the campaign are summarized below.

DASHBOARD – "THE TOOL YOU NEED TO HELP REELECT PRESIDENT OBAMA"
The Dashboard is technology developed and used by the Obama team to help bridge the gap between online supporters and offline field offices across the country. This innovation is one of most successful tools the campaign used during this election season. Volunteers who did not have a field office nearby or who wanted to call from their home, would logon

to the dashboard, download the script, get access to the prospective voters' list from the headquarters and call their target audience. The tool has tutorials in mulitiple languages to help volunteers and is by far more flexible than the MYBO (My Barack Obama) tool used in a similar fashion for the 2008 election. With the Dashboard, volunteers were able to find events, make calls, submit reports, call state and national updates, view individual or team members, learn about organizational best practices, connect with neighboorhood teams and affinity groups like Women for Obama, and check out what other volunteers were doing. Individuals' roles were clearly identified on this tool as staffer, neighborhood team leader, member, core team member, canvass capitain, phone bank captain, data captain, voter registration captain and supporter. According to the campaign source, 358,000 offline events were organized using the Dashboard.

Figure 5: Snapshot of the Obama Campaign Dashboard

MOBILE APPS

The mobile app helped users get national and state campaign updates, find events, register voters, connect to the dashboard, canvass, get voting information, read about campaign issues, share campaign contents, get local impact information, read state and national blogs and tweets. The new application had five major components (info, events, featured, action, and donate). The info button took the user to the issues page and provided updates on major areas including education, energy and environment, equal rights, health care jobs, economy, national security and taxes.

The 'latest news' button took users to the events, volunteer possibilities and other important information pages. The 'Event' feature provided users access to the events they had signed for, including a map option to show the exact location of the event. The 'featured' page reminded users to call voters, join online phone banks, or call from home, provided information of what Obama had accomplished in his first four years in office, and reminded visitors to call friends to vote. The 'action' option provided a link to register voters, connect to dashboard or Canvass. The 'donate' page allowed donors who used the mobile app to donate. This option also helped the campaign build a quick donate program by optionally saving credit card information on file. According to data released by Bloomberg BusinessWeek, one-click donors gave four times as often and three times as much money as those solicited the traditional way. The campaign also resulted in a record number of one-click donors contributing $115 million, the majority of these donations coming via phones. The 'canvassing' option automatically opened a Google map of the neighborhood around the volunteer's location with a little blue flag at each house where the campaign planned to knock on the door. Tips for canvassers including their safety were listed in the apps. Some of the materials the volunteers needed to read before knocking voters' doors included:

- Safety first!
- Read the script ahead of time for a guide. Make sure you have an idea about how the conversation should go before you knock on the first door. Be conversational!

- Be friendly. Smile when someone answers the door. Introduce yourself and ask how they are. If you meet someone who is hostile or disagrees with you, politely thank them for their time and move on to the next house.
- Record your data. Mark their answers to your questions before moving on to the next house to ensure you capture all of it.

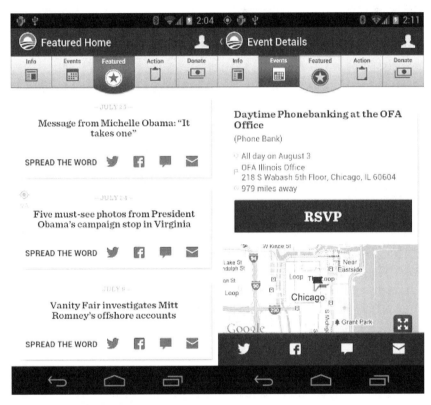

Figure 6: Some features of the Mobile Apps

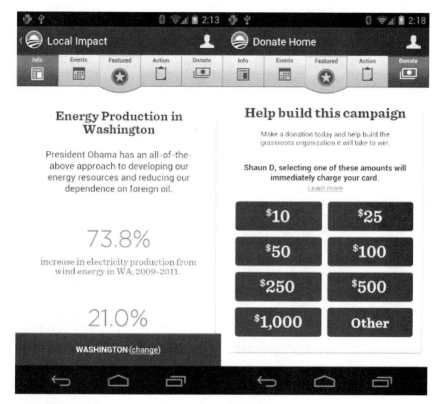

Figure 7: Additional features of the Mobile Apps

SOCIAL MEDIA

A few weeks after he launched the re-election campaign, the president wasted no time in jumping into the various social media networks. In April 2011, Obama joined Mark Zuckerberg, Facebook founder and CEO to host a town hall meeting answering questions on various issues, and reaching out to voters who were otherwise difficult to reach using traditional means. In June of the same year, he hosted the first "Twitter Town Hall" at the White House, answering questions about jobs and the economy with millions of young and tech-savvy followers, to test the potential of using social media for his campaign. The immense potential of social media was noted and the campaign began to develop various data mining tools and techniques to harvest millions of voters' information, for their fundraising, volunteering, as well as advertising efforts.

Facebook as a Virtual Door Knocking Tool: Utilizing a similar formula as the field organization, the use of Facebook to mobilize the get out the vote (GOTV) effort provided amazing results. The campaign developed various messages that could be shared with friends and family members who live in battleground states. These messages included information about registering to vote, where, when, and how to vote, why they should support the president and why these selected friends should vote, and information on the campaign activities with suggestions of ways friends can also get involved. Some of the contents of the messages were humorous, informative, included photos and videos, or charts and infographics. According to the campaign office, one in five people contacted through this method shared the content with friends and acted offline.

Facebook as a Platform for "Targeted Sharing": A protocol was developed by the campaign to search on Obama's supporters Facebook network to find voters, particularly those in the swing States and pursue them to register, volunteer, donate and vote. Hundreds of thousands of people downloaded the Obama for America app, and on the first page of the app, there was a disclaimer which stated, by clicking "visit Website" or "Send to Mobile" above, this app will receive your basic info, your email address, your profile info (birthday, likes and location), your photo your friends' profiles, their birthdays, likes and locations, photos shared with you. Anyone who visited the site or sent it to a mobile device got another request from the campaign to post on their behalf, including videos they watched, campaigns they donated to and access to posts in the newsfeed. This initiative resulted in over 1 million people downloading the campaign's Facebook App, which gave an ocean of information used to map voter files with friends' networks of its supporters. According to a report from Time magazine, in the final weeks of the campaign the Obama team used this information to ask supporters to directly contact their friends who were targeted voters in battleground States via Facebook, with specific requests to vote early, volunteer, donate and even watch a specific persuasion video. At the end of the campaign, more than 600,000 supporters shared items with an estimated 5 million individuals. The number of likes on Facebook pages for the campaign and the top three (Obama, Michelle and Joe Biden) shot up from 19 million to 45 million.

STRATEGY #6 RECRUITING THE BEST AND BRIGHTEST PEOPLE

The most innovative and surprising move by Messina was to surround himself with young, genius and energetic programmers, data analysts, statisticians, enterprise architects, content management experts, database administrators, marketing experts, pollsters, network infrastructure engineers and graphic designers, who spent their time experimenting different ways to scavenge and mine data from various sources, crunch them with different models and come up with tools and techniques used by field organizers, volunteers and campaign employees. Ben LaBolt, spokesman for the campaign called these people "Nuclear Codes". Jim Messina is quoted as saying, "Corporate Americaand Silicon Valley were knocking down the door trying to hire these guys". The day after the election, the president also acknowledged them by going to a campaign office and delivering the following tearful thank you message to staffers and volunteers around the country.

"So you guys ... I try to picture myself when I was your age. I first moved to Chicago at the age of 25 ... And so when I come here, and I look at all of you, what comes to mind is, is not actually that you guys remind me of myself, it's the fact that you are so much better than I was. In so many ways. You're smarter. You're better organized. And, you, you're more effective. And so I am absolutely confident that all of you are going to do just amazing things in your lives. And what Bobby Kennedy called the ripples of hope that come out when you throw a stone in the lake—that's going to be *you*.... I'm just looking around the room and thinking wherever you guys end up .... You're just going to do great things. And that's why even before last night's results I felt that the work that I had done, in running for office, had come full circle. Because what you guys have done proves that the work that I'm doing is important. What you guys accomplished will go on the annals of history and people will read about it .... but the most important thing you need to know is that your journey is just beginning… that is the source of my hope, the source of my strength and my aspiration. You lifted me up in each step. I'm really proud of that. I'm really proud of all of you."

The 4000+ people who worked tirelessly for the campaign were not only paid employees but dedicated soldiers who slept less, travelled more and delivered more than they were paid for. Even though it would be appropriate to list all of them, for the scope of this discourse, only the top twenty staffers' impressive political history as reported on public documents are summerized below.

CAMPAIGN MANAGER JIM MESSINA
Before leading the campaign, Messina was the White House Deputy Chief of Staff for Operations. He was Director of Personnel for the Obama-Biden Presidential Transition and National Chief of Staff for Barack Obama's 2008 presidential campaign.

SENIOR CAMPAIGN STRATEGIST/CONSULTANT DAVID AXELROD
Axelrod was a senior advisor to the President, the Obama-Biden Presidential Transition and senior strategist to Barack Obama's 2008 presidential campaign. He is considered the architect of the first election campaign and continued to be the lead advisor for the 2012 campaign.

DEPUTY CAMPAIGN MANAGER JEN DILLON O'MALLEY
O'Malley worked as executive director of the Democratic National Committee and was the 'battleground states' director on the Obama 2008 campaign. She also worked as deputy campaign manager on John Edwards' team when he ran for President after serving as state director on his Iowa caucus campaign.

DEPUTY CAMPAIGN MANAGER JULIANA SMOOT
Smoot was the White House social secretary, chief of staff to U.S. Trade Representative Ron Kirk, finance director on Barack Obama's 2008 presidential campaign as well as co-chair of the Presidential Inaugural Committee.

DEPUTY CAMPAIGN MANAGER STEPHANIE CUTTER

Before joining the 2012 campaign Cutter served as assistant to the President and deputy senior advisor at the White House, counselor to Treasury Secretary Geithner, chief spokesperson for the Obama-Biden Transition team, Senior advisor and chief of staff to Michelle Obama on the campaign, and communications director on both the Kerry-Edwards 2004 Presidential campaign and the John Kerry for President campaign.

SENIOR ADVISOR ROBERT GIBBS

Gibbs was the White House press secretary, senior strategist for communications and message on Obama's 2008 campaign, as well as communications director and senior traveling communications aide.

FIELD DIRECTOR JEREMY BIRD

Bird was the deputy director of Organizing for America, general election director on Obama's Campaign for Change in Ohio and during the primaries, he served as the Obama campaign's South Carolina, Maryland State and Pennsylvania field directors.

BATTLEGROUND STATES DIRECTOR MITCH STEWART

Stewart was the national director of Organizing for America, Virginia state director on the Obama 2008 campaign and Iowa caucus director during the 2008 primaries.

NATIONAL TRAINING DIRECTOR SARA EL-AMINE

Since joining the campaign during the Iowa caucuses in 2007, El-Amine has worked in 12 states, serving in every position within the field hierarchy at Organizing for America and Obama for America.

POLITICAL DIRECTOR KATHERINE ARCHULETA

Archuleta was one of the few staffers who did not work on the 2008 campaign. Prior to joining the campaign, she served as chief of staff to Labor Secretary Hilda Solis.

DEPUTY NATIONAL POLITICAL DIRECTOR YOHANNES ABRAHAM

Abraham was the national political director of Organizing for America at the DNC. He was also a field organizer on Obama's 2008 Iowa caucus campaign, served as GOTV director for the Virginia primary campaign, and as field director on the Virginia Campaign for Change.

POLICY DIRECTOR JAMES KVAAL

Kvaal was deputy undersecretary of education, special assistant to President Obama on the White House National Economic Council, senior fellow at the Center for American Progress Action Fund and policy director on John Edwards' 2007-08 presidential campaign.

COMMUNICATIONS DIRECTOR BRENT COLBURN

Colburn was Assistant Secretary for Public Affairs at the U.S. Department of Homeland Security, Director of external affairs at the Federal Emergency Management Agency and national spokesperson for the Presidential Inaugural Committee. He also served as the communications director on the Obama 2008 campaign in Michigan and Virginia.

PRESS SECRETARY BEN LABOLT

Before joining the campaign, LaBolt worked as communications director on Rahm Emanuel's run for Mayor of Chicago and assistant press secretary to President Obama. He Joined the Obama team in 2007 and held a variety of roles including spokesman for the primary in Ohio and deputy press secretary in the general election.

RESEARCH DIRECTOR ELIZABETH JARVIS-SHEAN

Before joining the campaign Jarvis-Shean worked as Special Assistant to the President and director of Research at the White House. She also worked as deputy director of content on the 2008 campaign.

CHIEF DIGITAL STRATEGIST JOE ROSPARS

Rospars worked as media director with Obama in 2008, and on Governor Howard Dean's presidential campaign Internet team, where he wrote and edited emails, worked on message development, online brand building and grassroots organizing.

DIGITAL DIRECTOR TEDDY GOFF

Goff led the creation and launch of the White House.gov website for the Obama-Biden presidential transition. He was a member of the new media team on Obama's 2008 campaign and director of new media for battleground states (Great Lakes and Ohio Valley). During the 2008 primaries Goff served on the campaign's mass email team.

DIGITAL ORGANIZING DIRECTOR BETSY HOOVER

Hoover worked as a field organizer in South Carolina and Pennsylvania primaries, and was a deputy field director on the Campaign for Change in Michigan in the general election.

The Dawn of a New Paradigm in Data Management, Forecasting and Voter Persuasion

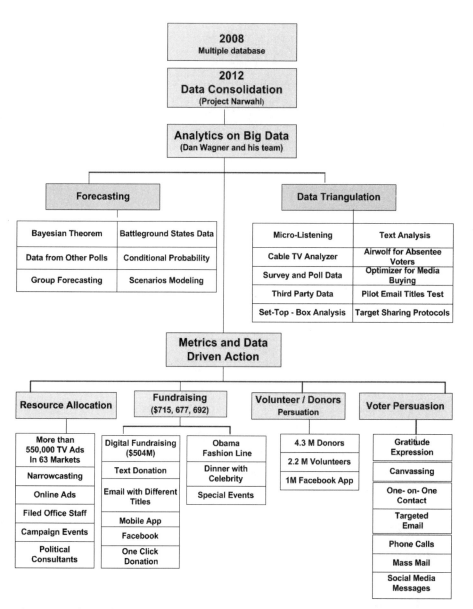

Figure 8: Obama's Campaign Data and Metrics Driven Decision Support System

"Data-driven predictions can succeed – and they can fail. It is when we deny our role in the process that the odds of failure rise. Before we demand more of our data, we need to demand more of ourselves" Nate Silver – Author of the Signal and the Noise

DATA AS THE NEW INTELLIGENT ENTERPRISE

THE NEXT WORLD WAR, (if it occurs) may not be only nuclear or biological but also Data Management Supremacy. Big data are the cornerstones for business, research, government and of course election campaigns. Analysis of big data has evolved from being a business initiative to a business imperative. As the population of a country grows, so too does the dataset used for everyday life, shopping behavior, customer interaction, social media and communications. Research reveals that organizations that achieve a competitive advantage with data analytics, are over two times more likely to substantially outperform their industry peers. In this global and dynamic world sometimes driven by intuitions, experience and gut instincts, data analytics may prove to be the GPS for success. As the industry becomes more complicated, so too does the size of data collected, in order to prevent any unplanned and unknown disasters. Modern passenger airplanes, according to an IBM report, are programmed with over one billion lines of code that generate about 10 terabytes (TB) of data per engine, during every half hour of operation. A single flight from London to New York generates about 650 TB of data giving the company a wealth of data mining opportunities for analyzing issues related to performance, disaster and optimizations. Political campaigns are also businesses that have objectives to achieve and the size, quality and quantity of data collected which is related to voter's history, preferences, donor's tendency and media coverage, are the starting point for success. The real issue here is how to identify, qualify, quantify and differentiate the noise from the signal, so as to be able to use the data for its intended purpose.

DATA TRIANGULATION

Triangulation is a method used to determine the location of a fixed point based on the laws of trigonometry. The law states that "if one side and two angles of a triangle are known, the other two sides and angles of that triangle can be calculated". Triangulation extends beyond its mathematical roots into social science research with a new definition: "a process of combining data from different sources to study a particular social phenomenon." Therefore, as one of the four basic types of triangulations identified in social studies (data, investigator, theory, and methodological), data triangulation is the use of multiple data sources in a single study. This was what was used by the Obama campaign - collecting seemingly unrelated personal data including voting records, Facebook friends and family information, twitted messages, consumer data, opinion polls data and social and professional networking information, into a single authoritative database to parse, dice, combine and uncover hidden relationship patterns and view trends over time. The team then transformed the data into information to produce tailored messages for the intended groups, motivate voters, design tools and techniques to capture supporters' attention and persuade them to vote for Obama.

OBAMA'S DATA MANAGEMENT - IT ALL STARTED IN 2007-2008

The data collection and management process for the 2012 campaign was founded on the complicated and vast data infrastructure developed for the Iowa primary in 2007, and later expanded for the 2008 general election. The work started months before the Iowa primary when cards signed by potential voters pledging to caucus for Obama were collected by canvassers and entered in the Voter Activation Network (VAN), a simple web application used as a front interface to input data to the main voter's database. In 2007, Dan Wagner, the chief analytics officer for the 2012 campaign, went to Iowa to work as deputy manager for voter files and he started to work on the VAN. This software uses a seven-digit identification code to track voters throughout their life. Isenberg called it "the political equivalent of a Social Security number" replacing the old clipboard voter lists and large wall maps used by previous campaigns. This was the first transformation of the voter data collection system from paperwork to digital. Once the data is entered in the system, the information is then synchronized with all associated databases to help canvassers avoid pursuing the same supporters twice. The information collected at the Iowa office along with that from many other states was uploaded daily to the central database. In his book "The Victory Lab", Sash Issenberg described Obama's 2008 campaign data collection and management system saying,

"Sandwiched between the heroic presidential candidate who positioned himself as uniquely able to loosen a nation's intellectually sclerotic politics, and the unrivaled hordes of volunteer activists and supporters who believed in him, sat one of the vastest data mining and processing operations that had ever been built in the United States for any purpose. Obama's computers were collecting a staggering volume of information on 100 million Americans and sifting through it to discern patterns and relationships. Along the way, staffers stumbled onto insights about not only political methods but also marketing and race relations, scrubbing clean a landscape that had been defined by nineteenth-century political borders and twentieth-century media institutions and redrawing it according to twenty-first century analytics that treated every individual voter as a distinct and meaningful unit."

As the caucus day approached, Wagner and his team developed an application that helped the campaign representatives to effectively manage the only public and complicated Iowa caucus in 1,784 precincts across the 99 counties, and helped Obama to be the winner. This practice was applied to the remaining primaries allowing the campaign to collect more delegates and Obama become the nominee. The campaign manager in 2008, David Plouffe reorganized the data management system to be effective for the general election. As a result, a two week long data mining and management training was organized in Oregon for sixty Obama staffers who had been involved in some form of data analysis task during the primaries, preparing them for the "dream job" of working in the data analytics department at the headquarters in Chicago. The boot camp was designed to walk participants through the existing database the campaign built as well as new analytical and forecasting techniques planned to be used to connect the dots, and show them how to provide strategic information to the campaign field offices. By the time the 2008 campaign came to a close, the Obama team had two million Facebook friends, 13 million email addresses, and 14.5 million hours of You Tube views. All the analysis tools, the massive voter database and a detailed 'lessons learned' document were used as the base for the 2012 election.

THE BEGINNING OF THE 2012 CAMPAIGN

The lessons learned document produced by the campaign after the 2008 election revealed that even though it was seen as one of the best and technologically advanced campaigns in political history, it did not use the massive amount of data collected to its maximallyin generating more votes and money. There were several disconnected databases owned by different departments and it was difficult to map information from one database to the other. The first step taken in the 2012 campaign was to establish a single authoritative database to allow seamless information transfer between major functions including voter registration, fundraising, GOTV activities, campaign ads, field operations, volunteer management, maintenance of potential voters in swing states, national database for voter's records, social media information and consumer behavior. This new consolidated database also helped the campaigners to allocate resources effectively, raise more money, recruit millions of volunteers and register many million voters. Based on publicly available data, the author provides a high level architectural roadmap – "*Data and Metrics Driven Decision Support System*"(figure 7) to help readers understand the process for gathering information, applying various analytic techniques and producing actionable information, which helped the campaign make informed decisions. The roadmap is grouped into three sections – data consolidation, use of analytic techniques and data and metric driven action. Each section is summarized below.

FIRST STEP – DATA CONSOLIDATION - PROJECT NARWAHL
Part of the lessons learned from Obama's 2008 campaign was that the team could have made even better use of the information they had during the campaign (records on 170 million potential voters, 15 million registered email addresses, 5 million friends on 15 social networking sites, 3 million donors, over a million volunteers and hundreds of field offices). Other than the email addresses of the 15 million supporters who signed up for online updates, little was known about their age, gender, voting record, how many of them had donated, how many had volunteered and what their preferences were. The campaign was sending mass generic emails again and again asking for donations to all these addresses. It was like a story of a bagger who sat for several years on a boxfull of gold but did not know of its contents until a stranger who passed by, asked him

what was inside. In the 2012 election using advanced technology like content analytics, the campaign was able to understand more about voters' preferences, fears and sentiments, and customized messages to address their issues were prepared. In order to accomplish this goal, the campaign launched what it called "Project Narwahl", to consolidate all stove piped databases into one giant authoritative database.

Before the Department of Homeland Security was created, over 15 intelligence and law enforcement agencies of the federal government, including the CIA and FBI, held enormous amounts of data on several variables, from terror suspects to tax evasion. These databases were kept separately and it was difficult to connect the dots to make proactive actions. Once the department was created, those databases were consolidated and agencies were able to share information to better coordinate their tasks. The objective of project Narwahl was similar to that of the Department of Homeland Security - to create one integrated data source. The next step Jim Messina took, was to build an analytic team five times the size of the 2008 campaign to find clues of voters' behaviors, their preferences, affiliations, age groups and others variables. Messina also established an in-house technology team that could do everything from designing the campaign applications, to developing and supporting the various web sites, analytic tools and applications. This effort was coordinated to track every conversation the volunteers had, every door they knocked on and every phone call they made.

SECOND STEP – USE OF ANALYTIC TECHNIQUES ON THE CAMPAIGN'S "BIG DATA"

At the beginning of the campaign, the team announced several data analytic positions to hire engineers and analysts. One advertisement listed on the Obama for America page read:

> "Obama for America is looking for Quantitative Media Analysts, Analytics Engineers, Battleground States Election Analysts and Modeling Analysts at all levels to join us now through November 2012 at our Chicago headquarters". The analytics department analyzes the quantitative, actionable insights that drive our decision making. We are a multi-disciplinary team of statisticians, mathematicians, software developers, general analysts and

organizers – all striving for a single goal: re-electing President Obama"

From the beginning of the campaign, statistical modeling experts built the data analytic team in order to help predict electoral outcomes. These models, in the campaign's view, were instrumental in helping determine the most effective use of its resources. Analytics engineers built the infrastructure that was used to efficiently produce accurate data products, including building data processing pipelines, integrating with new data sources, building web-based business process tools and generating reports to help monitor performance. Quantitative media analysts analyzed data to inform the paid media program including television and other outlets, throughout the campaign. The battleground state election analysts were responsible for analyzing and understanding campaign and political data, leveraging that understanding into strategic insights and communicating those insights to OFA state campaign leadership. They also helped to analyze data across channels by providing states with comprehensive strategic and tactical guidance based on the existing political database.

CONTENT ANALYTICS AS A DECISION SUPPORT SYSTEM

Content analysis is a technology developed to help organizations combine content gleaned from internal transactions with content from outside, including customer emails, blog comments and third party reports. The term content analysis has been coined to cover a range of advanced search, analysis and interpretation technologies used by organizations both in- house and on the Internet, to be competitive in a dynamic and complex economy. The challenges in searching for meaning across unstructured content from text email, tweets and social media conversations, forced the development of these smart analytic tools. They provide trend analysis, content assessment, pattern recognition and exception detection. As businesses and governments are increasingly engaging with employees, partners, vendors and other stakeholders across a range of electronic and social media to collaborate, find new ideas, measure sentiment, identify trends and predict future outcomes, the use of content analytic technology has become not only a necessity but also a must-have competitive tool.

The Obama 2012 team led by Dan Wagner worked on various content analytics tools including micro-listening to better understand individual voter's preferences and choices, dreamcatcher to analyze data from texts collected by the campaign and determine voters fears and hopes, cable TV(set-top box) analyzer to gather data about the TV programs viewed by voters, optimizer to help the campaign determinethe return on investment (ROI) for TV ads, Airwolf, a name used by the campaign for the software developed to map and match absentee ballot requests and inform the campaign who returned it on time and who did not, third party data analyzer to identify certain information from the consumer database and target sharing protocols to analyze Facebook users' networks to identify potential, persuadable voters in the battleground states. The following section summarizes these tools:

Project Dreamcatcher: How to identify voters' hopes and fears: Throughout the election period the campaign was asking voters to "share their stories" on why they want to be involved, how the work the president has done benefited them, stories about the economic crisis, the war in Iraq and Afghanistan, and many current issues. No-one thought that the thousands of memories would yield critical data on voter hopes, fears and aspirations. To materialize this vision a project called "Dreamcatcher" was initiated, with Rayid Ghani as a chief scientist. He specialized in building algorithms from various data sets including consumer shopping habits, to help businesses improve their sales. Even though there is little information about Dreamcatcher, it is believed to be a text analytic software designed to extract meaning from the unstructured contents of tens of thousands of personal stories sent to the campaign office, and to find out voters' sentiments towards the campaign, the opponent and the media. In industry, text analytics is used in conjunction with structured data to help explain results found. Some examples of where text analysis is used are sentiment analysis, fraud prevention and analysis of medical data to identify those patients most likely to be re-admitted. In sentiment analysis, text can be processed in dynamic mode allowing organizations to react to changes in real time.

Information from tweets and other social media can be collected, put through a sentiment analysis process, then sent to a database where it can be tracked over time to answer key questions like, whether a given tweet about the debate or any political ad was positive or negative and how voters' sentiments were changing over time.

Airwolf: This software was developed by the Obama campaign to help match the names and addresses of voters who requested mail -in-ballots and run searches with the email address in the campaign database. The exciting result according to Isenberg in his MIT article, was that "likely Obama supporters would get regular reminders from their local field organizers, asking them to return their ballots and once they had, a message thanking them and proposing other ways to be involved in the campaign. The local organizer would receive daily lists of the voters on his or her turf who had outstanding ballots, so that the campaign could follow up with personal contact by phone or at the doorstep".

Micro-listening and Micro-targeting – Treating one Voter at a Time: For several months, the Obama campaign built a massive database of almost everyone who voted for him in the previous election, picturing every voter in certain categories based on information obtained from public voter records, third party consumer data, social networking, conversations and others. This effort made targeting voters in certain geographical area, interest and age groups easy. It also helped the campaign office craft specific messages to either inform or educate voters on issues like auto bailout, the wars, equal pay, civil liberty and the new healthcare law. This technique was considered to be the best way to "treat voters one at a time" and is called micro-targeting. Below is a scenario the author built on how the campaign would have used micro-targeting to persuade voters.

"Mark Goldberg of Miami, 45 years old, is likely to donate online as he pays his bills online, shops online and uses mobile apps to download music and books. The best way to get his attention is to send an email by Jessica Parker offering him a chance to enter a raffle to eat dinner with her and the president. On the other hand

his neighbor Phil, will likely give more after receiving a phone call from a local Obama supporter, who can talk to him about common local issues surrounding the election. Using the set-top-box analyzer of cable TV usage, we found out that Susan, 38, a nurse from Aurora, Colorado watches Lifetime and Food channels in mid-late afternoons, so the best time to get her attention is to air campaign ads during these times. Tsigh, 40, lives in Las Vegas and did not register to vote. Her name was captured from her brother Berhanu's Facebook network. The best way to convince her to vote is to send a Facebook message to Berhanu who is a committed supporter and lead volunteer, to tell her and her friends in Las Vegas to register to vote and donate. Chris, 28, graduated from Ohio State, lives and works in Cleveland, Ohio and formed a book club with her 15 close conservative friends. At the beginning or end of their gathering, they discuss current political issues including women's reproductive rights. The best strategy to get her and her friends to commit to the new policy the Obama administration is pushing toward social issues, is to have a customized email sent by Stephanie Cutter, the campaign deputy manager, directly to their email addresses collected during the 2008 election."

With the 2008 campaign structure it was difficult, if not impossible, to send the above tailored messages to specific voters due to limitation of the database, or of the information in it and the techniques used. In this election, and derived from direct marketing and data mining techniques, political campaigners use micro-targeting as a method of tracking individual voters and to identify potential supporters. It is a predictive market segmentation tool that uses cluster analysis to segregate specific groups of voters, then prepare messages tailored to that particular group or individual to donate, take part in the discussion, fundraise, volunteer and ultimately vote. The means of communication for micro-targeting are direct mail, phone calls, canvasses, TV and Radio ads, social media messages, online ads, texts and tweets. Republicans were believed to have started the use of this technique when contacting voters for the 2004 presidential election. The Obama campaign used it for the 2008 election and *perfected* it for 2012. The method is used widely by big online companies like Amazon.com, which tracks purchasing habits of customers and recommends similar products, or Visa which focuses on consumer spending history. Both parties have their own databases - Voter Vault developed by the Republican National Committee and VoterBuilder, the Democratic National Committee's version. Third party databases used by the campaigns are Catalist, the left leaning database and Aristotle, the non-partisan version. Other third party sources of information used were Acxiom, Experian Americas, InfoUSA and Dun &Bradstreet. The political databases contained information about particular voters, including party affiliation, volunteer history, voting record and donation amounts. They were complemented with information from the third party databases on the identified voter's habits and preferences (as many as hundreds of variables), to create a profile for each person. Using this data, individual voter profiles were created and identified as "Likely Obama supporters", independents or "socially conservatives". Once the groups wre identified, tailored messages prepared for each was sent via several different means of communication.

STEP THREE – DATA DRIVEN DECISION MAKING
"A business decision based on actual data is priceless"

The last step in the Obama data and content analytics process was the application of the information extracted using all the tools and techniques above, to make informed decisions that would maximize the return on investment (ROI) on campaign money and time, and ensure that the goal the campaign set out to achieve was fulfilled. The result of this massive data analysis allowed the campaign to pinpoint the specific behaviors, preferences and needs of voters in age groups, neighborhoods and ethnic groups. The data analysis also guided the campaign in determining which special events (TV program, online forums, Podcasts and shows) to focus on, and especially which ones the president should appear on to appeal to certain groups of voters. This section covers how decisions were made to increase voter turnout, and donations and efficiently purchase TV ad-time from national and local media markets.

TELEVISION, RADIO AND ONLINE ADVERTISING

Presidential campaigns on average spend 80% of their budgets on broadcasting TV advertisements and, in this competitive market, having a strategy based on data analysis of the audience's preferred channels, type of shows and time of shows is a key to success. Comparing only campaign funds, Obama spent more money than his opponent. However, when combining the super PAC's and interest group's contributions, Romney spent more dollars on TV ads than the Obama group. The question raised by many was how the Obama team spent far less than Romney on ads aired by the same station during the same shows. For instance, $1,100 vs $200 were paid by the Romney and Obama campaigns respectively, for the ads aired the Sunday before Election Day on CBS's "Face the Nation" program on WRAL in Raleigh, North Carolina. The answer to this and other media buying strategies are summarized below.

1. *The use of "Optimizer"*, a very complicated program developed by the campaign, helped analyze and identify time slots that targeted persuadable users per dollar. According to many sources the Obama team had created its own television rating, based on the political leaning of categories of people the campaign was interested in reaching, thus allowing the campaign to buy its advertising on political terms as opposed to traditional industry terms. The Optimizer broke the day into 96 quarter-hour segments and assessed which time slots across 60 channels offered the greatest number of persuadable targets per dollar.

2. *Time of purchase:* While Romney battled the primaries, the Obama campaign locked those air times months before the election at cheaper prices, like airline tickets.

3. *Manpower to negotiate the labor intensive media market:* The Obama team had 30 full time media buyers who aggressively negotiated using their experience and connections, in contrast to the Romney campaign that had only one full time media buyer.

4. *GMMB's pioneering vision in media buying strategy:* During the 2008 elections, the Obama campaign hired GMMB, a

leading strategic advertising firm, to coordinate media advertising and campaign events. In this election, the company was again tasked with designing strategies to target TV media outlets, including TV Land which is often overlooked by political campaigns. TV Land is the home of original sitcoms and classic TV shows. Experts from GMMB were instrumental in finding the best deal and programs.

5. TV viewer's history from the "Set-Top Box": Set-top box is an information appliance device that contains a tuner and connects to a television set. Cable and Satellite TV companies track viewer history and analyze preferences and frequencies using third party companies. According to Jim Margolis, Obama's campaign senior advisor and managing partner for GMMB, the campaign used information from Rentrak Corp, a Portland based company that monitors digital boxes attached to TVs in households using satellite dishes, to get insight into viewer preferences.

NARROWCASTING

Narrowcasting is a method of dissemination of information to narrow audiences via radio or television broadcast, targeting specific segments of the public or geographical regions. In the final weeks of the campaign, polls showed a tight race in key counties of the swing states creating an environment to maximize the use of narrowcasting in these isolated regions. While the Romney campaign launched traditional TV ads across the board, the Obama team applied narrowcasting to target women on Lifetime, Food Network and shows like "2 Broke Girls", as well as on selected daily shows like ESPN for men. Millions of college football fans tuning in to watch various games weeks before the election, were bombarded by Obama advertisements, compared with the few ads aired by Romney. According to Tom Hamburger of Washington Post who cited a post-election analysis by Romney campaign operatives "from June through Election Day", the Obama campaign and its allies aired about 50,000 more ads than Romney and his associates. Another interesting report by Issenberg on how the Obama campaign used their narrowcasting techniques stated:

"Obama's media-buying strategy proved particularly hard to decipher. In early September as part of his standard review, Alex Lundry (who created Mitt Romney's data analytics unit), noticed that the week after the Democratic convention, Obama had aired 68 ads in Dothan, Alabama, a town near the Florida border. Dothan was one of the country's smallest media markets and Alabama, one of the safest Republican states. Even though the area was known to savvy ad buyers as one of the places where a media market crosses state lines, Dothan TV stations reached only about 9000 Florida voters and around 7,000 of them had voted for John McCain in 2008. This is a hard-core Republican media market", Lundry said. "It's incredibly tiny. But they were advertising there."

We do not know what the campaign saw when they advertised in this tightly Republican geographical zone. However, everyone including Romney's campaign staffers agreed that it was the smartest narrowcasting technique ever deployed and implemented by any political campaign.

FORECASTING
Can we trust the polls?

For the first time in recent U.S. presidential elections, the science of polling and its methodology (determining the population, use of sampling techniques and sampling frame, assumptions, lessons learned from the previous elections, analysis methods and the theory or framework underlining the technique), have come in question and were challenged by a young pollster, Nate Silver, who surprised the world by predicting 100% of the outcomes for both the presidential and senate races. Over 100 different pollsters crunched the poll numbers for 18 months feeding their results and analysis to news networks, campaign offices and the general public across the country. Polls taken the same weekend from the same state by two pollsters produced a wide margin of winning numbers for both candidates. Some of the pollsters were believed to have been (at least by many), influenced by their emotions and political views to favor one party or candidate over the other. After the election, one pollster who missed the prediction in a State poll by a wide margin, elegantly described it saying, "I was drinking the Republican Kool Aid". The election also reinforced the traditional data analysis question, "Is it the data or the statistician that lies?" The questions was why didn't a lot of people or groups pay attention to how Nate's prediction worked, even though they had been proven right in the 2008 elections? Was it partly because political analysts' and journalists' resistance or denial to learn a new concept? Or were they more comfortable in their own boxes focusing on the status quo approach of forecasting, which is based on covering events including speeches, conventions, voters enthusiasm level, debates, endorsements, image making, as well as political rhetoric, instead of examining the conditional variables iteratively as was done by Nate Silver and Dan Wagner to forecast the outcome.

On Election Day Jonah Goldberg, a conservative syndicated columnist, wrote an article on the American Enterprise Institute web page titled, *"Nate Silver's Number Racket"* to predict the outcome of the election as:

"The truth is any statistician can build a model. ... but ultimately, ... as the computer programmers like to say 'garbage in, garbage out'. Using his very complicated statistical model, which very few of his fans or detractors are said to understand, Nate predicted a decisive victory for Obama... I'm not saying Silver's just lucky or shoveling garbage. He is a serious numbers guy but so are folks at the University of Colorado's political science department whose own model is based on economic indicators. ... predict Romney will win, as do others..."

Who were the others that Jonah was referring to?

Since 1936, when Gallup correctly predicted Franklin Roosevelt's win over Alf Landon, hundreds of pollsters have been forecasting the outcome of political races for both the congress and presidential elections. In this election, over 42 pollsters (from ABC to Zogby), 21 poll blog sites (from Charles Franklin to Sam Wang), 30 plus academic pollsters (from ANES to Roper Centers including many universities), and more than six survey organizations (from AAPOR to WAPOR) have conducted surveys, interviewed voters, and crunched numbers to feed their results and predictions to news networks, election campaigns, special interest groups and others. The majority of these pollsters predicted Romney would win the election, while a handful of them thought otherwise. In the middle of this highly regarded and visible business, a young economist and statistician named Nate Silver who had developed a statistical model to forecast baseball performance and run the "Five-Thirty-Eight" blog in the New York Times, developed a statistical model to average and weigh many public polls, to produce probabilistic forecasts on which candidates was more likely to win. The model outperformed and proved wrong most traditional pollsters in its prediction of both the presidential and senate races which were found to be 100% correct. Nate had also predicted correctly, the outcome of the 2008 elections and only missed one out of the fifty states (Indiana by 1%). Not one of the well-respected traditional polls including Zogby, Rasmuss and Gallup had come close to the eventual results. On Election Night, according to a report by David Folkenflik of NPR, "*Nate stood tall while other prognosticators came up short*".

In the weeks and days before the election, Nate's daily tracking and predictions made Romney supporters uncomfortable and provided Obama supporters constant reassurance, even while being the center of media discussions. Joe Scarborough, in his Morning Joe show (MSNBC October 29, 2012), downgraded Nate's prediction saying, "Anybody who thinks that this race is anything but a toss-up right now is such an ideologue. They're jokes". Others called them "delusional wizards and citizens of Silly land". Fox News provided an analysis blasting Nate's method of forecasting, as a "simple excel sheet that tracks historic data and other polls and has no meaning." In an interview with the National Public Radio (NPR) days before the election, the managing director of Gallup also confirmed that their prediction was right and Nate's prediction would be proven false. Nate Silver's prediction on the nine battleground states days before the election is listed below.

	CO	FL	IA	NV	NC	NH	OH	VA	WI
POLLING AVERAGPPOLLING AVG.									
Dems	48.6	47.6	48.6	49.6	46.7	49.1	49.1	48.2	50.1
Reps	46.7	48.3	46.0	46.0	48.6	46.5	46.1	46.9	45.8
Margin	Obama +1.9	Romney +0.7	Obama +2.6	Obama +3.6	Romney +1.9	Obama +2.6	Obama +3.0	Obama +1.3	Obama +4.3
Adjusted Polling Average									
Dems	49.1	48.3	49.1	50.4	47.2	49.4	49.6	48.8	50.8
Reps	46.6	48.1	45.8	46.0	48.5	46.3	45.8	46.7	45.4
Margin	Obama +2.5	Obama +0.2	Obama +3.3	Obama +4.4	Romney +1.3	Obama +3.1	Obama +3.8	Obama +2.1	Obama +5.4
State Fundamentals									
Dems	48.8	46.2	49.2	50.1	45.5	50.9	47.7	48.2	50.9
Reps	46.7	49.3	46.3	45.1	50.1	44.3	47.7	47.4	44.4
Margin	Obama +2.1	Romney +3.1	Obama +2.9	Obama +5.0	Romney +4.6	Obama +6.6	Tie	Obama +0.8	Obama +6.5
New-Cast									
Dems	49.1	48.2	49.1	50.3	47.0	49.6	49.5	48.8	50.8
Reps	46.6	48.2	45.8	45.9	48.7	46.1	45.9	46.7	45.3

	CO	FL	IA	NV	NC	NH	OH	VA	WI
Margin	Obama +2.5	Tie	Oba-ma +3.3	Oba-ma +4.4	Rom-ney +1.7	Obama +3.5	Oba-ma +3.6	Oba-ma +2.1	Oba-ma +5.5
Projected vote share	+= 3.1		+=3.0	+=3.0	+=2.6	+=3.5	+=2.7	+=2.5	+=2.9
Dems	50.8	49.8	51.1	51.8	48.9	51.4	51.3	50.7	52.4
Reps	48.3	49.8	47.9	47.3	50.6	47.9	47.7	48.7	46.9
Margin	Obama +2.5	Tie	Oba-ma +3.2	Oba-ma +4.5	Rom-ney +1.7	Obama 3.5 +	Oba-ma +3.6	Oba-ma +2.0	Oba-ma +5.5
% of Winning									
Obama	80%	50%	84%	93%	**26%**	85%	91%	79%	97%
Romney	20%	50%	16%	7%	**74%**	15%	9%	21%	3%

Table 6: Nate Silver's prediction of the nine battleground states a few days before the election. Adapted from Nate Silver's Five Thirty Eight Forecast. Retrieved on January 6, 2012 from http://fivethirtyeight.blogs.nytimes.com/

Some of the conditional probabilities indicated in his daily simulated elections are listed below.

VARIABLE DESCRIPTION	PROBABILITY
Electoral College tie (269 electoral votes for each candidate)	0.2%
Recount (one or more decisive states within 0.5 percentage points)	6.4%
Obama wins popular vote	86.2%
Romney wins popular vote	13.8%
Obama wins popular vote but loses electoral college	0.6%
Romney wins popular vote but loses electoral college	5.3%

Variable Description	Probability
Obama landslide (double-digit popular vote margin)	0.3%
Romney landslide (double-digit popular vote margin)	<0.1%
Map exactly the same as in 2008	0.1%
Map exactly the same as in 2004	<0.1%
Obama loses at least one state he carried in 2008	99.6%
Obama wins at least one state he failed to carry in 2008	4.2%

Table 7: Conditional Probabilities Table. Adapted from Nate Silver's Five Thirty Eight Forecast. Retrieved on January 6, 2012 from http://fivethirtyeight.blogs.nytimes.com/

OBAMA'S 2012 CAMPAIGN INTERNAL FORECASTING MACHINE

After the 2008 election, Dan Wagner who built the data management and forecasting system for the campaign, joined the Democratic National Committee (DNC) as "Targeting Director" to replicate the success he had in the collection and analysis of voter information to help the president win the election. At DNC, Wagner used various statistical models (and later developed a software called Survey Manager), to identify voter's attitudes and preferences on how the party was doing, and he forecasted local and congressional election outcomes. According to Issenberg's report, Wagner's Survey Manager successfully predicted the result of special elections to fill an open congressional seat in upstate New York and the Massachusetts Senate seat election to replace the late Ted Kennedy. During his stay at the DNC, Wagner continued developing statistical models to predict Senate and congressional district races and his predictions' margin of error was 2.5%. When Obama launched his second re-election campaign, Dan Wagner returned to Chicago as Chief Analytics Officer to start what by many was called "the marvel of the campaign" – Data analysis. At the headquarters data center, Wagner and over 50 analysts used the huge amounts of data collected from various sources, to build different scenarios based modeling and run over 66,000 combinations of election scenarios every night, as they analyzed the probability of the President winning certain states, counties and cities. This type of conditional probability based on the Bayesian theorem was also the underlying architecture used in Nate Silver's predictions.

BAYESIAN STATISTICS – THE WAGNER AND SILVER FORECASTING METHODS

Forecasting of several presidential elections in the past, relied on one school of thought which dominated business – "Frequent Statistics" – that is, based on normal distribution, bell curves, few dependent and independent variables and assumptions. The approach used by Obama's campaign and Net Silver was the "Bayesian analysis". The theorem is based on conditional or evidential probabilities to identify what we know of the environment and past knowledge, to infer probabilities based on specific data to answer questions like "what is the likelihood of something happening, based on our knowledge of past conditions and the context of them in the world?" Net Silver defined this method as, "a mathematical formula" that helps us to think differently about our ideas and how to test them, help us become comfortable with probability and uncertainty and to help us think more carefully about the assumptions and beliefs that we bring to a problem. He continued "it is an algebraic expression with three known variables and one unknown one and this simple formula can lead to vast predictive insight". The formula contains prior probability, new event, and posterior probability. Bayes' Theorem is a simple mathematical formula used for calculating conditional probabilities.

VOTER PERSUASION

When Mr. Shawn Rux became a principle of Middle School 53, in Queens New York, the school was in disarray - with an F grade in performance from the New York Department of Education. The entire staff, including twenty-two teachers had quit, over 100 students had been suspended, and 50-60 played truant every day. To increase the level of attendance at the school, according to NPR reporter David Kestenbaum, the principle implemented new incentives for youngsters to come to school, incentives that were more obvious to middle school students – handing out raffle tickets to win an Xbox to anyone who showed up on time and issuing a type of currency called "Rux Buks", which teachers gave to students who behaved well in class. The currency was used to trade for school supplies and special lunches. In addition to these incentives, Mr. Rux stands outside school every morning, greeting students as they show up, a recognition and appreciation to the kids –and a subtle incentive to come to school. The result was amazing – the school went from an F to C, daily attendance went up to over 90% and one student said, "I like this school ... they treat me like home, they treat me nice, they always give me stuff. They always say "hi" in the morning".

Voters are like school children. They need incentives and convincing arguments to cast their vote. Today, when people have so little faith in one another, so little confidence in the willingness of elected politicians to get together, discuss and do what is right, winning every possible vote is critical to the success of a campaign. The voter turnout trend for presidential elections had been on the decline from 1960 until 2008. In addition to that, more and more voters identified themselves as independents and the search for more votes was a challenge for the campaigns.

The two major ways of attracting voters in recent presidential elections have been mobilization and persuasion. The debate by social study experts and political science scholars on how to develop new tools and techniques to attract voters to the presidential elections, started in the early 1920s when Harold Foote Gosnell, an American political scientist and author of many books on elections and political parties, ran field experiments to find out why people did not vote. His work was later picked up by Angus Campbell who studied the attitudes and opinions of the electorate in the 1948 election. Campbell's 1952 survey results were the source for the book "The American Voter", which later became a theoretical framework to base studies on electoral behavior on. This then yielded to the birth of the "The American National Election Studies", a leading academically run, national survey of voters conducted before and after elections to provide explanations of outcomes. A few decades passed before Samuel L. Popkin's book and theory *"The Reasoning Voter: Communication and Persuasion in Presidential Campaigns"* came to surface with a new approach, which argued that voters' activities also depended on behavioral psychology where, by and large, voters were uninterested in and not well informed about politics, yet they often voted in their best interests.

After the 1924 presidential election, Gosnell, who wrote the book, *"Negro Politician: The Rise of Negro Politics in Chicago"*, also considered whether not voting was a deliberate act or resulted perhaps from ignorance or a deficiency of public spirit or alienation. In his experiment, months before the presidential election, postcards were sent to selected sample voters underlining the importance of registering to vote. The people who received the postcards were found to be nine percentage points more likely to register. The experiment continued by sending two types of messages to those who did not react to the previous message. The first group received a non-partisan message to remind them of the urgency of registration, while the second received a cartoon describing non-voters as "slackers who failed their country when needed". The result was astonishing – both messages convinced voters to register and 75 percent of those who received at least one of the cards did so, compared with 65 percent who did not receive the messages.

In 2008, Donald P. Green and Alan S Gerber updated their book "Get Out the Vote", using various research findings from ten election cycles from 1998 to 2007. Their studies shed light on the effectiveness of the techniques used by consultants and campaign advisors and the potential for using new tools. They found that automatic (Robo) calls lead to only one vote per nine hundred calls, and that distributing flyers to neighborhoods and sending out mass emails to voters were old strategies that resulted in no or few voter turnouts.

In 2009, when Costas Panagopoulos, a researcher at Fordham University conducted a field experimental technique in a Staten Island New York special election to investigate the impact of gratitude expression on voting behavior, and whether thanking citizens for voting in the past stimulates their propensity to do again, he had no idea that his experiment would be groundbreaking for the new form of voter motivation tools, "Gratitude Expression". The result was astonishing – the mailer was far better at turning non-voters into voters than the traditional campaign election mail. This new phenomena caught the attention of Hal Malchow, the former Al Gore senate campaign guru who designed a political strategy and direct mail firm, in partnership with Panagopoulos and Our Community Votes, to explore the new adventure and replicate the experiment in more traditional election scenarios at New Jersey's 2009 Gubernatorial Election and Georgia's 2010 Primary Elections.

The experiment worked and the result matched the first one, validating it to be effective. After these findings, according to Issenberg, Hal Malchow used this technique and sent 1 million letters a few days before the Colorado U.S. Senate race to Democratic-leaning voters, resulting in the gain of 2,500 net votes. This was the tipping point for the Democrat Michael Bennett to retain the seat vacated by Ken Salazar who moved to Washington to become President Obama's secretary of the Interior. The letter had a similar message to that in the experiment, but the content was modified to thank the voters by name for having voted in 2008. It also stated that they looked forward to being able to express similar gratitude after the election. By the time of the 2012 elections, the technique had become a norm not only for political campaigns, but also for other Special Groups including Move On.org which used it to persuade voters to get active and engage in the political process. All of these techniques were used on potential voters by the Obama campaign.

Part Two

Variables That Affected the Election – Obama's First Term Presidency

_____

"You will be judged by your records
not by your rhetoric"

MY DAUGHTER WHO IS 9 at time of this writing, told me a story of a fifth grade boy at her elementary school who campaigned for the school presidency with the following promises:

1. I promise to put Coca Cola in water fountains throughout the school
2. I promise to make school days shorter
3. I promise to make class fun
4. I promise to get extra recess time to students

The majority of students voted for him and he became president. After a few months the students realized that nothing had changed and whenever they saw him in the school corridors, "they started to stick out their tongues at him and asked him to resign" my daughter continued. She said that "he was judged not by his rhetoric but by his records." At the beginning of the 2012 presidential campaign, some suggested that the election was a referendum on the incumbent while others lauded it as "the choice based on the accomplishments of the incumbent against the challenger", in other words, based on the record not rhetoric. This debate was the center point for the most part of the election season.

Two Paths - Prepared to Govern vs. Prepared to say NO

The story of Obama's first presidency started like this … on the evening of January 20, 2009 – Inauguration Day – when the president rolled from one ball to the other, with the expectation and hope that the next day he will start governing the country with a clear majority in both the House and Senate, *and* with a mandate from voters, 15 Republicans met at a restaurant in Washington DC to architect a strategy to deal with

Obama and his team. At the meeting they agreed to a number of measures: (a) challenge the president and democrats on every issue – say NO to every proposal, (b) stick together, (c) highlight any problem faced by a Democrat, (d) make Obama a "one term" president. According to Robert Draper's book *Do Not Ask What Good We Do: Inside the U.S. House of Representatives*, this group of 15 consisted of seven congressmen (Eric Cantor of Virginia, Kevin McCarthy of California, Paul Ryan of Wisconsin, Pete Sessions of Texas, Jeb Hensarling of Texas, Pete Hoekstra of Michigan and Dan Lungren of California); five senators (Jim DeMint of South Carolina, Jon Kyle of Arizona, Tom Coburn of Oklahoma, John Ensign of Nevada and Bob Corker of Tennessee); former House Speaker Newt Gingrich, Journalist Fred Barnes and communications specialist Frank Luntz.

Once readers revisit the conditions under which Obama's first term presidency started, part two of this book covers how the president handled various challenges from his own party and the Republicans, and how he was able to pass major legislation that later became variables for the 2012 election. These variables are the economy, the auto-bailout, financial regulations, health care, national security, civil liberties and campaign financing.

4

Chapter

The Economy

Imagine...
...The Sheriff of a small town asked you to rebuild a "looted store" and manage it. What do you do?

And imagine
...The Sherriff is you, the looted store is your country, the United States of America and the new store keeper is the person you have elected as President.
... Put yourself in his shoes and ride the wave he traveled on during the last four years to judge his performance.

WHEN PRESIDENT OBAMA took office on January 20, 2009, America was in the midst of a devastating economic collapse. The economy was in free fall, losing eight hundred thousand jobs per month. Unemployment was 7.8%, the auto industry was in bad shape, the deficit was $10.6 trillion (10,626,877,048,913.08 to be exact), the country was involved in two active wars that cost a few trillion dollars, stock markets were plunging, financial firms went under and once valuable securities lost most or all of their value, debt markets froze, good businesses shut down, big banks bet on people's saving and lost most or all of their value but the CEOs were rewarded with millions in bonuses while ordinary citizens were evicted from their homes, and a very hostile Congress seemed to put self-interest before the country and was poised to say NO to any effort to save the economy.

During the lame duck session, the first thing the president-elect did was to analyze the extent of the damage in order to find out ways to stop the bleeding by seeking advice from the country's respected economists, and to pick an economic strategy that would help pull the country out of the mess it found itself in.

WHICH SCHOOL TO CONSULT — FRESHWATER VS. SALTWATER ECONOMISTS — SMITH OR KEYNESIAN?

During this crisis there was a debate among economists to find the best way to pull the country out from the deep recession and into recovery. Economists fall into two main camps: saltwater economists (from universities located in the coastal region of the country like Harvard, MIT, and Stanford) and freshwater economists (from inland universities like the Chicago School of Economics), *or* followers of the Keynesian school of thought who believe in government intervention and neoclassical ideas such as Adam Smith's followers who believed in free market. The president and his close advisors sought professional opinions on the path forward and these two schools of thought gave two different options.

KEYNESIAN ECONOMICS: SUPPORT GOVERNMENT'S ROLE TO SAVE THE ECONOMY

During the 1936 Great Depression, a British economist John Maynard Keynes published a book titled *The General Theory of Employment, Interest, and Money,* where he argued that private sector decision sometimes lead to inefficient macroeconomic outcomes which require active policy responses by the public sector. In particular monetary policy actions by the central bank and fiscal policy actions by the government are taken in order to stabilize output over the business cycle. Economists under the Keynes umbrella argued that a lack of demand was the root cause of the economic problem shown during the Great Depression and as a result business had curbed their investment and production stalled. To re-energize the economy and give it a jumpstart, these economists called for a more robust fiscal policy, more government intervention and spending as a key solution. Keynes also argued against the idea of letting the market determine its own course and recover during a recession. Instead he favored active measures - the manipulation of public expenditure, taxes, and interest rates - to spur growth and employment. Keynes was not favored by neoclassical economists due to his disagreement with the Stock Market model which he labeled a "Casino", and his justification pointing out the danger of letting stock speculators dictate important business decisions for the market. His 1936 warning of too much dependency on speculation to the economy was confirmed during the 2007/2008 stock market and financial collapse. Here is what he had to say:

> "If I may be allowed to appropriate the term speculation for the activity of forecasting the psychology of the market, and the term enterprise for the activity of forecasting the prospective yield of assets over their whole life, it is by no means always the case that speculation predominates over enterprise. As the organization of investment market improves, the risk of the predominance of speculation does, however, increase. In one of the greatest investment markets in the world, namely, New York, the influence of speculation (in the above sense) is enormous.... Speculators may do no harm as bubbles on a steady stream of enterprise. But the position is serous when enterprise becomes the bubble on a whirlpool of speculation. When the capital development of a country becomes a by-product of the activities of a casino, the job is likely to be ill-done. The measure of success attained by Wall Street, regarded as an institution of which the proper social purpose is to direct new investment into the most profitable channels in terms of future yield, cannot be claimed as one of the outstanding triumphs of laissez-faire capitalism which is not a surprise."

THE NEOCLASSICAL ECONOMIC THEORIES – LET THE MARKET DECIDE ITS OWN COURSE

Many believed that the 2008 U.S and global recession was partly caused by interpretation of some neoclassical economic theories, which received plaudits over the last few decades and were used to help stabilize the economy allowing it to grow. However, the praise did not last long and the world saw an economic disaster from U.S to Greece, from Ireland to Italy, and in many Asian countries. The school of thought led by Milton Friedman of the University of Chicago, had a "monetarism doctrine" that underlined the importance of *less* government intervention. The argument from this group according to Paul Krugman, an economist and 2008 Nobel Prize winner for his work on *New Trade Theory*, and *New Economic Geography* is that a very limited, circumscribed form of government intervention – namely instructing central banks to keep the nation's money supply, the sum of cash in circulation and bank deposits, is all that is required to prevent financial depressions and that excessively expansionary policies would lead to a combination of inflation and high unemployment. In his New York Times article Krugman asked a question *How did economists get it so wrong?* and provided his assessments on the impact of following the neoclassical economic policy on the U.S economy as follows:

"It's hard to believe now, but not long ago economists were congratulating themselves over the success of their field. Those successes – or so they believed – were both theoretical and practical, leading to a golden era for the profession. On the theoretical side, they thought that they had resolved their internal disputes. Thus, in a 2008 paper titled *The State of Macro*, Oliver Blanchard of M.I.T, now the chief economist at the International Monetary Fund, declared that "the state of macro is good." The battles of yesteryear, he said, were over and there had been a "broad convergence of vision." And in the real world, economists believed they had things under control. The "central problem of depression-prevention has been solved," Robert Lucas of the University of Chicago declared in his 2003 presidential address to the American Economic Association. In 2004, Ben Bernanke, a former Princeton professor who is now the chairman of the Federal Reserve Board, celebrated the Great Moderation in economic performance over the previous two decades, which he attributed in part to improved economic policy making. Last year, everything came apart."

THE BATTLE OF THE MINDS: 200 ECONOMIST'S PETITIONED OPPOSING AND ANOTHER 200 IN FAVOR OF THE STIMULUS

On January 28, 2009, the New York Times and the Wall Street Journal posted full page advertisements sponsored by the Cato Institute against the quoted statement by President Obama, which stated that "there was no disagreement that we need action by our government, a recovery plan that will help to jumpstart the economy." The title of their petition was

With all due respect, Mr. President, that is not true. The content of the identical ads was:

> "Notwithstanding reports that all economists are now Keynesians and that we all support a big increase in the burden of government, we the undersigned do not believe that more government spending is a way to improve economic performance. More government spending by Hoover and Roosevelt did not pull the United States economy out of the Great Depression in the 1930s. More government spending did not solve Japan's "lost decade" in the 1990s. As such, it is a triumph of hope over experience to believe that more government spending will help the U.S today. To improve the economy, policymakers should focus on reforms that remove impediments to work, saving, investment and production. Lower tax rates and a reduction in the burden of government are the best ways of using fiscal policy to boost growth."

Ten days later on February 8, 2009, the Center for American Progress Action Fund submitted a letter to Congress signed by another 200 economists including six Nobel Prize winners in Economics, in favor of the stimulus. They argued that Obama's proposed stimulus plan would put the U.S back onto a sustainable long-term growth path. The six distinguished Nobel Memorial laureates among the 200 economists are Kenneth Arrow who won the Noble Prize in Economics in 1972 for his work on social choice theory and Arrow's impossibility theorem, as well as endogenous growth theory, Lawrence Robert Klein who received the Nobel Prize in 1980 for his work in creating computer models to forecast economic trends in the field of econometrics, Eric Stark Maskin who received the Nobel Prize in 2007 for his work in foundation of mechanism design theory, Daniel McFadden who shared the 2000 Nobel Prize for his work in developing the theory and methods for analyzing discreet choice, Paul Anthony Samuelson, the first American economist to win the Nobel Prize in 1970 for his work in developing many economic theories and Robert Solow who received the Noble Prize in 1987 in Economic Sciences for his contribution on the theory of economic growth that culminated in the exogenous growth model named after him. The content of their letter summarized the reason for their support:

"We the undersigned encourage Congress to pass quickly the American Recovery and Reinvestment Act of 2009 and stem the tide of rising joblessness. The United States is in a recession that threatens to be deep and protracted. Each month, employers are shedding hundreds of thousands of jobs. To stop the hemorrhaging of jobs and pull the economy back from the edge, policymakers must act quickly and decisively. A critical needed action is significant fiscal stimulus specifically designed to boost employment and economic growth. To this end, Congress and the new administration have put together an economic recovery plan of unprecedented scope and size. The $825 billion American Recovery and Reinvestment Act of 2009, is of the scale and breadth necessary to begin tackling the mounting problems faced by our economy. The plan proposes important investments that can start to overcome the nation's damaging loss of jobs by saving or creating millions of jobs and put the United States back onto a sustainable long-term growth path. We do not have the luxury of lengthy debate over the best course of action. This legislation may not be enough to solve all the economy's problems, but it is urgently needed and an important step in the right direction."

THE DECISION WAS TO USE *KEYNESIAN ECONOMIC THEORY TO STIMULATE THE ECONOMY*

During the Great Depression, the F.D.R administration launched a massive government investment plan as part of the "New Deal" using Keynes' economic principles. These policies helped the country to pull itself out of the Depression and into prosperity. Seventy three years later President Obama had no choice but to follow F.D.R's path to give the economy a jumpstart by using Keynesian economic theory – active government intervention, printing more money, spending heavily on public works to fight unemployment, giving tax breaks to the middle class and so on. Two European countries, France and Britain, also followed the same logic to support their economy.

THE STIMULUS PACKAGE

Two weeks before taking office, the president-elect went to Capitol Hill to build a bipartisan coalition for his stimulus package, which proposed to pump money into the economy to stabilize the sudden and sharp contraction of spending by consumers and businesses. He met with both Democrats and Republicans and underlined the urgency of the need for action with his message as "right now, the most important task for us is to stabilize the patient. The economy is badly damaged – it is very sick. So we have to take whatever steps are required to make sure that it is stabilized. This is not a Republican problem or a Democratic problem at this stage. It is an American problem and we're going to all have to chip in and do what the American people expect." On January 15, 2009, the House of Democrats presented the stimulus bill which included aid to all/some/various states for Medicaid costs, temporary increase in unemployment benefits, public work projects to create jobs, federal spending on schools and a temporary, new health care entitlement under which people receiving unemployment would become eligible for Medicaid. The bill was passed by the House on January 28, 2010 with a vote of 244 to 188, and not a single Republican voted for it. The Senate bill which differed somewhat from that of the House, included additional $70 billion to protect middle-class families who would otherwise have been hit by the alternative –minimum tax as well as tax credit for first-time home buyers. After days of debate, on February 9, 2009 the Bill passed with the help of three Republicans – the Senate voted 61 to 37 to pass their version of the bill. After a series of discussions between the House and Senate reconciled the difference and On February 17, 2009 the President signed the *American Recovery and Reinvestment Act* (the Recovery Act). At the signing, the president underlined the challenges to repair the economy that lay ahead saying:

> "None of this will be easy. The road to recovery will not be straight. It will demand courage and discipline and a new sense of responsibility that's been missing from Wall Street and the

way to Washington. There will be hazards and reverses along the way. But I have every confidence that if we are willing to continue doing the critical work that must be done – by each of us, by all of us – then we will leave this struggling economy behind us, and come out on the other side, more prosperous as a people."

WHAT WAS INCLUDED IN THE PACKAGE?

The bill was planned to preserve and create jobs, promote economic recovery, assist those most impacted by the recession, provide investments needed to increase economic efficiency by spurring technological advances in science and health, invest in transportation, environmental protection and other infrastructure that will provide long-term economic benefits, stabilize State and local government budgets, in order to minimize and avoid reductions in essential services and counterproductive states, and local tax increases. The three major categories of the bill with associated dollar amounts are tax cuts and benefits for millions of working families and businesses constituting $290.7B, funding for entitlement programs such as unemployment benefits with $244.0B and funding for federal contracts, grants and loans with $250B. A more refined category of the spending is outlined by the Congressional Budget Office (CBO) as:

- Providing funds to States and localities by raising federal matching rates under Medicaid, providing aid for reduction and increasing financial support for some transportation projects
- Supporting people in need by extending and expanding unemployment benefits and increasing benefits under the supplemental Nutrition Assistance program
- Purchasing goods and services – by funding construction and other investment activities that could take several years to complete, and
  - Providing temporary tax relief for individuals and businesses by raising exemption amounts for the alternative minimum tax, adding a new Making Work

Pay tax credit and creating enhanced deductions for depreciation of business equipment. Table 8 provides the detailed breakdown by category.

FUND DESCRIPTION	AMOUNT IN BILLIONS
Individual Tax Credits (First time Homebuyers. Transportation Subsidy Education benefits and Earned income tax credits)	131.8
Education State Fiscal Stabilization Fund. Student Aid , Training And Employment services, Aid for the Disadvantaged Special Education and Rehabilitative Service	91.9
Medicaid/.Medicare Medicaid Grants to States; Medicare HITCH Incentive Payments; Program Management	98.1
Making Work Pay $400 tax credit for working individuals; $800 for working Married couples	104.4
Transportation Highway Infrastructure. High Speed Rail Corridors. Grants For Railroads and Airports	37.2
Family Services Foster Care and Adoption Assistance; Child Support Food Stamp Program; Assistance for Needy Families	45.9
Energy Incentives Tax credits for energy efficient improvements to residences. Tax credits for alternative energy equipment. Electric Vehicles Tax Credit	10.9
Energy/Environment Energy Efficient and Renewable Energy Program Defense Environmental Clean-up. Electricity Delivery and Energy Reliability Program. Water and Related Resources Superfund Program	28.7

Fund Description	Amount in Billions
Economic Recovery Payments One-time $250 payments to Social Security beneficiaries. Railroad Board payments, Veterans payments	13.8
Manufacturing & Economic Recovery; Infrastructure Refinancing, Other Tax-exempt bonds to expand industrial development Bonds for investment in Infrastructure, job training, and education in high unemployment areas. Increased available New Market credits	7.3
Research & Development /Science Fossil Energy R&D. National Science Foundation. National Institute of Health	14.7
Housing Grants to States for Low-Income Housing in Lieu of Low-Income Tax Credits	5.6
COBRA Assistance with Continuation of Health Coverage	3.7
Housing Public Housing. Rental Assistance Programs. Homelessness Prevention Programs. Homeowner Assistance Fund	13.9
Agriculture Assistance for Farm and Aquaculture Revenue Losses Due to Natural Disasters and Trade Adjustment Assistance for Farmers	1.0
Health Centers for Disease Control & Prevention. Indian Health Services. Food &Nutrition Services	11.6
Other programs (public Safety; Family; Job Training/Unemployment	20.9

Table 8: Breakdown of Funds Paid Out by Category: Source
    http://www.recovery.gov

THE RESULT OF THE STIMULUS PACKAGE – DID IT REALLY WORK?

Four years after the bill was passed, many have argued and are still debating whether the stimulus had an impact on the economy or not. The answer depends on who provides the analysis. The report from the Obama campaign leading to the 2012 election showed that before the president took office, the economy was losing 800,000 jobs a month and that after the bill was passed the country saw 32 consecutive months of job growth, including the creation of more than 5 million new private sector jobs.

Scholarly research analysis on the impact

Many research institutions and universities have investigated the impact of the various components of the law on job creation/preservation, economic growth and other benefits. A meta-analysis of this research showed that the majority confirmed the positive impact of the bill in improving the economy ... some found a slight positive influence while others showed little or no difference on the economy. Researchers from University of California, Berkley, Massachusetts Institute of Technology (MIT) and Stanford University conducted a study to find out whether State fiscal relief during the recession had increased employment or not. The researchers found a significant positive effect on employment and that the matching funds they received from the federal government had increased employment. The National Bureau of Economic Research also published their findings of a study on the effect of the stimulus on the economy. Their cross-State analysis suggested that one additional job was created by each $170,000 in stimulus spending, and that aid to low-income people and infrastructure spending showed a significant positive impact. The Federal Reserve Bank of San Francisco published its research showing that the stimulus created two million jobs in its first year and 3.2 million by March 2011. The study also showed that spending in the private sector, States and local government, as well as the construction sector showed a significant positive effect. The Congressional Budget Office analysis also supported the same trend. A report from CBO showed that through the first quarter of 2011, the stimulus created between 1.6 million and 4.6 million jobs, increased real GDP by between 1.1 and 3.1 percent and reduced unemployment by between 0.6 and 1.8 percent. This study was in line with the Executive Office of the President Council of Economic Advisers' November 2010 report which showed the following contribution of the stimulus package on the overall economy: (a) Real GDP began to grow steadily starting in the third quarter of 2009 and private payroll employment increased on net by nearly 1 million from the start of 2010 to the end of the third quarter, and (b) The stimulus raised the level of GDP as of the third quarter of 2010, relative to what it otherwise would have been, by 2.7 percent.

A survey of over 40 economists across the country by the University Of Chicago's Booth School of Business showed that 80% of the survey participants said that the unemployment rate at the end of 2010 was lower than what they believed it would have been without the stimulus. Another question the economists were asked was whether the cost of the stimulus exceeded the benefit and nearly half of the respondents answered 'no', while 27 percent were uncertain about the effect. These economists were from the major universities in the nation including Harvard, MIT, Yale, Berkeley, Chicago, Princeton and Stanford.

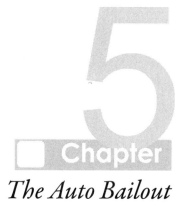

Chapter 5

The Auto Bailout

Public support for the bailout:

2009 – 37%

2012 – 56%

2008

"Spending billions of additional federal tax dollars with no promise to reform the root causes crippling automakers' competitiveness around the world, is neither fair to taxpayers nor sound fiscal policy." *John Boehner, Speaker of the House, November 12, 2008*

—

"These rescue loans are necessary – not to reward bad decision-making in Detroit, but to protect 3 million American jobs, 3 million livelihoods, 3 million families depend on the automakers. Are we really willing to put those workers at risk in this deep recession, after a month in which our country just lost 533,000 more jobs?" *House Majority Leader Steny H. Hoyer*

—

"Let Detroit Go Bankrupt." – *Mitt Romney, November 18, 2008*

—

"With one in 10 American jobs tied to the auto industry, we must provide this jump-start for an industry that is essential to our nation's economic health.." *Nancy Pelosi, December 10, 2008*

—

"While government has a responsibility not to undermine the private enterprise system … If we were to allow the free market to take its course now, it would almost certainly lead to disorderly bankruptcy and liquidation for the automakers." *President Bush*

2009

"We cannot, and must not, and we will not let our auto industry simply vanish. This industry is like no other – it's an emblem of the American spirit; a once and future symbol of America's success. It's what helped build the middle class and sustained it throughout the 20th century.." *President Obama, March 2009*

2012

"My plan was to rebuild the auto industry and take it through bankruptcy" … *Mitt Romney September 2012*

—

"Bin Laden is dead and General Motors is alive." – *Vice President Joe Biden*

—

"I said I believe in American workers. I believe in this American industry, and now the American auto industry has come roaring back." – *President Obama at the DNC*

—

THE YEAR 2009 was a historic one for the auto industry like many sectors of the U.S. economy. The bankruptcy of General Motors Corporation, Chrysler LLC and hundreds of parts suppliers caused the closing of many assembly plants and worker buyouts, crippling more than 1,700 suppliers with close to a million employees, the market domination of foreign cars, the collapse of world credit markets and less demand for new cars, increasing fuel price and less demand for SUVs and a 20-30% decline in car sales for the big three from the previous years. The crisis in the housing and financial market spilled over to the auto industry and as the Congressional Research Services report indicated, the swift demise of the credit market alone would have precipitated a crisis for automakers, because auto sales are heavily dependent on adequate financing for dealers and consumers. In addition, General Motors and Chrysler were in a precarious financial state before the fall of 2008, and the tightening of credit made it impossible for them to raise private funds to keep their operations afloat. Executives from GM, Chrysler and Ford submitted a request for federal financial assistance to help the auto manufacturing sector. Ford later dropped its request after the company got a private investor to support its production. The two remaining companies asked for $25 billion in loans from the federal government. Leading to the decision on the loan in November 18, 2008 before the Senate Banking, Housing and Urban Affairs Committee, two different views to solve the problem were discussed.

The first was presented by the then Chairman and CEO of GM, Rick Wagoner, who argued that the failure was mainly due to the global financial crisis and that if the loan was granted, GM would use it effectively to pay for essential operations, new vehicles and power trains, wages and benefits, as well as for research development of new models that are fuel efficient. The second view came from scholar and economist Peter Morici from the University of Maryland, who argued for Chapter 11 as the solution saying, "it may not be fair, it may not be what we would want to see but it is inevitable ... and I don't think giving these guys $25 billion right now is a smart idea.." Governor Romney also wrote an article on the New York Times opinion page on November 18, 2008 opposing the bailout. This was believed by some to be the key factor for him losing Ohio and the presidency.

"LET DETROIT GO BANKRUPT"

"If General Motors, Ford and Chrysler get the bailout that their chief executives asked for yesterday, you can kiss the American automotive industry goodbye. It won't go overnight, but its demise will be virtually guaranteed. Without that bailout, Detroit will need to drastically restructure itself. With it, the automakers will stay the courses – the suicidal course of declining market shares, insurmountable labor and retiree burdens, technology atrophy, product inferiority and never-ending job losses. Detroit needs a turnaround, not a check. I love cars, American cars. I was born in Detroit, the son of an auto chief executive.... You don't have to look far for industries with unions that went down that road. Companies in the 21st century cannot perpetuate the destructive labor relations of the 20th. This will mean a new direction for the U.A.W., profit sharing or stock grants to all employees and a change in the Big Three management culture. A managed bankruptcy may be the only path to the fundamental restructuring the industry needs. It would permit the companies to share excess labor, pension and real estate costs. The federal government should provide guarantees for post-bankruptcy financing and assure car buyers that their warranties are not at risk. In a managed bankruptcy, the federal government would propel newly competitive and viable automakers, rather than seal their fate with a bailout check." *Governor Romney ,November 18, 2008*

In reaction to the September 2008 market panic, the *Troubled Asset Relief Program* (TARP) was created by the Emergency Economic Stabilization Act and signed into law by President Bush on October 2008. The act authorized the Secretary of the Treasury to either purchase or insure up to $700 billion in troubled assets owned by financial firms, for a maximum of two years from the date of enactment. The general concept according to the Congressional Research Service was that by removing such assets from the financial system, confidence could be restored and the system could resume functioning. The four major areas the fund was allocated to were banking support, credit markets, housing and other programs. A fraction of this fund was allocated to the auto bailout project. To have a better understanding of the fund allocation and the portion of the auto bailout, a brief summary of major funds covered under this program is listed below.

Banking Support program: (a) Capital Purchase Program (CPP) – $205 billion used to purchase preferred shares in banks, (b) Targeted Investment Program (TIP) – $40 billion used only for Citigroup and Bank of America exceptional preferred share purchase, (c) Community Development Capital Initiative (CDCI) – $0.57 billion for banks that target their lending to low-income, underserved communities and small businesses.

Credit Market Programs: (a) Public Private Investment Program (PPIP) – $21 billion allocated to provide funds and guarantees for purchases of mortgage-related securities from bank balance sheets, (b) Term Asset-Backed Securities Loan Facility (TALF), (c) Section 7(a)

Securities Purchase Program – $0.37 billion used to support the Small Business Administration's (SBA) Section 7(a) loan program.

Other Programs: (a) AIG Assistance (Systemically Significant Failing Institution Program) $67.84 billion, (b) Automobile Industry Support$79.7 billion – initially provided loans to support General Motors (GM) and Chrysler and later included preferred share purchase from the auto financing company (GMAC), now called Ally Financial and a loan for Chrysler Financial. This program resulted in a majority government ownership of GM (60.8%), GMAC (74%) and small portion of Chrysler (9.9%).

Housing Programs: (a) Home Affordable Modification Program (HAMP) – $29.9 billion planned and as of 2012 only $4 billion was disbursed. This program was supposed to reduce the financial burden on homeowners, (b) Hardest Hit Fund (HHF) provides aid to State housing finance programs in States with high unemployment rates, as well as for the eighteen States and DC which were experiencing steep declines in house prices. Unfortunately, out of the $7.6 billion planned to be used in 2012, only $1.5 billion has been used, and (c) FHA Short Refinance – planned to promote refinancing of mortgages on "underwater" properties, to those where the mortgage balance is greater than the current value of the house, if lenders agree to forgive some of the principal balance owed on the mortgage. This program also used only $0.06 billion out of the planned $8.1billion.

In November 2008, the House and Senate leadership requested that the auto companies needed to provide more detailed plans including how they would use the loan, as well as information on the scope of their restructuring plan. On December 2, 2008, these companies presented their plans outlining their vision for their companies. Below is a summary of the restructuring plans presented to Congress.

General Motors: the company representatives announced that GM had begun its business process re-engineering (BPR) by designing more fuel-efficient and world class competitive vehicles. They had already spent $62 billion for research and development and for corporate transformation. They pointed out that had it not been for the collapse of the U.S. economy, the company would not have needed the government loan. GM estimated the planned spending for the remaining weeks of

2008 and through 2009 to be a total of $18 billion with a substantial downsizing of the labor force using various means including buyouts. The company's workforce in 2000 was close to 191,000 and by the end of 2008, the number was 96,500. The management planned to eliminate 20-30 thousand more by 2012. The plan also called for closing nine powertrain, stamping and assembly plants in the US reducing the total number of plants to 38. The other key aspect of their restructuring was to sell or downsize four of the eight brands (Hummer, Saab, Saturn, and Pontiac).

Chrysler: According to the Chrysler restructuring plan submitted to Congress, the company would focus on implementing cost reduction and modifications to its capital structure to improve its balance sheet, and on developing a fuel-efficient production portfolio that would meet customer expectations and governmentally imposed environmental requirements. In addition, the company signed a non-binding letter of intent to establish a "global strategic alliance" and give Fiat an initial 35% equity interest. The restructuring action also included workforce reduction of 32,000, discontinuation of 4 models, reduction of 12 manufacturing shifts, 30% capacity reduction to 1.2 million units and sale of $700 million in non-earning assets. Many concessions from key stakeholders of the companies were also identified including suspending the 401 K match, performance bonuses, merit increase, and eliminating retiree life insurance benefits, various forms of dealers, suppliers and shareholders concessions.

Ford: Unlike GM and Chrysler, Ford did not ask for the bailout money. Instead the company requested a "stand-by" line of credit in the amount up to $9 billion at government borrowing rates, for a 10 year term to support the restructuring plan which included the acceleration of products that consumers want and value. Unlike the GM CEO who blamed his company's situation on the financial crisis rather than the failure of leadership vision, Ford officially admitted that they took a shared responsibility for the crisis saying, "as a company and as an industry, we readily admit that we have made our share of mistakes and miscalculations in the past. We would ask congress to recognize, however, that Ford did not wait until the current crisis to begin our restructuring effort, and that much of what we describe below are actions we have taken and decisions we have made about the future that have already put us on a path to long-term viability." Some of the steps in Ford's restructuring included selling three brands (Aston Martin, Jaguar, Land Rover) and majority ownership of Mazda, negotiating a transformational labor agreement with the United Auto Workers (UAW) to lower wages and flexible work rules, cutting operating costs in North America by $5 billion, closing 17 plants and downsizing 12,000 salaried and 45,000 hourly employees in North America alone and converting three truck assembly plants to small car production.

In support of this request, a bill to provide auto companies with up to $25 billion in direct loans from the TARP was proposed by Harry Reid, the Senate Majority Leader. The bill was approved by the House on December 10, 2008 authorizing $14 billion in direct loans with the creation of the "Car Czar" to oversee compliance by borrowing companies. However, it did did not get Republican support in the Senate, forcing President Bush to issue presidential action to support the troubled auto industry. In his December 19, 2008 speech, the president broke ranks from the traditional Republican stand to support the aid as he stated, "while government has a responsibility not to undermine the private enterprise system ... if we were to allow the free market to take its course now, it would almost certainly lead to disorderly bankruptcy and liquidation for the automakers."

This action allowed $13.4 billion in loans ($4 billion each for GM and Chrysler) for December 2008 and January 2009 and in January GM received an additional $5.4 billion. According to the Congressional Research Service, these three loan installments were taken from the remaining $350 billion TARP fund. Later the administration made the third projected loan of $4 billion "contingent on Congress action" and approved by the Senate.

ACTION BY THE OBAMA ADMINISTRATION – "MANAGED BANKRUPTCY WITH THE BAILOUT OPTION"

Bankruptcy helps troubled companies to rearrange their capital structure so as to allow those that should survive to continue service and those that should fail to fail. The fundamental criteria for bankruptcy are economic and based on whether the troubled company, with the help of reorganization and capital injection, could become profitable or not. Bailout, on the other hand is considered a means of rescuing failing companies where other variables including social implications, unemployment as well as politics tend to mix with and override fundamental economic considerations.

The choice the new Obama administration was faced with when the president took office in January 2009, was whether "to let the auto industry vanish or bail it out." There was sharp disagreement among politicians on how to solve the problem – some said 'let Detroit go bankrupt' and others argued for restructuring and saving the three million jobs involved. This was a choice between applying the pure economic decision and letting the companies go bankrupt or taking a more broader approach that considered other variables including restructuring the organization and their social support system. Obama's first significant decision was not to appoint the 'Car Czar' as planned by the previous administration. Instead he created a "Car Industry Task Force" and appointed Steven R. Rattner to lead the team, asking him to come up with recommendations for the next step. In his book "*Overhaul: An Insider's Account of the Obama Administration's Emergency Rescue of the Auto Industry*", Rattner recounts that he was given only five weeks to bring a 'path forward' plan for the crisis. The second decision Obama took, was to force the resignation of the General Motors Chairman, Rick Wagoner, followed by rejecting both of the company's recovery plans which had been submitted to the previous administration.

Announcing his rescue plan for the auto industry, Obama summarized the importance of supporting it saying:

"We cannot, and must not, and we will not let our auto industry simply vanish. This industry is like no other – it's an emblem of the American spirit, a once and future symbol of America's success. It's what helped build the middle class and sustained it throughout the 20th century. It's a source of deep pride for the generations of American workers whose hard work and imagination led to some of the finest cars the world has ever known. It's a pillar of our economy that has held up the dreams of millions of our people. And we cannot continue to excuse poor decisions. We cannot make the survival of our auto industry dependent on an unending flow of taxpayer dollars. These companies – and this industry – must ultimately stand on their own, not as wards of the State. And that's why the federal government provided General Motors and Chrysler with emergency loans to prevent their sudden collapse at the end of last year – only on the condition that they would develop plans to restructure. In keeping with that agreement, each company has submitted a plan to restructure. But after careful analysis, we've determined that neither goes far enough to warrant the substantial new investments that these companies are requesting. And so today I'm announcing that my administration will offer GM and Chrysler a limited additional period of time to work with creditors, unions and other stakeholders to fundamentally restructure in a way that would justify an investment of additional taxpayer dollars. During this period they must produce plans that would give the American people confidence in their long-term prospects for success."

His task force team also informed GM to come up with an agreement to reduce debt to bondholders by two thirds, and strike a deal with the United Auto Workers to shift some of the health care costs to the union within 60 days. On the other hand, the task force recommended that Chrysler may not have the necessary resources to continue as an independent company and was given one month to complete the partnership plan with Fiat which had been submitted at the end of 2008. Moreover, the company was told to take tougher decisions similar to those made by GM. On April 30, 2009 Chrysler filed for bankruptcy with the plan to enter into an alliance with Fiat and a few months later in June, Chrysler completed the deal with Fiat and came out of bankruptcy – quick in and quick out. The move was considered by some to be one of the fastest bankruptcy trips. For GM, it was a more painful decision. As a result of the extreme conditions imposed by the government, the company filed bankruptcy on June 1 with the president promising to create a more dynamic company. The new GM in which the government now had a 60% share, was designed to have just 12 factories with less than 40,000 workers in the US. In addition to the $19.4 billion they received, new federal aid in the amount of $30.1 billion from the US government and only $9.5 billion dollars from the Canadian government was pumped in to revitalize the new company. The 40-day bankruptcy period for GM ended on July 10 after the company sold its assets to a new GM along with the three top brands – Chevrolet, Cadillac, and GMC . They got rid of Saturn, Hummer, Opel and Pontiac, and established a smaller network.

THE RESULT

The result of the auto bailout has been interpreted in different ways. For the conservative, the action was considered part of Obama's government power consolidation to increase government's role in controlling the economy and interfering in the movement of the free market. On the other hand for the liberal and progressive, the action was considered as selecting the better of two bad choices. A comment from the American Prospect summarized the reaction as:

> "While he (Obama) did not particularly want the government running car companies, the alternative was to let them go out of business right at the moment when the economy was reeling from the worst downturn since the Great Depression. At stake were not only the jobs of all GM and Chrysler employees, but the jobs of people who worked for hundreds of suppliers, from stereo manufacturers to steel and rubber producers. Estimates of the potential job losses topped one million. So he did what had to be done."

ON THE ECONOMY

Some numbers indicative of the effect of the bailout on the economy are summarized below.

- The Center for Automotive Research found that the government's involvement in the automotive industry saved 1.14 million jobs and $96.5 billion in personal income in 2009.

- The same study indicated that in 2010 around 314,400 jobs were saved by the bailout, and that the loans to GM and Chrysler allowed $28.6 billion in social security and income taxes to be paid back to the federal government.
- Public opinion survey conducted by Pew Research on the bailout [by the government] found a 19% increase in support from 37% in 2009 to 56% in 2012.
- In the first quarter of 2011, GM reported its first profit in three years and Chrysler reported a positive cash flow.
- In 2012 through September, GM's and Ford's North American operations earned a combined $11.95 billion in pretax profit pushing their shares to the highest level since April. U.S. light-vehicle sales rose 14 percent in 2012 (through October) and Ford reported that the company is on pace to produce 14.5 million units, the best achievement since 2007.
- The auto industry contributed 18 percent of the 2.2 percent average rate of growth for gross domestic product (GDP) in the recovery which began from the third quarter of 2009 to the second quarter of 2012.
- The unemployment rate in Ohio which had reached 10.6 percent went down to 7 percent in September 2012. In Michigan, it went from 14.2 percent in August 2009 to 9.3 percent in September 2012.
- According to the Bloomberg report, auto jobs have increased about 15 percent in Ohio and 33 percent in Michigan from July 2009 to September 2012 when GM was emerging from bankruptcy.
- The January 2013 data from the Bureau of Labor Statistics shows the auto industry employs 3.6 million Americans.

On the 2012 election - without the auto bailout, Ohio would have been leaning in favor of Republican challenger.

Michigan and Ohio hosted 65 percent of General Motors (GM) and Chrysler factories, and in Ohio one in eight people worked in auto related businesses. The impact of the bailout on the election was clear.

Many analysts, including Peter Brown, assistant director of the Quinnipiac University Polling Institute, agreed that without it, Ohio would most likely have been leaning in favor of Republican challenger Mitt Romney and that it could ultimately decide the presidency. At the Democratic National Convention in Charlotte, North Carolina, when the president told the crowd, "I said I believe in American workers, I believe in this American industry, and now the American auto industry has come roaring back", few had anticipated that he was ready to take the auto bailout deal to Ohio and battle ground States. It seems apparent that the decision by the president to bailout GM and Chrysler, Romney's comment "Let Detroit Go Bankrupt" and the last TV ad about Jeep taking its production to China, was a deal breaker to win Ohio and ultimately the presidency. In one of his weekly addresses president Obama summarized the path to success of the auto industry with the help of the government saying:

"Just a few years ago, the auto industry wasn't just struggling – it was flat-lining. GM and Chrysler were on the verge of collapse. Suppliers and distributors were at risk of going under. More than a million jobs across the country were on the line – and not just auto jobs, but the jobs of teachers, small business owners and everyone in communities that depend on this great American industry. But we refused to throw in the towel and do nothing. We refused to let Detroit go bankrupt. We bet on American workers and American ingenuity, and three years later, that bet is paying off in a big way. Today, auto sales are the highest they've been in more than four years. GM is back. Ford and Chrysler are growing again. Together, our auto industry has created nearly a quarter of a million new jobs right here in America. And we're not just making more cars and trucks – we're making better ones."

Chapter 6

Financial Crisis and Regulation

"In the fall of 2008, America suffered a devastating economic collapse. Once valuable securities lost most or all of their value, debt markets froze, stock markets plunged and storied financial firms went under. Millions of Americans lost their jobs, millions of families lost their homes and good businesses shut down. These events cast the United States into an economic recession so deep that the country has yet to fully recover."

—Report from the United States Senate Permanent Subcommittee on Investigations titled *Wall Street and the Financial Crisis: Anatomy of Financial Collapse" April 13, 2011*

CLOSING THE FLOOD GATE IN THE WALL STREET HISTORY

WITH AN OVER $4.9 trillion contribution to the 2011 Gross Domestic Product (GDP), the finance and related sectors (insurance, real estate, rental and leasing industry) play a central part in the nation's economy. When the U.S economy was hit by a wave of crises in the final two months of the 2008 presidential election, the financial sector was in the eyes of the hurricane, the scale and severity of a damage seen in many decades. This led millions of Americans to become unemployed, customer confidences dropped to its lowest point, and precipitated the loss of trillions of dollars in wealth. The law in place to regulate this sector according to a White House report was "fragmented, antiquated, and allowed large parts of the financial system to operate with little or no oversight".

60 YEARS OF PROTECTION AND TWO DECADES OF ASSAULT ON FINANCIAL REGULATIONS

In 1929, the U.S. stock market collapsed as a result of banks mixing commercial and investing activities, and taking high risks with depositors' money thereby causing the country to drift into the Great Depression. In 1933, Congress passed the Banking Act of 1933, later called the Glass Steagall Act after the co-sponsors of the Bill – Senator Carter Glass and Representative Henry B. Steagall – and was signed by President Franklin D. Roosevelt. For over sixty years the legislation enforced banks, investment banks, securities firms and insurance companies to operate separately. This meant that commercial banks would only accept depositors' money and make loans and investment banks would only underwrite and sell securities. The Act also created the Federal Deposit Insurance Corporation known as the FDIC to insure bank deposits of commercial banks. In addition, federal and State laws limited federally-chartered banks from branching across State lines giving opportunity for the mid-sized banks to flourish and as a result over 15,000 regional, local and thrift banks, as well as over 13,000 regional and local credit unions were serving their local communities across the county.

Under tremendous lobbying pressure by the banking industry to elected officials in Congress, starting mid-1990 substantial changes were made to the law, including relaxing the rules under which banks operated and the level of risk they could take. In 1994, Congress authorized interstate banking permitting federally chartered banks to open branches nationwide. This action alone shrank the regional and local banks from 15,000 to 8,000 and regional and local credit unions from 13,000 to 7,500. In November 1999, Congress reversed what a New York Times reporter called "one of the key elements of the Depression-era banking law", by knocking down the firewall between commercial banks which take deposits and make loans, and investment banks which underwrite securities. The same law also exempted investment bank holding companies from direct federal regulation. The biggest change of all came in 2000 when Congress enacted the Commodity Futures Modernization Act which barred federal regulation of the trillion-dollar swap markets allowing U.S banks, broker-dealers and other financial institutions to develop, market and trade these unregulated financial products including credit default swaps, foreign currency swaps, interest rate swaps, energy swaps and total return swaps. The reason given by Republicans was that it would provide "ways to help American banks grow larger and better compete on the world stage."

In 2002, the Treasury Department, along with other federal bank regulatory agencies, altered the way capital reserves were calculated for banks, and encouraged the retention of securitized mortgages with investment grade credit ratings by allowing banks to hold less capital in reserve for them, than if individual mortgages were held directly on the banks' books. In 2004, the Security and Exchange Commission (SEC) relaxed the capital requirements for larger broker-dealers, allowing them to grow even bigger, often with borrowed funds. These rules according to SEC, permits a broker-dealer to use mathematical models to calculate net capital requirements for market and derivatives-related credit risk. In 2006, the Federal Court of Appeals issued an opinion to invalidate an SEC rule which required most hedge fund operations (the major causes of the financial crisis), to register their names and open their books for inspection.

All these changes resulted in the collapse of smaller and regional saving banks and credit unions, opened the flood gates for merges and acquisitions, and allowed a few banks and broker-dealers to rule the industry. According to a Levin and Coburn report, these "giant financial conglomerates were involved in collecting deposits, financing loans, trading equities, swaps and commodities, and issuing, underwriting, and marketing billions of dollars in stock, debt instruments, insurance policies, and derivatives." These banks received a free pass to try many experiments, including creating "innovative" financial products which embedded risks that are difficult to analyze and predict, namely, collateralized debt obligations, credit default swaps, exchange traded funds, and commodity and swap indices. The subjects for their experiments were couples who saved their money to buy their first house, families who wanted to refinance their homes, employees who saved their 401 K and other retirement money for a rainy day deciding to invest in those "once in a life time" investment opportunities, celebrities, investors, and others who were seeking references and recommendations to invest in one of the worst Ponzi schemes of the century – Bernard Madoff Investment Securities LLC.

THE SCOPE OF THE PROBLEM

On April 13, 2011the United States Senate Permanent Subcommittee on Investigations led by Senators Carl Levin and Tom Coburn, produced a 639 page report called "*Wall Street and the Financial Crisis: Anatomy of Financial Collapse.* The report was compiled after two years of bipartisan investigation using many interviews, dispositions and close collaboration with experts from the government, academic and private sectors. The committee had also reviewed tens of thousands of pages of documents including court pleadings, filings with the Securities and Exchange Commissions, trustee reports, corporate board and committee minutes, mortgage transactions and other sources. The report summarized the cause under four major categories: high risk lending, regulatory failure, inflated credit rating and investment abuse. The report selected visible banks and regulatory agencies as a case study to show the magnitude of the crisis. A brief summary of each identified cause is listed below:

HIGH RISK LENDING

High risk lending is a strategy involving the origin and sale of complex mortgages that differ from the traditional 30-year fixed rate home loans. According to the bi-partisan report, between 2000 and 2007, banks involved in high risk lending originated 14.5 million high risk loans. Out of this number 59% were used to refinance an existing loan and 55% were for cash out refinancing. The total amount of high risk loans jumped from $125 billion in 2000 to $1 trillion in 2006. Examples of high risk lending strategies used by the banks a few years before the crisis are shown below:

Securitization: financial institutions bundled a large number of home loans into a loan pool and calculated the amount of mortgage payments that would be paid into that pool by the borrowers. The loan company then formed a shell corporation or trust, often offshore, to hold the loan pool and use the mortgage revenue stream to support the creation of bonds that make payments to investors over time. These bonds which were registered with SEC were called residential mortgage backed securities (RMBS) and were sold in a public offering to investors.

High Risk (subprime) Mortgages: this was the lending practice of banks to high risk borrowers referred to by some as subprime borrowers. Banks took major risks to lend to borrowers who did not fulfill the requirements even though the Office of the Comptroller of the Currency had provided a clear definition of subprime borrowers as those with certain credit risk characteristics, including one of the following: (a) two or more 30-day delinquency in the last 12 months, or one 60-day delinquencies in the last 24 months, (b) a judgment or foreclosure in the prior 24 months, (c) a bankruptcy in the last five years, (d) a relatively high default probability as evidenced by, for example, a credit score below 660 on the FICO scale or a debt service to income ratio of 50% or more.

Hybrid ARMs: these were mortgage loans created from a fixed-rate mortgage and a regular adjustable-rate mortgage. It had an initial fixed interest rate period followed by an adjustable rate period. After the fixed interest rate expired, the interest rate was adjusted based on an index plus a margin. These high risk loans were offered primarily to subprime borrowers and referred to as "2/28", "3/27" or "5/25" loans. The loans gave borrowers a break for the selected two, three, or five years by paying interest only and after the fixed period of the teaser rate expires, the monthly payment was recalculated using the highest floating rate to pay off the remaining principal and interest owed over the course of the remaining period. This resulted in a dramatic increase in the monthly payment forcing the debtor to default on the loan. According to a GAO report, between 2000 and 2007, close to 70% of subprime loans were Hybrid ARMS.

Pick-A-Payment or Option ARMs: As the profit from different innovative mortgages increased, so too did the types of products offered to trap borrowers. The pick-a-payment or option ARMs allowed borrowers to pay low teaser rates, sometimes as low as a 1% annual rate for the first month, and then imposed a much higher interest rate linked to an index, while also giving the borrower a choice each month on how much to pay the outstanding loan balance. The four alternative payment options were (a) paying the full amortized amount needed to pay off the loan in 30 years, (b) paying an even higher amount to pay off the loan in 15 years,

(c) paying only the interest owed that month and no principal or (d) making a "minimum" payment that covered only a portion of the interest owed and none of the principal.

Home Equity Loans: This is a type of loan secured by the borrower's equity on his or her home, which served as the loan collateral. This type of loan provided a lump sum loan amount that had to be repaid over a fixed period of time, such as 5, 10, or 30 years using a fixed interest rate.

Alt a Loans: These were loans issued to borrowers with relatively good credit histories. However the loans were underwritten aggressively to increase the risk. The target group were self-employed individuals who could not produce documentation to support their income level such as W-2 tax return forms or pay stubs. The loans allowed them to obtain 100% financing of their homes ... an unusually high debt-to-income ratio. A GAO report indicated that between 2000 to 2006, the percentage of Alt A loans with less than full documentation of the borrower's income or assets increased from 60% to 80%.

Stated Income Loans: One of the many strategies the bank used to lend money to folks with no documentation at all, and no effort made by the lender to verify the borrower's income, was called stated income loans. These loans according to the Senate report allowed borrowers simply to "state" their income, with no verification from the bank. This type of loan was reserved at the beginning, for wealthier borrowers who were not required to provide documentation, but later became common to others. According to the GAO report, between 2000 to 2006 assets from this type of loan rose from 20% to 38%.

THE STORY OF WASHINGTON MUTUAL BANK AND ITS RISKY LENDING PRACTICES
Almost all banks were involved in providing millions of high risk loans between 2000 and 2007. The Washington Mutual Bank, once believed to be the number one thrift and sixth largest bank in the U.S., with $300 billion in assets, $188 billion in deposits, 2,300 branches in 15 States, and over 43,000 employees, engaged in designing a high profit lending architecture by giving high risk loans. According to the case study in the senate bi-partisan report, during 2005 the bank began to see high rates of delinquency and default, and the following year its mortgage backed securities began incurring losses due to a portfolio that contained poor

quality and fraudulent loans and securities. Its stock price dropped as shareholders lost confidence and depositors began withdrawing funds, eventually causing a liquidity crisis at the bank. In 2008, the bank was seized by the Office of Thrift Supervision and sold to JPMorgan Chase for $1.9 billion. The decision to sell it to JP Morgan saved its $45 billion Deposit Insurance Fund. Some interesting numbers are: in the four years leading up to the collapse, the bank's high risk loans jumped from 19% to 55% whereas the low risk loans fell from 64% to 25%. The Open Adjustable Rate Mortgages (Open ARMs) believed to be the cause for mortgage collapse, was $42.6 billion while home equity loans were $63.5 billion, 27% of its home loan portfolio. This number had increased 130% from 2003. By the end of 2007, stated income loans made up 50% of Washington Mutual Bank's subprime loans, 73% of its Option ARMs and 90% of its home equity loans.

REGULATORY FAILURE

The fundamental failure in the regulatory architecture for the financial system is that the government reacted to past events and created several agencies or offices to make sure that those failures would not be repeated again, instead of developing a proactive strategy to avoid issues. Some regulatory entities in the US were created as a result of events in the market. The panic of 1907 which led to the creation of the National Monitory Commission, and later in 1913, the Federal Reserve was triggered according to Burner and Carr, in the "curbside" stock market that was organized outside the formal confines of the New York Stock Exchange. The Great Depression and microeconomic shock was the cause for the creation of the Federal Deposit Insurance Corporation (FDIC) The Security and Exchange Commission was created in 1934 to regulate the stock market and prevent corporate abuses relating to the offering and scale of securities and corporate reporting. For nearly fifty years the market was controlled and regulated by these agencies and in the early 1980s a new challenge to the agencies arose. The Continental Illinois bank lost its value due to aggressive marketing practices and as a reaction to this event, the government (FDIC) issued the first bailout package to save the bank. The saving and loan crisis of the late 1980s led to the creation of risk based deposit insurance. Many other laws and regulations were passed as a result of the reaction to the market rather than in anticipation of the risk.

During this time, regulators were struggling to tighten policy and control this dynamic and complex sector but in the process some did not succeed. One of the visible examples cited for this case was the failure of the Office of Thrift Supervision (OTS) established in 1989 to supervise and regulate all federal and State chartered savings banks and loan associations. The agency's role was later expanded to oversee not only banks, but also insurance and security companies like the American International Group (AIG), Washington Mutual and IndyMac, all of whom found themselves in the center of the crisis. OTC's did not act to stop the irresponsible business practice when it found over 500 deficiencies with the Washington Mutual Bank, and instead of imposing tough fines and down grade its rating, it continued to give the bank a financial sound rate. This was a serious regulatory failure.

Another big regulatory failure during the financial crisis was the Security and Exchange Commission's (SEC) reaction to the case of Bernard Madoff who ran a Ponzi scheme. The SEC was charged by the Congress with the mandate to preserve the national public interest through fair and honest markets. There were many different occasions over a long period when the SEC could have acted on multiple credible complaints including the one by Harry Markopolos who later published a book with the title *No One Would Listen*, about Madoff's scheme. However, it failed to respond quickly and adequately. According to Markopolos report, the SEC missed opportunities to investigate and uncover Madoff's fraud, save billions of his clients' money and thereby protect thousands of innocent investors, had it reacted to the reports on time.

INFLATED CREDIT RATINGS: GIVING UNDESERVED HIGH RATINGS TO BANKS

According to a Senate bi-partisan report, the same companies, Standard and Poor Financial Services LLC (S&P) which downgraded the US credit rating from AAA (outstanding) to AA+ (Excellent) in August 2011, and Moody Investment Service Inc., were involved in illegal activities including inaccurate ratings as well as conflicts of interest, These companies placed achieving market share and increased revenues ahead of ensuring accurate ratings. The report continued,

"Between 2004 and 2007, Moody's and S&P issued credit ratings for tens of thousands of U.S. residential mortgage backed securities (RMBS) and collateralized debt obligations (OCD). Taking in increasing revenue from Wall Street firms, Moody's and S&P issued AAA and other investment grade credit ratings for the vast majority of those RBMS and CDO securities deeming them safe investments, even though many relied on high risk home loans. In late 2006, high risk mortgages began incurring delinquencies and defaults at an alarming rate. Despite signs of a deteriorating mortgage market, for six months Moody's and S&P continued to issue investment grade ratings for numerous RMBS and CDO securities."

Conflicts of Interest were seen as one major factor for these ratings, as these ratings companies were paid by the Wall Street firms that sought their ratings and profited from the financial products being rated. Under this "issuer pays" mode, according to the Senate report, the rating agencies were dependent upon those Wall Street firms to bring them business, and were therefore vulnerable to threats that the firms would take their business elsewhere if they did not get the rating they wanted. Thus the rating agencies weakened their standards as each competed to provide the most favorable rating to win business and greater market share. Furthermore the rating models used by these companies were not complete as they failed to include relevant mortgage performance data, used unclear and subjective criteria to produce ratings, failed to apply updated rating models to existing rated transactions and failed to provide adequate staffing to perform rating and surveillance services.

INVESTMENT BANK ABUSES

A core component of the U.S financial sector's investment banking are financial institutions which were involved in assisting individuals, corporations and governments to raise capital by underwriting, acting as the client's agent in the issuance of securities. Approximately 2,000 investment banking firms of various types work with millions of customers garnering business of trillions of dollars. According to

Morrison and Wilhelm, between the early 1980s and early 2000s, the number of professionals employed by the top five investment banks rose from 56,000 to 205,000. The 2009 revenue of the top 10 investment banks (Goldman Sachs, JP Morgan Chase, Morgan Stanley, Citigroup, Bank of America, Barclays, Lazard, Credit Suisse, Deutche Bank and UBS) was estimated to be over $500 billion. With this power and influence in the economy, these banks over-stepped their boundaries and responsibilities, and designed complex high risk financial products that were at the center of this crisis. These products included residential mortgage backed securities (RMBS), collateralized debt obligations (CDO), credit card default swaps (CDS) and CDS contracts linked to the ABX index. According to the report from the Senate bi-partisan investigation from 2004 to 2008, the U.S financial institutions issued nearly $2.5 trillion in RBMS and over $1.4 trillion in CDO securities, backed primarily by mortgage related products.

THE CARNAGE TO THESE BANKS BEGAN

Starting in 2005, housing prices started to fall and in the second quarter of 2007, and the widespread decline in the value of mortgage backed securities caused Bear Stearns' two funds concentrating in MBS to file bankruptcy, a decline in the portfolio of Citibank, Morgan Stanley and Merrill Lynch, as well as the failure of banks including New Century Financial. By 2008, the Bank of America acquired the near bankrupt Countrywide Financial, one of the largest Subprimelenders, JP Morgan Chase purchased Bear Stearns (the fifth largest U.S investment bank) at $2 a share, Fannie Mae and Freddie Mac went into insolvency, Lehman Brothers failed to be rescued, Merrill Lynch was acquired by Bank of America, AIG was taken over by the U.S Treasury with the aid of the Federal Reserve and Morgan Stanley and Goldman Sachs became bank holding companies under the Federal Reserve System's supervision after their stocks plummeted by double digits. In September 2008, the Dow-Jones industrial index plummeted by over 4 percent.

One country two worlds: Golden Parachutes for the CEOs and employees - eviction and unemployment for the ordinary Americans –

Since the compensation and bonus structure of these investment banks were based on annual performance and the largest share was paid out in advance, there was no incentive for executives to pay attention to the problem the banks were in. As the Financial Crisis Inquiry report indicated, the motto used by employees of these banks was "I will be gone and you will be gone. Let's get our fair share". According to Lawrence and Patrick's book *A Colossal Failure of Common Sense"*, the New Century Bank's mortgage brokerage team (the bank was bankrupted in 2008) was making between $300,000 - $600, 000, on commissions *per annum*. Some members of the bank expressed their positions saying, *"Our job is to sell the mortgage policy. Period. Right after that it's someone else's problem."* Here are a few examples of the incredible payments employees received that make ordinary people living from pay-check to pay-check think that all of this is content from a movie and not real stories from Wall Street:

- In his book *Street Freak: Money and Madness at Lehman Brothers*, Jared Sillian who was a trader for Lehman wrote about his bonus surprise in 2005 and his conversation with his boss – "Last year your total compensation was two hundred seventy-five thousand dollars and this year it will be six hundred and fifty thousand dollars... That is an insane amount of money... What the hell am I going to do with all this money?"
- The head of Citigroup's energy-trading unit reportedly received over $100 million in 2008 and was in line for a similar payment in 2009.
- Joseph J. Cassano, who led AIG's Financial Products division from 2002-2008 and was responsible for the failure of the company was fired, but walked out with a $34 million bonus and a $1 million monthly consulting contract in addition to the $280 million he received over the year he was working at AIG.

Fraud and Ponzi schemes - *Bernard Madoff the pioneer of Impression Management*

The financial crisis in 2008 not only brought a new era of financial imprudence and exposed failures of many institutions of society, it also revealed the most scandalous malfeasance of this new era – The Bernard Madoff Ponzi scheme. The scheme gets its name, according to Perkins and Dilbar, from Charles Ponzi, an Italian-born American immigrant who became known in the early 1920's as a swindler in North America, and for his most famous "get rich quick" scam where he swindled around $15 million out of 40,000 investors. Ponzi was allegedly buying coupons in a nation with a weak currency, trading them for American postage stamps, then converting the stamps into cash at a huge profit. When the scam was exposed, Ponzi possessed only $30 in postal coupons. He promised a 50 percent return on monies invested for a period of three months - or 200 percent over the course of a year. Surprisingly, U.S. postal officials, local prosecuting attorneys and several Boston newspapers were said to be suspicious of Ponzi's operations almost from the outset. But, "until he was finally unable to meet the payments on his maturing liabilities with fresh inflows of funds from new investors, officials were powerless to intervene in his dubious and rather nebulous, business venture."

Bernard Lawrence Madoff was known by many of his investors under his many accomplishments as "an American businessman, highly respected, well-established, esteemed financial expert, large broker dealer and former chairman of NASDAQ", when in fact he was a white collar criminal and master in impression management. He used his skills, ingratiation (conveying happiness and pleasantness to elicit good will), intimidation (to get others to obey) and supplication (so that others will be helpful), to attract billions of dollars into his fake investment portfolio. Lewis' paper *Madoff's victims and their day in court* summarized Madoff's behavior: "Madoff was a master at ingratiation and intimidation. He is someone with discretion. He does not give the show away by involuntarily disclosing its secrets. He is someone with 'presence of mind' who can cover up on the spur of the moment for inappropriate behavior. That is how he managed his Ponzi scheme so well for so long.

Madoff's Ponzi scheme is considered to be the largest financial fraud in the U.S history with over $65 billion of funds invested by innocent investors. This scam came on the heels of the biggest credit crisis in decades and is believed to have wiped out generations of wealth and savings of many hard working people. It has negatively affected numerous investors at all levels of the economic strata. Thousands of individuals lost their retirement savings and others, large parts of their investments. Harry Markopolos who consistently tried to report Madoff's scheme to government officials responsible for overseeing the financial sector summarized Madoff's action and its impact on our society and economy in his book, *No One Would Listen* :

> "We're going to be living with Bernie Madoff for the rest of our lives. He has become so much a part of our culture that he has achieved a certain kind of infamy – his name has become a metaphor for a brilliant and heartless criminal …This is a story that will have an impact for generations … But for me, of course and the Fox Hounds, Bernie Madoff will always be the one who got away. … On paper, Madoff defrauded an estimated three million investors of $64.8 billion … In 2000, I turned over everything I knew to the SEC. Five times I reported my concerns, and no one would listen until it was far too late. I was a whistleblower taking on one of the most powerful men on Wall Street and at some points through the nightmarish journey, I feared for both my safety and that of my family. I was convinced the crime he was committing was going to be the worst in market history. Ten years later, Madoff is now behind bars and we all know why."

IS IT NOT COMMON SENSE TO REFORM THE FINANCIAL SECTOR CONSIDERING WHAT HAPPENED?

Before taking office, the then candidate Obama outlined his vision to reform the financial regulation in his speech, *Renewing the American Economy* at Cooper Union (New York):

> "A regulatory structure set up for banks in the 1930's needed to change. But by the time the Glass-Steagall Act was repealed in 1999, the $300 million lobbying effort that drove deregulation was more about facilitating mergers than creating an efficient

regulatory framework. ... Unfortunately, instead of establishing a 21st century regulatory framework, we simply dismantled the old one, thereby encouraging a winner take all, anything goes environment that helped foster devastating dislocations in our economy."

After taking office, the Obama administration started working with Democrats in Congress to craft a radical reform for the financial sector to control the abuse. There were many oppositions to this initiative citing "control kills innovation", "government intervention will not help the economy", let the market decide its own path" and others. The Dodd-Frank Wall Street Reform and Consumer Protection Act referred to by the Washington Post as "the most ambitious overhaul of financial regulations in generations" was passed by Congress and signed in to law by the president on July 21, 2010. . At the signing ceremony the president said:

"Over the past two years, we have faced the worst recession since the Great Depression. Eight million people lost their jobs. Tens of millions saw the value of their homes and retirement savings plummet. Countless businesses have been unable to get the loans they need and many have been forced to shut their doors. And although the economy is growing again, too many people are still feeling the pain of the downturn. Now, while a number of factors led to such a severe recession, the primary cause was a breakdown in our financial system. It was a crisis born of a failure of responsibility from certain corners of Wall Street to the halls of power in Washington. For years, our financial sector was governed by antiquated and poorly enforced rules that allowed some to game the system and take risks that endangered the entire economy. Unscrupulous lenders locked consumers into complex loans with hidden costs. Firms like AIG placed massive, risky bets with borrowed money. And while the rules left abuse and excess unchecked, they also left taxpayers on the hook if a big bank or financial institution ever failed. Now, even before the crisis hit, I went to Wall Street and

I called for common-sense reforms to protect consumers and our economy as a whole. And soon after taking office, I proposed a set of reforms to empower consumers and investors, to bring the shadowy deals that caused this crisis into the light of day, and to put a stop to taxpayer bailouts once and for all. Today, thanks to a lot of people in this room, those reforms will become the law of the land."

57 Democratic and only three Republican senators (Scott Brown of Massachusetts, Olympia Snowe and Susan Collins of Maine) voted to pass the bill from the senate after it cleared the house with a 237 to 192 vote. The Act introduced regulation in three areas - consumer protection, banking regulation and Wall Street Reform –and would affect the oversight and supervision of financial institutions, provide for a new resolution procedure for large financial companies, create a new compliance with consumer financial laws, introduce more stringent regulatory capital requirements, effect significant changes in the regulation of over the counter derivatives, reform the regulation of credit rating agencies, implement changes to corporate governance and executive compensation practices, incorporate the Volker Rule, require the registration of advisers to certain private funds and effect significant changes in the securitization market. A brief summary of these three sections is listed below.

CONSUMER PROTECTION

The Act created an independent bureau, the Consumer Financial Protection Bureau (CFPB), within the Federal Reserve. The CFPB wrote the rules for consumer protection governing all financial institutions - bank and non-bank - which offer consumer financial products and services. The CFPB will have the authority to examine and enforce regulations for banks and credit unions with assets over $10 billion, as well as all mortgage-related businesses, payday lenders and student lenders. Large non-bank financial institutions, such as debt collectors and credit reporting agencies, will also be regulated and examined by the CFPB. Banks with assets under $10 billion will be examined for consumer complaints by the appropriate bank regulator. The CFPB will oversee federal laws intended to ensure the fair, equitable and nondiscriminatory access to credit for individuals and communities. The bureau would monitor consumer financial products and services, so that consumers do not have to wait for congressional action in order to be protected from bad business practices.

BANKING REGULATION

The Act established a simple federal standard for home loans: institutions must ensure that borrowers can repay the loans they are sold. First, providing financial incentives to steer customers to more expensive loans is prohibited. Second, yield spread premiums-bonuses paid to brokers who inflate the price of loans are specifically prohibited. Third, pre-payment penalties are also prohibited. Moreover, the Act lowered the interest rates, points and fee triggers on high-cost mortgages. Lenders must disclose the maximum a consumer must pay on variable rate mortgages and also advise clients that payments will vary based on interest rate changes. The Act makes sure that lenders and mortgage brokers who do not follow the new rules will be penalized, gives the Security and Exchange Commission (SEC) the authority to impose a fiduciary duty on brokers who give investment advice (a fiduciary duty requires investment advice to be in the best interest of the client), created an Investment Advisory Committee that will be composed of investors who will advise the SEC on regulatory priorities and practices, and amended the Sarbanes-Oxley Act of 2002 (SOX) to require auditors of all broker-dealers to register with the Public Company Accounting Oversight Board (PCAOB) - this Board is authorized by the Dodd-Frank Act to adopt rules for the inspection of audit reports of broker-dealers.

WALL STREET REFORM

The Dodd-Frank Act also made significant changes to the Federal Reserve. The Government Accountability Office (GAO) conducted a one-time audit of the emergency lending by the Federal Reserve, and that took place during the current financial crisis. The GAO will have the power to audit on an ongoing basis two areas of the Federal Reserve that it had never been allowed to audit before – discount window lending and open market transactions. In addition, the Federal Reserve will be required to periodically disclose information about its discount window lending and open market transactions, including the counterparties, amounts and terms. The discount window allows eligible institutions to borrow money to meet short-term cash shortages. The Dodd-Frank Act implemented a strong version of the Volcker Rule (a proposal named after its architect, former Federal Reserve chair and chair of the President's Economic Recovery Advisory Board, Paul Volcker). Paul Volker was later appointed by president Obama as the chair of the President's Economic Recovery Advisory Board. Based on its provisions, banks are prohibited from proprietary trading and investing their money in hedge funds. The Act requires regulators to establish regulations for banks, their affiliates and holding companies that prohibit proprietary trading in, investment in and sponsorship of hedge funds and private equity funds. Banks will also be required to limit their relationships with hedge funds and private equity funds. However, they will still be allowed to engage in certain derivative trades on behalf of clients. Specifically, banks will be able to conduct client trades in interest rate swaps, foreign currency swaps, derivatives referencing gold and silver and high-grade credit-default swaps. Banks will also be able to trade derivatives for themselves if hedging existing positions.

The Dodd-Frank Act is said to be the most comprehensive financial reform bill since the Glass-Steagall Act of 1933. However, the Act has been criticized by some for being too lenient, and by others for being too strict. While the Act is indeed lengthy, much of the reform and regulatory work is left up to new and existing regulators. It does, however, provide a clear mandate for drafting the rules and regulations to implement the legislated financial reforms. Upon release of the Act, sponsor Senator Christopher J. Dodd (D–CT) commented: "It is a great moment. I'm proud to have been here ... No one will know until it is actually in place how it works. But we believe we have done something that has been needed for a long time. It took a crisis until we could actually get this job done."

REACTION TO THE REFORM — WALL STREET THREATENED — SHIFTED SUPPORT FROM OBAMA TO ROMNEY

The market performed well during the first term of president Obama's administration – Dow doubled, S&P rose over 60%. Wall Street and financial services, however, were not comfortable with the Obama presidency and felt threatened mainly due to the introduction of *The Dodd-Frank Wall Street Reform and Consumer Protection Act* whichdictated how much of a cash cushion banks must store, regulated on the use of derivatives and limited banks risk taking capacity. The law generally restricted banks from making speculative investments that do not benefit their customers. In the 2008 election, many banks and Wall Street firms had supported the president by pouring close to $3.5 million into his campaign. In this election cycle, their contribution dropped to $650,000 while the Romney campaign cashed out $3.3 million. Employees from Goldman Sachs whose company benefited from bailout funds through the Troubled Asset Relief Program, made a surprise shift from their tradition of supporting Democrats in the past several elections and became top contributors to the Romney campaign, indicating their unhappiness with the Obama "Regulatory attack." According to the Wall Street Journal, at Goldman the switch goes beyond the presidential contest. In 2008, its employees gave 75% of their $6 million in donation to Democrats. In this election, 75% of their $6.5 million in contributions went to Republicans. This resentment is said to be partly because they were not consulted when the administration crafted the financial regulation and because they became a target for the campaign. According to the Center for Responsive Politics, in 2008, financial services were the second-largest source of the Obama campaign donating $43 million. This time round, the industry donated only $12 million while doubling their support to the Romney campaign.

CORPORATION	2008 ELECTION	2012 ELECTION
JP. Morgan	808,000	155,000
Citigroup	735,000	101,000
Bank of America	395,000	132,000
Morgan Stanley	517,000	134,000

| Goldman Sachs | 1,013,000 | 136,000 |
| Total | 3, 470,000 | 658,000 |

Table 9: Financial Services Contribution to the Obama Campaign - 2008/2012Source: Wall Street Journal October 10, 2012

On the day of the 2012 election, there were no earning reports from companies and the market was quiet until the news that Romney may win the election started circulating in reaction to which, the Dow shot up 130 points. As the election results rolled in, Dow features went down by more than 100 points. The next day with the realization that Obama will be here for another four years, the market tanked over 300 points. It is worthwhile to note that shortly after the president took office in March 2008 the DOW was at 6,300 points and that over the last four years the DOW had doubled to 13,000 points and performed as well as the S&P 500 which is considered a better measure of the largest U.S. companies.

The question here is, if the market performed well under this administration, why did Wall Street and the financial sector feel uncomfortable and threatened by the Obama presidency? The answer again takes us back to the limitation in wiggle room imposed by the *Dodd-Frank Wall Street Reform and Consumer Protection Act*. One section of the law which affects the revenue source is the Volker Rule which may have cost these big banks including Goldman as much as 10% of their revenues by crippling the proprietary trading market.

7 Chapter

Health Care – The Law of the Land

219 Democrats Yes
212 Republicans No
0 Republicans supported the bill

—

"Today, I'm signing this reform bill into law on behalf of my mother, who argued with insurance companies even as she battled cancer in her final days … I'm signing this bill for all the leaders who took up this cause through the generations – from Teddy Roosevelt to Franklin Roosevelt, from Harry Truman to Lyndon Johnson, from Bill and Hillary Clinton, to one of the deans who's been fighting this so long, John Dingell, and Senator Ted Kennedy." **President Obama at the signing ceremony, March 23, 2010**

FIRST, THE NUMBERS

- The United States has the highest health care costs in the world, far higher than other countries including Germany, Switzerland, Netherlands, Sweden, Norway, and Denmark.
- In 2011 we spent $2.7 trillion in national health expenditure, ($8,680 per person) accounting for 17.9 percent of the Gross Domestic Product (GDP of $15.1 trillion). Nearly one in every 5.6 dollars spent are in health care related expenditure.
- In the 2010 Census report 49.9 million residents, 16.3% of the population was uninsured.
- A national study of 2,314 bankruptcy filers in 2007, showed that 62.1% were due to high medical expenses. Illness and medical bills contribute to a large and increasing share of bankruptcies.
- U.S is 50th in the world in life expectancy - below most developed nations and some developing nations.
- U.S ranks close to the bottom compared to other industrialized countries on several health issues (low birth weight and infant mortality, injuries and murder, teen pregnancy, STDs, HIV and AIDS, deaths resulting from drug overdoses, obesity and diabetes and heart disease).
- U.S is among the few industrialized nations in the world that does not guarantee access to health care for its population.
- With the exception of Mexico, Turkey, and the United States, all OECD countries have achieved universal or near-universal health coverage for their population.
- A Harvard 2009 study reported that 44,800 deaths are due annually to lack of health insurance.

Looking at the numbers above, one would think it would be common sense to reform our health care system. With 14 million people – close to nine percent of the work force – engaged in the health care related industry generating close to 1.7 trillion dollars in revenue (as of 2010), health care is one of the few critical sectors of the U.S economy. As the population gets older, the cost of keeping health care in control becomes a challenge and if no action is taken, the economy will be in trouble. In 1960 with a population of 186 million, the health care cost was $27.1 million and 51 years later in 2011 with a population of 311 million, the health care cost had sky-rocketed to $2.7 trillion. This means that while the population increased three-fold, the cost of health care rose by over 100-fold. On March 23, 2010 the long drawn-out debate on health care came to a conclusion when President Barack Obama signed into law the *Patient Protection and Affordable Care Act* (PPACA), now often referred to simply as the *Affordable Care Act*, a sweeping measure to make health care affordable to ordinary citizens and also to control the costs. The enactment of this law represented the culmination of many policy advocates' strenuous efforts to establish a federal mandate that all individuals purchase health insurance, create federally subsidized health insurance exchanges, expand eligibility for Medicaid, reduce the growth of Medicare payments and cover millions of Americans who do not have health insurance. The magnitude of the challenge to pass the bill was generally reflected by the enormous cost associated with health care, lack of support by a single Republican vote and the record number of lobbyists working hard to either curb the content or kill parts of the provisions of the bill.

THE 100 YEAR ATTEMPT TO REFORM THE U.S. HEALTH SYSTEM
In the past, over seven presidents and many congressmen and senators have attempted to curb and control the ever-expanding cost of health care by introducing several initiatives. Since 1798 when the first Public Health Service Act was passed by the 5th Congress authorizing marine hospitals for the care of American merchant seaman, the debate on the role of government in regulating and guiding health care has been challenging. Fifty years later in 1847 the American Medical Association (AMA) was founded and became a national force for organized medicine influencing Congress and law makers on behalf of its members, all of whom are medical doctors . Even though the time between 1850 and the end of the century was marked with steady growth in the development of medicine, it was in the first years of 1900 that surgery became a common procedure especially for removing tumors, infected tonsils and gynecological operations. As a result of these expensive procedures, doctors were no longer expected to provide free services to all hospital patients. At that same time, working Americans did not receive compensation for sick days or maternity leave and as a result in 1905, a

small group of economists formed the American Association for Labor Legislation (AALL) which first started to study the labor conditions and labor legislation in the United States, later becoming activist for major changes in worker's compensation, occupational health and safety laws. By 1909 and under the leadership of John Andrews, this group became influential and the movement forced President Theodor Roosevelt to call for a universal health care system in his August 6, 1912 speech at the Progressive Party Convention. Unfortunately, his initiative failed to materialize. That was the first major attempt to reform the health care by a politician from the highest office of the land.

The second effort was made by the American Association of Labor Legislation (AALL) in early 1920s. They proposed a "standard bill" for health insurance for working-class Americans making $1,200 or less a year. The bill included benefits to their families, hospital care, sick pay, maternity leave and death benefits. Strong opposition from AMA and other groups, together with the beginning of the First World War were considered to be the cause of the failure of this effort. In 1929 President Herbert Hoover mentioned how public health service should be fully organized universally and incorporated into the governmental system. He was believed to be the first president to openly support a nationalized health program. Unfortunately, nothing was done to advance this idea throughout his term. The 1920s, was also a decade where the American middle-class saw higher costs of medical care as a result, companies like General Motors signing an agreement to purchase life insurance for its employees.

In 1935 Roosevelt signed the Social Security Act, into law without including health coverage. Acknowledging the pressure from many interest groups who opposed the establishment of a health care system, Roosevelt explained his rational for the decision saying that the financial aid given to the States by the Public Health Service through Social Security funds would be enough to improve health care, and that no special program of medical care for the elderly was needed. In 1939, the Interdepartmental Committee assigned by the president to co-ordinate health and welfare activities recommended a national health program but was rejected by FDR. Six years later in 1945, President Harry Truman created a five-point plan calling for more health care providers in rural areas, better hospital quality, the creation of a board of doctors and public officials to maintain hospital standards, better sick day payments and an optional national health insurance plan to compete with the private sector. Again the national health insurance initiative failed. Truman in the last months of his second term, created the *President's Commission* to recommend steps towards improving the health of the nation. The commission decided to pass on the discussion to the Eisenhower administration after which Eisenhower officially rejected the concept of universal health care.

When Kennedy became president in the early 1960s, he called for a bill to provide health care insurance for the elderly that would be financed through Social Security. In 1965, president Lyndon Johnson extended the Social Security Act to provide full health care coverage for all Americans over the age of 65. This was the first law that covered at least a part of society. At the beginning of the 1970s, Nixon announced the National Health Strategy to promote equal access to health care. However his initiative was far from supporting a national health care system. It was in 1974 that States started to promote some form of mandated insurance and Hawaii became the first State to require employers to pay a portion of the insurance premium. The law stated that employee's share would be no more than 2.5 percent of their annual salary. 35 years later Hawaii still enforces employers to provide health insurance. In 1977, President Jimmy Carter proposed reducing spending on health care and in 1979, he initiated a National Health Plan to provide coverage for low-income and disabled Americans, as well as to consolidate the different Medicare and Medicaid programs into a federal "Healthcare" program. Like the previous other plans, this one was also killed prematurely. Two decades later in 1993, president Bill Clinton embarked on a new plan to overhaul the country's health insurance system with universal coverage, as well as to allow Americans to choose their own doctors and health plans from private insurers. The Republicans filibustered and killed the bill. In 2010 after a bitter battle that cost many House Democrats and Senators' their jobs, president Obama was able to pass a comprehensive bill to address many issues the country was facing. Even though the final bill was a "watered down version of the original bill" submitted, it was one of the landmark decisions in the US health care history.

WHY WAS IT DIFFICULT TO REFORM HEALTH CARE?

Special Interest groups (Lobbyists) and their power – Eight Lobbyists for Each Member of Congress
As the debate over health care intensified according to OpenSecrets.org and Center for Public Integrity which analyzed Senate lobbying disclosure forms, 1,247 organizations were registered to lobby the health care bill and they hired about 4,525 lobbyists – on average eight lobbyists were assigned for each member of Congress. The price tag for this huge task was approximately $1.2 billion and there were 207 hospitals, 105 insurance companies, 85 manufacturing companies, as well as trade, advocacy and professional organizations involved to influence the bill. Some of the visible organizations were AARP (56 lobbyists), U.S. Chamber of Commerce (47 lobbyists), Titans (40 lobbyists) and American Medical Association (33 lobbyists). The American Medical Association (AMA) alone spent $20 million in 2009 lobbying on behalf of doctors and was able to influence the Congress to avoid cuts from doctors' pockets, including killing a $300 yearly fee for doctors who participate in Medicare or Medicaid, tax on cosmetic surgery, five percent Medicare payment cuts to the 10 percent of Medicare billers and Medicare payment cuts for primary care physicians.

The lobbyists were from all sectors of the economy including companies like Campbell's Soup which paid money to lobby against the public insurance option, Dunkin Donuts against soda tax, Cigar Association against tobacco tax to fund health insurance expansion and the medical equipment industry against the $20 billion medical device tax. The number of lobbyists working on health reform more than doubled throughout 2009 from 1,400 in the first three months to nearly 3,700 in the final quarter when attention was focused on the Senate bill. The question was, did those lobbyists get what they wanted? The answer was considered to be a "BIG yes." Even though the bill was passed by Congress and signed by the president, the content of the bill was squeezed to much less than it set out to accomplish. Countless provisions were omitted including the public option and the scope of the bill shrank significantly to the extent that some provisions were left just as a place holder, rather than an actual law. Julian Zelizer Professor of public affairs at Princeton University commented on the power of the lobbyists to water down the health care reform effort and summarized it as *"They cut it. They chopped it. They reconstructed it. They didn't bury it. I don't think they wanted to."*

CHALLENGES OF THE LAW AT THE U.S. SUPREME COURT

Twenty-six States, several individuals and the National Federation of Independent Business brought their cases in Federal District Court, challenging the constitutionality of parts of the law. The two key provisions that were brought to the court's attention were individual mandate and Medicaid expansion. The individual mandate according to the court's decision transcript requires most Americans to maintain "minimum essential" health insurance coverage. This means for individuals who are not exempt and who do not receive health insurance through an employer or government program, the means of satisfying the requirement is to purchase insurance from a private company. Beginning in 2014, those who do not comply with the mandate must make a "shared responsibility payment" to the Federal Government. The act provides that this "penalty" will be paid to the Internal Revenue Service with an individual's tax, and shall be assessed and collected in the same manner as tax penalties. The second provision - "Medicaid Expansion" states that the current Medicaid program offers federal funding to States to assist pregnant women, children, needy families, the blind, the elderly and the disabled in obtaining medical care. The Affordable Care Act expands the scope of the Medicaid program and increases the number of individuals the States must cover, to up to 133 percent of the federal poverty level, whereas many States now cover adults with children only if their income is considerably lower and they do not cover childless adults at all. The law increases federal funding to cover the States' costs in expanding Medicaid coverage. However if a State does not comply with the Act's new coverage requirements, it may lose not only the federal funding for those requirements, but all of its federal Medicaid funds.

The case was argued before the U.S Supreme Court on March 26, 27, 28, 2012, and on June 28, 2012 the court delivered a stunning decision to uphold individual coverage. Chief Justice Roberts concluded in part III-A that "the individual mandate is not a valid exercise of Congress' power under the Commerce clause and the Necessary and Proper Clause. The chief Justice delivered the opinion of the Court with respect to Part III-C concluding that "the individual mandate may be upheld as within Congress's power under the Taxing Clause." Four of the eight justices (Justices Ruth Bader-Ginsburg, Stephen Breyer, Sonia Sotomayor, and Elena Kagan) supported the decision and the other four (Justices Antonin Scalia, Anthony Kennedy, Clarence Thomas and Samuel Alito) joined in a dissent. David Von Drehle in his report summarized the Supreme Court's action saying "With his fellow supreme court Justices split 4-4 between two extreme outcomes – blessing the sprawling health care law or killing it – Roberts maneuvered half of the court into signing half his ruling and the other half into endorsing the rest. By doing so, he gave the liberals their long cherished dream of government led reform while giving his fellow conservatives a new doctrine to limit congressional power, which they have been seeking since the New Deal".

While this decision gave the Obama administration and his campaign the necessary fuel to justify the two-year-long battle to reform health care, it also gave the Romney campaign a convincing reason to use as his primary campaign slogan "Repeal Obama Care" and energize his base. A blog posted on "Syracuse.com" concluded the court's decision as a gateway to victory for the Romney campaign and summarizes the way Republicans translated the decision. The content of the blog is provided on the next page:

To the Editor:

Gov. Mitt Romney:

> Chief Justice John Roberts has just handed you the presidency of the United States. Since its inception, the Democratic Party and President Barack Obama have insisted that the Affordable Care Act is not a tax. The bill was

rammed through Congress under the provisions of the Commerce Clause. The bill was then sent to the Supreme Court and the constitutionality challenged under the Commerce Clause. The Supreme Court ruled the law was constitutional not under the Commerce Clause, but under Congress' "authority to levy taxes." Failure to comply with the provisions of the bill will result in fines levied against individuals and businesses. The fines will then be collected by the IRS as a provision of our tax returns. This is a tax, and the American people have been lied to once again. Well known is the fact you instituted a health care program while you were governor of Massachusetts. It is less well-known that the State Legislature was controlled by the Democrats during your term in office. You demonstrated tremendous agility and skill in the art of compromise to secure the best program for the people of Massachusetts. You have the knowledge and experience to know what worked and what didn't in the Massachusetts program. This is a tremendous advantage over your opponent. This is your watershed moment. It is Obama's Waterloo. The time for true leadership is now. You have just been handed the keys to the White House by the Supreme Court. Do not shy away from this issue. It is yours for the taking. Health care and the economy are intertwined. Increased taxes and mandates mean decreased disposable income for the average family. An economy already in recession will result in further downturns and a possible depression. It is time to make your stand. This is the issue that will win you the presidency. Now is the time for bold leadership. It's time to lead. The people are counting on you to do just that.

The Health care law and the way it was interpreted by the public was the number one reason for the Democrats losing 63 seats in the House giving the majority to Republicans in the 2010 mid-term election.

A FLAW IN THE DESIGN OF THE CURRENT HEALTH CARE SYSTEM

The U.S. health insurance system is "the costliest and most wasteful system on the face of the earth." *President Bill Clinton, September 22, 1993 during his speech proposing to overhaul the bleeding health care system before a joint session of Congress on Capitol Hill.*

Why was it costly and wasteful? - Fraud and Corruption – A White-Collar Crime

Fraud and corruption in the US health care system also called by some "white collar-crime", is considered to be one of the worst and difficult crimes to control. In 1993, Clinton's Attorney General Janet Reno declared health care fraud and corruption as the "number two crime problem" of the nation next to violent crime. Fraudulent billings to health care programs are estimated between 3-10 percent of total health care expenditure. This means that out of the $2.7 trillion spent in 2011 the fraudulent billing amounts from $81 - 270 billion, a big hole. Despite the outcry by the opponents of Obama care labeling it as a "government takeover", the U.S health care system involves comparatively few public sector officials or employees in frontline service delivery roles. In this case, some argue that instead of taking the definition of corruption as "abuse of public authority" the definition of the U. S *health care* corruption should be "abuse of entrusted authority" or dishonest actions of physicians, hospitals and other health care professionals who are generally afforded high social and professional status, and are expected to exercise professional medical judgment, unbiased by private financial interest. The reality is that these big companies breach their trust and steal money from the public.

Some of these frauds are well orchestrated by big insurance, hospitals, drug companies and service providers and are often times invisible to detect, causing concern about the integrity of the system. According to an FBI Financial Report to the Public, in FY 2011, 2,690 health care fraud cases were investigated resulting in 1,676 information/indictments and 736 convictions. Some of the more prevalent schemes include, billing for service not provided, duplicate claims medically unnecessary services up coding of service or equipment and kickbacks for referring patients for service paid by Medicare/Medicaid. The report underlined the increasing involvement of organized criminal groups in many of these schemes

(2,493 cases for 2007, 2,434 for 2008, 2,494 for 2009, 2,573 for 2010 and 2,690 cases for 2011). Only in 2011, did the FBI manage to achieve $1.2 billion in restitutions, $1 billion in fines, $96 million in seizures, $320 million in civil restitutions and over $1 billion in civil settlements.

In his article *Corruption and Health Care Systems: the US Experience,* Malcolm Sparrow noted that despite the extraordinary level of spending ($2.7 trillion in 2011), health care economists have paid very little attention to corruption, fraud, waste and abuse in the US health care delivery system. He continued "they do not factor into their cost models," they say, " because there is no data on that." There is certainly a paucity of reliable data on the extent of corruption in the system and few reliable estimates of how much of each health care dollar is actually lost to criminal enterprises. This is because like any white collar crime, these frauds and other acts of corruption are well orchestrated criminal schemes and are invisible by design. As a result, they often go undetected. As a flaw in its own design, the current US health care system has many features that make it easy for fraud and corruption. Some of these weak links include:

1. *The health care delivery is outsourced:* Health care in the US is mostly delivered by the private sector or independent not-for-profit entities. However, the services are paid for by government programs including Medicare, Medicaid or by commercial insurers who offer health insurance to individuals, groups or to employers. The problem with this approach, according to Sparrow's report, is that neither the government nor private payers have reliable information about which services were performed other than the word of the providers. FBI identified fraud associated with this arrangement as "billing for service not rendered" and this includes instances where no medical service of any kind was provided, the service was not rendered as described in the claim for payment or the service was previously billed and the claim had been paid.

2. *Automated payment system that focuses less on verification and more on processing accuracy:* Unfortunately, the design of the entire system was based on the assumption that physicians would

act honestly and the built-in automatic processing check and balance system was focused on payment accuracy rather than controlling whether in fact the services were rendered.

3. *Submitting false or inflated bills:* The existing fee for services payment structure encourages providers to submit false or inflated bills. FBI calls this "up-coding of services", where the health care provider submits a bill using a procedure code that yields a higher payment than the code for the service that was actually rendered. Examples of this type of dishonest services include a routine, follow-up doctor's office visit being billed as an initial or comprehensive office visit, group therapy being billed as individual therapy, unilateral procedures being billed as bilateral procedures and 30-minute sessions being billed as 50+ minute sessions.

4. *Fee-for-Service Structure and payment on trust* – The majority of services in the U.S health care system are reimbursed on a fee-for-service basis and under this agreement health care providers (doctors, hospitals, specialists) are trusted to determine the appropriate level of care, and to bill the insurer for the service they perform. Unfortunately the reality has been shown to be different.

5. *Improper Payment.* According to the US Government Accountability Office (GAO) testimony before the Subcommittee on Government Organization, Efficiency and Financial Management, in 2010 alone, $125.4 billion was wasted through improper payments. Out of this amount, health care related payments ranked in the first 10 (Medicare Fee for Service program with $34 billion for medically unnecessary services and insufficient documentation, Medicaid with $22.5 billion for insufficient or no documentation provided for conducting medical services and Medicare Advantage with $13.6 billion with errors in the transfer of data and payment calculations).

WHAT IS INCLUDED IN THE NEW BILL?

The law has three major components and many sub-components. The major components include elimination of the denial of health coverage due to a preexisting condition, expanding access to care through State Medicaid programs to over 30 million uninsured Americans and mandates that individuals carry health insurance coverage. A summary of these major components is provided below:

ELIMINATION OF DENIAL OF COVERAGE DUE TO PRE-EXISTING CONDITIONS

In 1998 when my family moved to the United States from Germany, my wife was six months pregnant and before we all moved to the U.S, I wanted to purchase insurance to cover her delivery. I shopped around between various insurance companies and was denied by all with the explanation that -"a pre-existing condition is any health condition you had and were aware of before the effective date of a health insurance policy, and pregnancy is a preexisting condition." Thus she would not be enrolled. I had to leave her behind in Germany where she had insurance as a student until I got a job that would cover her insurance. Months later, she joined me after I got my first job that covered her from day one of my employment. When the Affordable Health Care Act passed through the congress and was signed by the president, it reminded me of the agony I had gone through 14 years ago. Prior to the passage of the ACA, it was impossible for a person with a pre-existing condition to purchase coverage leaving them with little resources, or with the option of going to the emergency room, adding to the burden of tax payers. According to the timetable for the law, by 2014 no one will be denied access to health insurance. In the meantime, the government has developed a temporary solution to bridge the gap and cover those with preexisting conditions by creating the Pre-Existing Condition Insurance Plan (PCIP), with a new health coverage option for people who have been without health coverage for at least six months and have a pre-existing condition, or have been denied health coverage because of their medical condition. The PCIP is run by either State or the Federal government. As of 2012 over 50,000 uninsured people with pre-existing conditions have already gained coverage and the number is expected to increase.

INDIVIDUAL MANDATE TO PURCHASE HEALTH INSURANCE

The law requires all Americans to have healthcare coverage, either through their employer, a private insurer or a government program. One of the main reasons for the law was that millions of Americans had no insurance coverage because it was expensive to purchase. The 1986 Emergency Medical Treatment and Labor Act (EMTALA) requires any hospital that accepts payments from Medicare to provide care to any patient who arrives in its emergency department for treatment. So when people got sick, they would go to emergency rooms to get treatment and won't need to pay their medical bills resulting in taxpayers' covering the bill.

MEDICAL CARE FOR SENIORS - MEDICARE AND THE DISCUSSION ON THE DONUT HOLE

The law helps seniors get access to the preventive and screening services they need, save money on prescription drugs, as well as eliminate the 'donut hole' to make drugs affordable. According to the 2012 government report, over 3.6 million seniors have saved $2.1 billion on their prescription drugs. That is an average saving of $600 for every senior in Medicare's prescription drug coverage, often called the 'donut hole'. Seniors now receive 50 percent discounts on covered brand name drugs in the donut hole and new discounts on generic drugs. The donut hole is expected to be closed in 2020.

COVERAGE FOR CHILDREN AND YOUNG ADULTS

One of the early implementation of the law was to allow children under the age of 26 to get coverage under their parents plan. The law came into effect on September 23, 2010, six months after the president signed the law. Before this law, young adults would lose their insurance as soon as they graduated from college or high school. According to the 2012 government report, 3.1 million young adults have already secured their health insurance through their parents' plans.

PREVENTIVE CARE

The law also allows adults and children to have access to preventive screenings and tests at no cost over and above that of their insurance premiums. The screenings that do not require any co-pay or co-insurance include diabetes, blood pressure problems, HIV and other sexually transmitted diseases, cholesterol related illnesses, breast cancer screening and others. According to government sources, since the law took effect in 2012, over 54 million Americans have received coverage for preventive services free of cost. Furthermore, as of January 2013, 32.5 million people with Medicare used free preventive services. The new health reform law eliminated any deductible or co-pay for many preventive services or for a new annual Wellness Visit. In 2011 alone, more than 20 million seniors received cardiovascular screening free of charge.

EXPANDING MEDICAID TO LOW INCOME ADULTS:

The law bridged the gap in coverage for the poorest Americans by creating a minimum Medicaid income eligibility level across the country. Beginning in January 2014, individuals under 65 years of age with income below 133 percent of the federal poverty level (FPL) will be eligible for Medicaid. For the first time in the U.S. health care history, low-income adults without children will be guaranteed coverage through Medicaid in every State without need for a waiver, and parents of children will be eligible at a uniform income level across all States. A study from Harvard School of Public Health (HSPH) published in the New England Journal of Medicine (year) underlined the importance of this law in saving lives, pointing out that "expanding Medicaid to low-income adults leads to widespread gains in coverage, access to care and most-importantly improved health and reduced mortality." Eligibility and enrollment to this program will be much simpler and will be coordinated with the newly created Affordable Insurance Exchanges.

HEALTH INSURANCE EXCHANGE:

Health Insurance Exchange (HIX) is a governmental or quasi-governmental entity established to help insurance agencies comply with consumer protections and allow them to compete, as well as to enable the expansion of insurance coverage to millions of Americans. These exchanges will use a certain set of criteria to determine the insurance companies that are allowed to participate in them, facilitate transparency, accountability and increased enrollment, as well as delivery of subsidies.

In addition, the exchanges help to spread risk so as to ensure that costs associated with high medical needs are shared broadly across large groups.

When Congress passed the Affordable Health Care Bill, the law gave States the choice to either join together to run multi-state exchanges or to opt out of running their own exchange, in which case the federal government would step in to create an exchange for use by the State's residents. This type of practice is not new and when the Bill passed, there were already a few functioning health insurance exchanges including the Massachusetts Connector, the Utah Health Exchange and the New York-based Health Pass. Since the U.S is utilizing an employer-based healthcare payment system which singles out millions who either work for companies not offering health insurance benefits, or are self-employed and/or have no access to affordable insurance programs, the need to have a market place where individuals can shop around for insurance was a requirement. The highlight of the health insurance marketplace was to create an arena where competitive insurance companies would offer their health plans to those who need them within any given State. Citizens would be able to compare all their health insurance options in one place.

TIMELINE OF THE HEALTH CARE IMPLEMENTATION

The implementation of the law is to be phased in from September 2010 until January 2015. A brief summary of tasks to be completed during the implementation phase is listed below.

2010

- The Affordable Care Act becomes law
- Providing small business health insurance tax credit
- Allowing States to cover more people on Medicare
- Relief for seniors from high prescription drugs
- Cracking down on health care fraud
- Expanding coverage for early retirees
- Eliminating the pre-Existing condition requirement
- Extending coverage for young adults
- Providing free preventive care
- Prohibiting insurance companies from rescinding coverage
- Eliminating lifetime limits on insurance coverage
- Regulating annual limits on insurance coverage
- Prohibiting denying coverage of children based on pre-existing conditions
- Holding insurance companies accountable for unreasonable rate hikes
- Rebuilding the Primary Care workforce.

2011

- Establishing Consumer Assistance Programs in the States
- Funding for preventing disease and illness
- Strengthen community health centers
- Payments for rural health care providers
- Offering prescription drug discounts
- Providing free preventive care for seniors
- Effective January 1, 2011 Bringing down health care premiums
- Effective January 1, 2011 Addressing overpayment to big insurance companies and strengthening Medicare advantage
- Improving health care quality and efficiency
- Improving care for seniors after they leave the hospital

- October 1, 2011 administrative funding becomes available for new innovations to bring down costs
- Effective beginning October 1, 2011 increasing access to services at home and in the community

2012

- Effective January 1, 2012 encouraging integrated health systems
- Effective March 2012 understanding and fighting health disparities
- First regulation effective October 1, 2012 reducing paperwork and administrative costs
- Linking payment to quality outcomes
- Providing new voluntary options for long-term insurance

2013

- Effective January 1, 2013 improving preventive health coverage
- Effective January 1, 2013 increasing Medicaid payments for primary care doctors
- Effective no later than January 1, 2013 expanded authority to bundle payments
- Effective October 1, 2013 additional funding for the Children's Health Insurance Program (CHIP)

2014

- Effective January 1, 2014 establishing the Health Insurance Market Place
- Effective January 1, 2014 promoting individual responsibility
- Effective January 1, 2014 increasing access to Medicaid
- Effective January 1, 2014 make care more affordable
- Ensuring coverage for individuals participating in clinical trails
- Effective January 1, 2014 eliminating annual limits on insurance coverage
- Effective January 1, 2014 no discrimination due to pre-existing conditions or gender
- Increasing small business health insurance tax credit

2015
- January 1, 2015 paying physicians based on value not volume

Both the Supreme Court and the American people have rejected the arguments of the challengers and Obama care has become the law of the land.

Both the Supreme Court and the American people rejected the arguments of detractors of the Affordable Health Care Bill and accepted the fact that reforming the health care system would serve the country well. Realizing this hard fact, the House speaker John Boehner, in an interview with Diane Sawyer of ABC News, called the Patient Protection and Affordable Care Act *The Law of the Land*. Excerpts from transcripts of his interview are shown below:

Sawyer: A couple of other questions about the agenda now. You have said next year you would repeal the healthcare vote. That's still your mission?

Boehner: Well, I think the election changes that. It's pretty clear that the president was reelected. Obama.care is the law of the land. I think there are parts of the healthcare law that are gonna be very difficult to implement. And very expensive. And as the time when we're tryin' to find a way to create a path toward a balanced budget everything has to be on the table.

Sawyer: But you won't be spending the time next year trying to repeal Obama care?

Boehner: There certainly may be parts of it that we believe – need to change. We may do that. No decision at the point.

The re-election of the president marks the first time since its inception that Obama care is no longer considered a what-if. It is the future of health care in America. Winning the 100 year battle to reform the U.S health care system was one of the major milestones of the president's first term accomplishments. However, this same law became a variable or topic of the 2012 presidential campaigning and was still used to energize the opposition.

National Security

_____

Winding down the two costliest wars
and killing Osama Bin-Laden

The Human Cost of the Two Wars: As of 3/1/2013 over 6,700 U.S. military deaths (4,488 in Iraq and 2,178 in Afghanistan), 33,000 military wounded and 500,000 Iraqi and Afghan civilian deaths have been reported.

The Monetary Cost of the Two Wars: As of March 1, 2013, $1.4 trillion ($807 billion for Iraq, $571 billion for Afghanistan) has been spent on the two wars.

Cost Trade Off - Many have argued that for the same amount of money the country could have built many infrastructure projects - high tech research centers, hospitals, schools, airports and other major initiatives that would have made the U.S. more competitive on the global market.

THE IRAQ WAR

"What I am opposed to is a dumb war. What I am opposed to is a rash war. What I am opposed to is the cynical attempt by Richard Perle and Paul Wolfowitz and other armchair, weekend warriors in this administration to shove their own ideological agendas down our throats, irrespective of the costs in lives lost and in hardships borne. What I'm opposed to is the attempt by political hacks like Karl Rove to distract us from the rise in the uninsured, a rise in the poverty rate, a drop in the median income - to distract us from corporate scandals and a stock market that has just gone through the worst month since the Great Depression." *Obama's October 2, 2002 speech against going to war with Iraq*

THE "PROJECT FOR THE NEW AMERICAN CENTURY" AND THE WAR IN IRAQ

O N FEBRUARY 17, 1941, Henry Luce the founding editor of TIME Magazine published an article entitled *The American Century* where he anticipated that the United States would emerge from World War II as the world's greatest superpower. He argued that "it was time for the U.S. to accept wholeheartedly our duty and our opportunity as the most powerful and vital nation of the world and in consequence to assert upon the world the full impact of our influence, for such means as we see fit". Fifty six years later in the spring of 1997 a conservative 'think tank' *Project for the New American Century* was formed to "promote American global leadership", the same principle as Henry Luce envisioned. The organization underlined the importance of shaping circumstances before crisis emerges, and meet threats before they become dire. The primary goal of this think tank was to remind Americans that (a) the need to increase defense spending significantly if the country is to carry out its global responsibilities as well as modernize the armed forces for the future, (b) to strengthen U.S. ties to democratic allies and to challenge regimes hostile to the nation's interest and values, (c) to promote the cause of political and economic freedom abroad and (d) to accept responsibility of America's unique role in preserving and extending an international order friendly to the nation's security, prosperity and principles.

This think tank (PNAC) with it's over 20 neo-conservative members started to influence U.S. policies in different directions. On January 26, 1998, PNAC wrote a letter to President Clinton urging war against Iraq and the removal of Saddam Hussein arguing that he is a "hazard" to "a significant portion of the world's supply of oil". The letter also called for the U.S. to go to war alone, attack the United Nations and it suggested that the U.S. should not be crippled by a misguided insistence on unanimity in the UN Security Council. On May 29, 1998, in a letter to the leadership of the U.S. House of Representatives and U.S. Senate, this group continued to try to influence policy makers by painting scenarios of how to attack Iraq. An excerpt from the letter is shown below:

> "U.S. policy should have as its explicit goal removing Saddam Hussein's regime from power and establishing a peaceful and democratic Iraq in its place. We recognize that this goal will not

be achieved easily. But the alternative is to leave the initiative to Saddam, who will continue to strengthen his position at home and in the region. Only the U.S. can lead the way in demonstrating that his rule is not legitimate and that time is not on the side of his regime… We should establish and maintain a strong U.S. military presence in the region, and be prepared to use that force to protect our vital interest in the Gulf – and if necessary, to help remove Saddam from power."

WHO WERE THE KEY PLAYERS OF THIS NEO-CONSERVATIVE GROUP?
When George Bush became President, 10 out of the 18 people who signed the two letters to Clinton and the Congress joined the Bush administration and continued to plan the invasion of Iraq. They included Vice-President Dick Cheney, Defense Secretary Donald Rumsfeld, Assistant Defense Secretary Paul Wolfowitz, Deputy Secretaries of States Richard Armitage and Robert Zoellick, under-secretaries of State John Bolton and Paula Dobrinansky, presidential adviser for the Middle East Elliott Abrams, Defense Policy Board chairman Richard Perle and George W. Bush's Special Iraq envoy Zalmay Khalilzad. Others who remained influential were Jeb Bush, William Bennett, Jeffrey Bergner, Gary Bauer, Eliot A. Cohen, Midge Decter, Steve Forbes, Aaron Friedberg, Francis Fukuyama, Frank Gaffney, Robert Kagan, William Kristol, Peter Rodman, William Schneider, Vin Weber and James Woolsey.

JUSTIFICATION TO ATTACK - LINK IRAQ WITH WEAPONS OF MASS DESTRUCTION (WMD)
The people who signed the petition to attack Iraq under the New American Century Think Tank in 1998 took strategic positions in the Bush Administration starting from the Vice- President, Secretary of Defense, national security and other key positions and started to build their case to justify and convince the American people why they wanted to invade Iraq. Even though Saddam Hussein's regime was known for its repression and crime against humanity, going to war for this reason alone was not compelling enough, so there was a need to find other reasons that could be used to link U.S. national and international security to his

activities. The search for information yielded documents linking Iraq to WMD and training of Al-Qaida and despite warning signals from the intelligence community that the information was not creditable, these documents ended up as supporting evidence. With these in hand, the next step was to have the Secretary of State present Iraq's alleged possessions of nuclear, biological and chemical weapons, and the potential of transferring those weapons to al-Qaeda operatives at the United Nations Security Council meeting. The same information was given to the president to present his case to the American people.

In the meantime, the intimidation of people and undemocratic enforcement of the law in Iraq encouraged locals to produce false claims, and key officials from the U.S. administration jammed the airwaves to justify the reason for going to Iraq. Vice-President Dick Cheney said it was "pretty well confirmed that 9/11 hijacker Mohammed Atta met with Iraqi intelligence officials". Defense Secretary Donald Rumsfeld suggested that "the war in Iraq would be short and swift." Assistant Defense Secretary Paul Wolfowitz predicted that, "the U.S. would be greeted as liberators and Iraqi oil money would pay for the reconstruction". Defense Policy Board chairman Richard Perle suggested that Iraq had a hand in 9-11. On the other hand Scooter Libby, Vice-President Dick Cheney's chief of staff, repeatedly pressured CIA analysts to report that Iraq had weapons of mass destruction and links to Al Qaeda. John Hannah, deputy national security advisor to Vice-President Cheney who served as the conduit between Ahmad Chalabi's Iraqi National Congress and the Bush administration continued passing along false information about Iraq's alleged weapons of mass destruction that the administration relied upon to justify the invasion. Stephen Hadley, Deputy National Security Advisor disregarded memos from the CIA director George Tenet warning that the references to Iraq's pursuit of uranium be dropped from Bush's speeches. Condoleezza Rice, the National security advisor, disregarded at least two CIA memos and a personal phone call from Director George Tenet who suggested that the evidence behind Iraq's supposed uranium acquisition was weak. She said "we don't want the smoking gun to be a mushroom cloud".

THEN WE WENT TO WAR

March 18, 2003 – Bushes War Ultimatum Speech "My fellow citizens, events in Iraq have now reached the final days of decisions….We have passed more than a dozen resolutions in the United Nations Security Council. We have sent hundreds of weapons inspectors to oversee the disarmament of Iraq. Our good faith has not been returned…"

March 19, 2003 The Invasion Began: "My fellow citizens, at this hour, American and coalition forces are in the early stages of military operations to disarm Iraq, to free its people from grave danger".

THE RESULT - NO WEAPONS OF MASS DESTRUCTION

Over 4,000 of young soldiers gave their lives, tax payers took the burden of paying trillions for the cost, over a hundred thousand Iraqi citizens were killed, no weapons of mass destruction were found, no link with Al Qaida was found, American global leadership (the main purpose of the war according to the new American Century's letter to Congress) went down, instead of being greeted with flowers, shoes were thrown (the worst form of disrespect in the Iraqi culture) at our leaders. The world saw the worst form of human abuses (including torture), and the people who orchestrated all of this got promoted to different positions in the administration.

PRESIDENT OBAMA'S ACTION

As the public's support for the war hit bottom low, many Congressional proposals were presented to the Bush Administration to end the war and outline a withdrawal schedule. On 17 November 2005, Representative John Murtha introduced a resolution calling for the U.S. force in Iraq to be redeployed .The resolution was voted down. On June 2006 after the Republican majority House voted against establishing a deadline for the withdrawal of troops from Iraq, the then House Majority Leader John Boehner argued that "achieving victory is our only option and we must not shy away". The House Minority leader Nancy Pelosi warned that "stay(ing) the course' is not a strategy, it is a slogan and it's time to face the facts". On March 2007, Congress passed the resolution for the withdrawal of U.S. troops in Iraq by March 2008. President Bush vetoed the Bill.

To fulfill his presidential campaign promise to end the war in Iraq, shortly after he took office, on February, 27, 2009, President Obama outlined the schedule for withdrawing combat troops and ending the war he opposed from the beginning. At Marine Corps Base Camp Lejeune in North Carolina, he announced a deadline for the withdrawal of U.S. combat troops from Iraq. In his visit to Baghdad, he explained his plan to the troops there stating that "it was time for Iraqis "to take responsibility for their country and for their sovereignty". He urged Iraq's leaders to unite the country and include every ethnic faction into their new government. Ten days before the deadline, the last American combat brigade, the 4th Stryker Brigade, 2nd Infantry Division left Iraq marking the end of seven and a half years of U.S. military engagement in that country. On 15, December 2011, an American military ceremony was held in Baghdad to officially mark the end of the U.S. mission in Iraq.

WORLD REACTION TO THE COMPLETION OF THE WAR IN IRAQ

On the day the president announced the completion of the withdrawal from Iraq, many international newspapers provided their view of the decision and the impact of the war on the global economy and geo political stability. Antonio Cano a journalist for one of Spain's newspapers wrote an article summarizing the event - *"Over is an era in which the U.S. tried to impose democracy through force, and concluded that it was the most unfortunate and tragic military venture since the Vietnam War"*. He continued:

> "Finally, mission accomplished. After nearly nine years, America's war in Iraq will be over", President Barack Obama announced yesterday. He didn't do it from the solemnity of an aircraft carrier, like George Bush did on May 1, 2003, but in the modest White House Briefing Room. The primary difference between the two moments is that this time truly 'the rest of our troops will be home for the holidays.'… It is the end of a cycle that has affected U.S. foreign policy and global security for a decade. … This nation has already left in Iraq more than 4,400 men, more than $1 trillion and tons of prestige with the pretext of destroying an arsenal of weapons of

mass destruction that never existed…Obama runs the risk that this measure will be interpreted as a withdrawal of American foreign policy, as proof that the U.S. currently cannot deal with several conflicts at the same time. In part it is this. The economic crisis weights in more than anything and the U.S. needs to invest its money at home. But equally important is the fact that Obama wants to develop a new conception of the U.S' role internationally without the burden involved in an operation like Iraq… The definitive end of American presence in this conflict has another relevant aspect that connects it to the next phased exit from Afghanistan."

AFGHANISTAN – "THE OTHER WAR" "THE LONGEST U.S. WAR"

Located in a strategic point between the Middle East, Central Asia and the Indian sub-continent, Afghanistan has been the center for many conflicts that involved many countries including the British Empire, Imperial Russia, United States and neighboring Pakistan since 1838. The U.S. involvement in Afghanistan started in the late 1970s to support the mujahedeen movement during their fight against Babrak Kamal, the USSR installed ruler. In 1986 U.S. began supplying the mujahedeen with Stinger missiles, enabling them to shoot down Soviet helicopter gunships. Two years later in 1988 Afghanistan, USSR, Pakistan and the U.S. signed peace accords after which the Soviet Union began pulling out troops from Afghanistan. Between 1992 and 1996 the country collapsed into civil war and the situation helped the Taliban to seize control of Kabul allowing Afghanistan to be a safe haven for Osama bin Laden and his terror group. On August 7, 1998 simultaneous attacks organized by al Qaida were made on the U.S. embassies in Tanzania and Kenya, killed hundreds of people and in retaliation the U.S. launched missile strikes at suspected bases of their leader, Osama bin Laden.

On October 15, 1999, the United Nation Security Council adopted Resolution 1267, creating the al-Qaeda and Taliban Sanctions Committee, linking the two groups as terrorist entities and imposing sanctions on their funding, travel and arms shipments, in order to force Afghanistan to hand over Osama bin Laden for trial. A few days before 9/11, Ahmad Shah Massoud, commander of the Northern Alliance an anti-Taliban coalition, was assassinated by al-Qaeda operatives believed to have given a safe haven to bin Laden. On September 11, 2011 Al-Qaeda operatives hijacked four commercial airliners, crashing them into the World Trade Center and the Pentagon killing close to three thousand people. President George W. Bush promise to bring the people behind the attack to justice resulted in overwhelming support by the American people. One week after the attack on September 18, 2001, President Bush signed into law, a joint resolution authorizing the use of force against those responsible for attacking the United States on September 11. This resolution allowed the administration to take sweeping measures to combat terrorism, from invading Afghanistan to eavesdropping on U.S. citizens without a court order, to setting up the detention camp at Guantanamo Bay, Cuba. On October 7, 2001, the U.S. officially launched "Operation Enduring Freedom", an international bombing campaign against Taliban forces. A few months into the war in Afghanistan, the Taliban were in disarray and in mid-November, 2001, the UN Security Council passed resolution 1378 calling for a central role for the United Nations in establishing a transitional administration. The following month an interim government was created and Hamid Karzai was installed as administrator, with the help of international peacekeeping forces to maintain security in Kabul. December 2001 marked the end of the Taliban regime after Mullah Omar fled the city. In the same month it was reported that Osama bin Laden had escaped to Pakistan

MARCH 2002 - SHIFTING PRIORITY FROM AFGHAN TO IRAQ

In mid-March, during the largest international ground operation against many hundreds of al-Qaeda and Taliban fighters, Pentagon planners began shifting military and intelligence resources away from Afghanistan in the direction of Iraq. Barton Gellman and Dafna Linder, staff writers of the Washington Post, reported that CIA was scaling back operations in Afghanistan and was focusing on Iraq. The announcement according to this report marked "a year-long decrease of specialized military and intelligence resources from the geographic center of combat with Osama bin Laden. As Jihadist enemies reorganized, slipping back and forth from Pakistan and Iran, the CIA closed forward bases in the cities of Heart, Mazar-e Sharif and Kandahar. The agency also put off an $80 million plan to train and equip a friendly intelligence service for the new U.S-installed Afghan government ... and Task Force 5 – a covert commando team that led the hunt for bin Laden and his lieutenants in the border region - lost more than two thirds of its fighting strength." On May 1, 2003, the day President Bush declared "mission accomplished" for the war in Iraq, the Defense Secretary also declared an end to "major combat" in Afghanistan. Many events happened after this declaration including several counter-offensives by the U.S. and coalition forces. Thousands of soldiers were killed or wounded, a new president was sworn into the White House and the war continues until now, 2013, marking it as the longest U.S. war in history.

OBAMA'S NEW APPROACH: RETURNING AMERICA'S FOCUS TO THE CENTRAL FRONT AGAINST AL QAEDA AFTER YEARS OF DISTRACTION IN IRAQ

After taking the Oval office, the president and his administration conducted a thorough review of the U.S. objectives in Afghanistan and Pakistan and developed a new approach – instead of an indefinite military mission committing large numbers of U.S. troops, the new approach would increase assistance and training of Afghan forces to ensure that the Afghans take responsibilities for their own country's security. Although Americans will be essential partners of the Afghans, the understanding under the new approach would be that U.S. assistance should be targeted, result based and tied to clear and achievable metrics including establishing a benchmark to determine how many Afghan security forces can operate independently of the U.S. and the coalition force support. In the meantime however, a temporary increase in troop numbers was required to stabilize the political climate so that there was a proper transfer of military control. In addition the U.S. could finish the work of hunting Osama bin Laden – a process that had been stalled when the war effort's focus was changed to Iraq. This meant that attention had to be shifted back to Afghanistan by expanding the ground intelligence work. In the past, intelligence-sharing and close cooperation with foreign law enforcement and intelligence agencies had been effective in capturing suspected terrorists, which was more effective than deploying large numbers of soldiers.

THE PLANNED WITHDRAWAL FROM AFGHANISTAN

After the United States Special Forces killed Osama bin Laden, President Obama declared that America had largely achieved its goals in Afghanistan, reassuring the nation of the aggressive timetable for the withdrawal of troops by 2014. On February 1, 2012 the secretary of Defense, Leon Panetta announced that American forces would step back from combat roles there as early as mid-2013, a year before all troops were scheduled to come home. On May 1, 2012, nine years to date after Donald Rumsfeld declared the completion of major combat in Afghanistan, President Obama made a surprise trip to Kabul to sign a landmark strategic partnership agreement between the U.S. and Afghanistan, marking the beginning of the end of a crisis that had lasted for more than a decade. This strategic partnership agreement outlined both U.S. and Afghanistan's acceptance of certain conditions including pledges of American support to Afghanistan for 10 years after the withdrawal of the last American soldiers at the end of 2014. This step paved the way for the U.S. to make the transition of what the New York Times reported *"from the largest foreign military force in Afghanistan to a staunch, if far away, ally"* In September 2012, the military completed the withdrawal of the 33,000 troops that were deployed during the surge in 2009. As the New York reporter underlined, American officials entered 2013 with their eyes on the exit sign in Afghanistan, hoping to accelerate a process of winding down the nation's longest war.

"LIGHT FOOTPRINT STRATEGY" – NO BOOTS ON THE GROUND – OBAMA'S LESSONS LEARNED

With the end of the Iraq war and winding down in Afghanistan, president Obama may have reviewed the U.S. approach to intervening in crises across the globe as - "No boots on the ground". The analysis by the New York time reporter on Obama's 'lessons learned' summarizes this:

> "Behind the narrowed commitment laid out in the agreement (between U.S. and Afghanistan) lie lessons that have not only shaped Mr. Obama's Afghanistan strategy but also much of his foreign policy. Fatigue and frustration with the war have defined the strategies his administration has adopted to guide

how America intervenes in the world's messiest conflicts. Out of the experience emerged Mr. Obama's "light footprint" strategy, in which the United States strikes from a distance but does not engage in years–long, enervating occupations. That doctrine shaped the president's thinking about how to deal with the challenges that followed – Libya, Syria, and nuclear Iran."

THE HUNT FOR BIN-LADEN

CULMINATION OF YEARS OF INTELLIGENCE GATHERING

"The road to bin Laden's house in Abbottabad was being built, not 'brick by brick' but 'pebble by pebble". *Michael V. Hayden, former Director of the National Security Agency, and CIA.*

The Obama presidency is also remembered by the careful and secretive mission to kill America's number one enemy. A lot has been written on this subject and most agree that this action was done based on the intelligence information collected during the Bush Administration and a new focus and priority set by President Obama to kill or capture Osama bin Laden. Several attempts were made to track and kill him but he managed to stay alive for ten years after he killed thousands of innocent civilians and thousands more who went to Afghanistan to hunt him down. Finally the work was done and justice was served.

THE HUNT BEGAN

According to a detailed report from Washington Post three months after the 9/11 attack, the CIA field commander and his team believed to have spotted Osama in Afghanistan and called for action. The "Blue-82", a 15,000 pound daisy cutter bomb that could flatten a forest into a helicopter-sized landing zone, was delivered from a C-130 plane on the cave he was believed to be hiding in, killing many al-Qaeda fighters including the man the team believed was Osama bin Laden. A few days later, the same CIA team heard Osama addressing his soldiers through the radio of a dead al-Qaeda soldier and realized that he had escaped. Using his connections from the time of his fight along with the mujahidin against the Soviet invasion force, he created a temporary safe heaven along the Afghanistan-Pakistan border and stayed with Yunis Khalis, who he knew from their fight in the 1980s in Jalalabad. Khalis was an elderly Afghan warrior who controlled the territory along the border. When the U.S. intensified the attack, bin Laden then fled to the caves of Tora Bora.

HE FLED INTO PAKISTAN - CIA PULLED ITS RESOURCES TO IRAQ

A few days after he fled to the mountains, the CIA operatives spotted him and asked for action and there was an intensive bombardment that lasted two days. Unfortunately he escaped deeper into the mountain and later crossed the border into Pakistan. After the Tora Bora attempt, the Bush Administration pulled out many of the Special Operations and CIA forces as part of the preparation for the war in Iraq, including the drones that the U.S. forces depended on to track movements of terrorists. According to the Washington Post report citing an interview with Lt. Gen. John Vines, once, when Vines' troops believed they were within half an hour of catching up with bin Laden, the general asked for drones to cover three possible escape routes. But only one drone was available – others had been moved to Iraq. The target got away.

A SHIFT IN THINKING – FOCUS NOT ONLY ON HIS LOCATION BUT ALSO HIS COMMUNICATION STYLE

Several years passed without any convincing leads on the whereabouts of bin Laden including al-Qaeda's top people yet the group still managed to get instructions from him. This mystery forced the intelligence community to take a holistic view and approach the search from a different corner – "not only to focus on his location but his communication style" – how does he communicate? The four-year investigation and data triangulation started with a vague reference to a "trusted courier" believed to be obtained from the enhanced interrogation of one of the detainees. Here is what BBC called "the pivotal moment in the process".

So the hunt took a different twist – to think out of the box or think like him however tedious and complicated the job was. Ten years later on May 1, 2011 the job was completed by brave American soldiers who put their lives on the line. The leadership discipline exercised across the board, keeping the secret operation to only a handful of trusted advisors until it was completed, was a new discipline in Washington DC.

In 2002 following the 9/11 attacks, the CIA and U.S. military began rounding up suspected al-Qaeda members and interrogating them and officials began compiling information about major players, foot soldiers, couriers and money men. Some prisoners revealed that bin Laden had a trusted courier whose pseudonym was 'Abu Ahmed al-Kuwaiti". In 2003, the alleged mastermind of 9/11 Khalid Sheikh Mohammed was captured in the Pakistan city of Karachi and sent to a secret prison in Thailand. After weeks of interrogation he provided information on the courier and confirmed knowing al-Kuwaiti. In January 2004, the top al-Qaeda operative Hassan Ghul was captured in northern Iraq and confirmed that al-Kuwaiti was someone crucial to al-Qaeda and its leader and was close to Abu Faraj al-Libi, who succeeded Khalid Sheikh Mohammed. Hassan Ghul was considered to be the "linchpin". In May 2005, Abu Faraj al-Libi was captured in the northern Pakistan city of Mardan and he stated that when he was promoted to succeed Khalid Sheikh Mohammed, he received the word through a courier. He denied knowing al-Kuwaiti. Later on, he admitted knowing al-Kuwaiti and provided key information including that the courier carried messages from bin Laden to the outside world once every two months. Officials discovered the courier's family name and the National Security Agency (NSA) set to work intercepting telephone calls and emails between his family and anyone inside Pakistan. From these conversations, according to the report, they got his full name, Sheikh Abu Ahmed, a Pakistani man who was born in Kuwait. Four years later in 2009, U.S. intelligence agencies finally identified an area of Pakistan where the courier and his brother were operating but could not specify the exact location. In July 2010, satellite phone calls that the courier made to known al-Qaeda associates in the cities of Kohat and Charsada in Pakistan's Khyber Pakhtunkhwa province were monitored by the U.S. National Security Agency (NSA). A Pakistani agent working for the CIA spotted al-Kuwaiti driving his vehicle near the northern city of Peshawar and the team began tracking his movements. In August 2010, Al-Kuwaiti unknowingly led the agents to a compound in Abbottabad, 35 miles north of Islamabad and less than a mile from the Pakistan Military Academy, with a three story building inside and concrete walls as high as 18 ft. The CIA Director Leon Panetta briefed President Obama and his most senior national security aides, including Vice-President Joe Biden, Secretary of State Hilary Clinton and Defense Secretary Robert Gates. In autumn 2010, a safe house was set up in Abbotabad, from which CIA officers were able to observe daily activities at the compound for some months using cameras with telephoto lenses, infrared imaging equipment and high tech eavesdropping tools. The National Geospatial-Intelligence Agency (NGA) also developed highly detailed maps of the area and imagery of the compound for the CIA. By mid- February 2011, it was determined that there was a "sound intelligence basis" for developing courses of action to pursue bin Laden at the location and to plan a strike. The commander of the U.S. military Joint Special Operations Command (JSOC), Vice-Admiral William McRaven came up with three alternatives, a high-altitude bombing raid by B-2 Bombers, a "direct shot" with cruise missiles and a helicopter assault using a team of U.S. commandos. On March 14, 2011, the President chaired the first of five National Security meetings to discuss the options presented by Admiral McRaven and the administration officials were split on whether to launch a commando assault, order of an air or missile strike or wait and continue monitoring to gather more information. On March 22, the president asked his advisers their opinion and according to the report, Mr. Gates was skeptical of a helicopter assault calling it risky and he suggested that military officials look at using smart bombs. Finally, the helicopter assault was chosen as the favorite alternative using the Navy Seal team. Seal Team Six began rehearsing the operation at training facilities without knowing the target. On April 26, the CIA chief after discussions with dozens of aides concluded that the evidence was strong enough to risk the raid and two days later on April 28 told the president and his national security advisors to decide. The room, according to the report, was split 50-50 on which option to pick. The president concluded the meeting by saying: "*I'm not going to tell you what my decision is now – I'm going to go back and think about it some more but I'm going to make a decision soon*".

"IT'S A GO": A BITTER DECISION WITH LOTS OF IMPLICATIONS
On April 29, shortly before he boarded a helicopter that would take him to tour the tornado damage in Alabama, President Obama called his senior aides to the White House Diplomatic Room and handed over a

signed order instructing them to proceed with the helicopter assault. "It's a go", he said. The order was communicated to Admiral McRaven by Panetta to undertake the mission saying *"go in there and get bin Laden, and if bin Laden isn't there, get the hell out!"* On April 30, the president took a break from rehearsing for the White House Correspondents Dinner to call Admiral McRaven and wish him luck.

MAY DAY, 2011: THE MESSAGE WAS SEALED AND DELIVERED
On May 1, all West Wing tours were cancelled so that tourists and visiting celebrities would not see high-level national security officials gathered in the Situation Room monitoring the feeds they were getting from Mr. Panetta, who was coordinating the event from CIA headquarters in Langley. That night White House officials told major news anchors to stay put for an important security briefing from the president and the tension mounted with speculation. In the meantime the president and his aides started calling members of the Senate and Congress to brief them on what had happened after which came the big announcement:

> "Good evening. Tonight I can report to the American people and to the world that the United States has conducted an operation that killed Osama bin Laden, the leader of al Qaeda, and a terrorist who's responsible for the murder of thousands of innocent men, women, and children... And yet we know that the worst images are those that were unseen to the world. The empty seat at the dinner table. Children who were forced to grow up without their mother or their father. Parents who would never know the feeling of their child's embrace. Nearly 3,000 citizens taken from us, leaving a gaping hole in our hearts... Shortly after taking office, I directed Leon Panetta, the director of the CIA, to make the killing or capture of bin Laden the top priority of our war against al Qaeda, even as we continued our border efforts to disrupt, dismantle and defeat his network. Then, last August, after years of painstaking work by our intelligence community, I was briefed on a possible lead to bin Laden... Today, at my direction, the United States

launched a targeted operation against that compound in Abbottabad, Pakistan... After a firefight, they killed Osama bin Laden and took custody of his body. ... The American people did not choose this fight. It came to our shores, and started with senseless slaughter of our citizens. After nearly 10 years of service, struggle, and sacrifice, we know well the costs of war. These efforts weigh on me every time I, as Commander-in-Chief, have to sign a letter to a family that has lost a loved one, or look into the eyes of a service member who's been gravely wounded.... The cause of securing our country is not complete. But tonight, we are once again reminded that America can do whatever we set our mind to."

REACTION TO THE EVENT AND ITS IMPACT ON OBAMA'S BID FOR REELECTION

There was a sigh of relief from the American people especially from the families of the men and women who died in the U.S. because of Osama bin Laden's atrocities and fighting the war. Finally they had a sense of closure at the end of the 10-year long chapter of hunting bin Laden. Many political analysts thought "Obama ate the Republican's lunch and dinner", their stronghold of being tough in national and homeland security. President George W. Bush said "this momentous achievement marks a victory for America, for people who seek peace around the world and for all those who lost loved ones on September 11, 2001". President Bill Clinton described it as "a profoundly important moment for people all over the world who want to build a common future of peace, freedom and cooperation for our children. The Chinese government released their statement "a milestone and a positive development for the international anti-terrorism efforts". "We woke up in a safer world" was the comment from Jerzy Buzek, the president of the European Union Parliament. "A massive step forward in the fight against terrorism and the news of the death will bring great relief to people across the world" - comment by David Cameron, British Prime Minister; "Last night the forces of peace were able to report a success but international terrorism has not been yet defeated" – comment by Angela Merkel, German Chancellor. The secretary general of NATO, Andres Fogh Rasmussen, called the action "a significant success for the security of NATO allies and all the nations which have joined us in our efforts to combat the scourge of global terrorism".

Obama did not make it a campaign event or immediately use it in his bid for reelection but he did deliver on his promise that he would bring Osama to justice. He ended the war in Iraq, shifted resources back to Afghanistan, beefed up the intelligence work to connect dots by sharing information from the field to various offices, coordinated and directed one of the top secretive tasks in modern U.S. history and put his political career on the line when he decided to send Americans to get Osama. If anything had gone wrong with this last action, he would most likely have been criticized for his decision. But despite this possibility, he took time to decide the best strategy to bring this to closure. 10 years after the former President Bush who stood on the smoldering wreckage of World Trade Centers, bullhorn in hand and declared "the people who knocked these buildings down will hear [from] all of us soon" after the killing of Osama bin Laden, the President went to New York to meet members of the New York firefighter and police departments and visited Ground Zero to meet with family members of some of the fallen. He said *"the killing of bin Laden told the world that when we say we will never forget, we mean what we say"*. After meeting with the firefighters at the "Pride of Manhattan" firehouse, the president said "I wanted to just come here to thank you. This is a symbolic site of the extraordinary sacrifice that was made on that terrible day almost 10 years ago. It didn't matter who was in charge, we were going to make sure that the perpetrators of the horrible act - that they received justice". Obama had invited President Bush to join him at Ground Zero but Bush declined the invitation and said through his spokesman that he preferred to remain out of the spotlight since leaving office in 2009. At Ground Zero Obama made no comments about this, but rather, simply greeted relatives of victims.

The Obama Presidency and the Roberts Court

A Roller-coaster Ride

"From the awkward swearing-in of President Obama by Chief Justice Roberts to Obama's caustic reaction to the Citizens United ruling to Robert's support of Obama's health care law, the tumultuous relationship between the administration and the Supreme Court has been increasingly evident." *Vanessa Bush, The Booklist*

THE BALANCING FORCE OF THE COUNTRY – THE SUPREME COURT

AS THE JUDICIAL BRANCH of the government, the Supreme Court via court cases, explains the meaning of the Constitution and laws passed by Congress and rules whether something is constitutional or unconstitutional. It has nine justices (eight associate justices and one chief justice) nominated by the President and approved by the Senate. There is no term limit. Its decisions are final and no other court can overrule them. In most cases, these decisions set precedents to look at new ways of interpreting the law. Over one hundred and ten justices have served the Supreme Court since its first session in 1790, made decisions that shaped and affected how we live today. Some of the decisions are still hard to understand for ordinary people but as the highest law enforcer of the land, its decisions have been respected and they continue to be the law of the land. Some of the significant decisions involving so-called watershed cases made by the court include (a) the 1857 Dred Scott V. Sanford case where the court declared that a slave was not a citizen and that Congress could not outlaw slavery in U.S. Territories. The decision explained that federal government had no power to regulate slavery in the territories and that people of African descent both slave and free, were not protected by the Constitution and were not U.S. citizens, (b) the 1896 Plessy v. Ferguson where the court upheld the constitutionality of state laws requiring racial segregation in public facilities under the doctrine of "separate but equal", (c) the 1954 Brown v. Board of Education where the court made racial segregation in schools illegal, (d) the 1966 Miranda v. Arizona where the court stated that criminal suspects must be informed of their rights before being questioned by the police, (e) the 1973 Roe v. Wade where the court made abortion legal and (f) the 2003 Grutter v. Bollinger and Gratz v.

Bollinger where the court ruled that colleges can, under certain conditions, consider race and ethnicity in admissions. The latest two decisions, on healthcare and campaign financing, were made under President Obama's first term and made the relationship between the judicial and executive branches of the government interesting.

The selection of a new president always raises questions on how his decision on nomination of the justices affects the composition of the court, as well as the political landscape of the country. With two successful appointments to the Supreme Court of the United States in his first term in office, the relationship between the Supreme Court and the president and every decision made by both during the Obama presidency, was marked as historic. Even though the two heads have similar educational backgrounds – Harvard law school and served in Harvard Law Review – they came from different walks of life, different political views and different paths to take the country to the next level. This relationship was described by some as a "roller coaster ride" where it started back in the day when the then senator Obama opposed the nomination of justices Alito, the second Bush nominee to the bench, Obama's first day in the office when he was sworn in by Chief Justice Robert who stumbled administering the oath process and had to redo it, the nomination of the first Hispanic on the Supreme Court, assigning two women to the court, decisions that lead to the rise of the super PACs as well as giving the president a constitutional validation for the healthcare law that had cost two full years of his presidency, the power transfer in the house and the rise of the Tea Party movement, all of which were some of the visible interactions between the executive and the judiciary branches of the government . Supreme Court members also knew that if Obama was elected, he would have a chance to put his signature on the composition of the justices and he would not shy away from expressing his views on how the Court should handle cases. During his 2008 campaign at the Planned Parenthood Action Fund event, he summarized his intention when he became the president with the statement:

"I think the Constitution can be interpreted in so many ways. And one way is a cramped and narrow way in which the constitution and the courts essentially become the rubber stamps of the powerful in society. And then there's another vision of the court that says that the courts are the refuge of the powerless. Because often times they can lose in the democratic back and forth. They may be locked out and prevented from fully participating in the democratic process. And we need someone who's got the heart – the empathy – to recognize what it's like to be a young teenage mom. The empathy to understand what it's like to be poor or African-American or gay or disabled or old – and the criteria by which I'll be selecting my judges."

In his book *The Oath*, Jeffrey Toobin explained the relationship between the two branches of the government and their heads (Obama and Roberts) as:

"From the moment John Roberts, Chief Justice of the United Sates, fumbled the oath of office at Barack Obama's inauguration, the relationship between the Court and the White House has been tense and confrontational. The president and the chief justice are young, brilliant, charismatic, charming, and determined to change the course of the nation – and completely at odds on almost every major constitutional issues. And now they are also linked in history because of Robert's stunning vote to uphold Obama's health care plan. The battle between the two branches of government has often been bitter, and public. In his 2010 State of the Union address, in an unusual breach of protocol, Obama criticized the controversial ruling in the Citizen United case, which removed decades old restrictions on political spending by corporations, freeing them to flood the airwaves with anti-Obama advertising. As Obama spoke, Bush appointee Justice Samuel Alito muttered, "Not true." With an election on the horizon – and the possibility that the conservatives may lose their 5-4 majority – the Roberts Courts has accepted cases on many issues dear to the heart to the conservative movement."

The rift was clearly seen by the reaction of Justice Alito during the 2011 State of the Union speech by the president opposing the court's decision to revert its own ruling and allow corporations to enjoy uncontrolled and unregistered campaign contributions to candidates that could influence the political election process. Justices Samuel Alito was whispering "Not true, not true" and shook his head after the president said "special interest" which some believed was him reacting to the speech. It was also not clear whether the Justice was recalling the then Obama's remarks at his confirmation hearing by the senate where he said "Alito is an accomplished jurist, but when you look at his record – when it comes to his understanding of the Constitution, I have found that in almost every case, he consistently sides on behalf of the powerful against the powerless, on behalf of strong government or corporation against upholding American's individual rights." After his confirmation, according to the Washington Post report, he has expressed unhappiness with the confirmation process and did not show up when President-elect Obama and Vice-President-elect Biden accepted Chief Justice John Roberts's invitation to pay a courtesy call on the court. He was also the only member who did not attend the afternoon event.

SUPREME COURT'S WATERSHED DECISION — CAMPAIGN FINANCING — OPENING THE FLOODGATES FOR DARK MONEY

"With all due deference to separation of powers, last week the Supreme Court reversed a century of law that, I believe, will open the floodgates, to spend without limit in our elections. I don't think American elections should be bankrolled by America's most powerful interests or worse, by foreign entities. They should be decided by the American people. And I urge Democrats and Republicans to pass a bill that helps correct some of these problems." *President Obama at the 2011 State of the Union Speech*

Hillary: The Movie was the center point of argument that resulted in a controversial decision by the Supreme Court. In January 2008, Citizens United, a nonprofit organization, released a 90 minute documentary *Hillary: The Movie* which was based on whether the then senator Hillary Clinton, a candidate for the Democratic presidential nomination, was fit for the presidency. The movie was distributed in theaters and on DVD as well as through video on demand. Anticipating that the movie would be made available on cable television through video-on-demand within 30 days of primary elections, Citizens United produced television ads to run on broadcast and cable television. Citizens United planned to use general treasury funds to pay for the ad expense. However federal law prohibits corporations and unions from spending general treasury funds on "electioneering communications" or for speech that expressly advocates the election or defeat of a candidate. According to the interpretation of the law, electioneering communication includes any broadcast, cable or satellite communication that (a) refers to a clearly identified candidate for federal office, (b) is made within 30 days of a primary election or 60 days of a general election and (c) is publicly distributed. Suspecting that the movie would be blocked under the third option, Citizens United filed an injection request in federal district court against the Federal Election Commission (FEC) arguing that the law is unconstitutional. Furthermore, Citizens United also submitted a request to the court to reject the Bipartisan Campaign Reform Act's (BCRA) disclaimer and disclosure requirements, as they are unconstitutional as applied to the movie they plan to release. Part of the law for the Bipartisan Campaign Reform Act 311 requires that televised electioneering communications funded by anyone other than a candidate for office must include a clear, readable disclaimer displayed on the screen for at least four seconds. The disclaimer also must identify the person or organization responsible for the advertisement, that the person or organization's address or website and a statement that the advertisement "is not authorized by any candidate or candidate's committee. The other part of the BCRA 200 states that any person who spends more than $10,000 on electioneering communications during a calendar year must file a disclosure statement with the FEC and the statement must identify the person making the expenditure, the amount, the election to which the communication was directed and the names of the contributors. The district court denied these motions and granted summary judgment to FEC so Citizens United appealed to the U.S. Supreme Court. The case was argued on March 24 and September 9, 2009 and decided on January 21, 2010.

AND THE DECISION WAS

That corporations and labor unions have a First Amendment right to engage in independent spending to influence elections. By a vote of five to four, the Justices overturned their own precedents and struck down a portion of federal election law that prohibited corporations and labor unions from spending their own funds directly, to urge support for political candidates. Under the Supreme Court's decision corporations, unions and issue advocacy organizations may now spend unlimited amounts of money from their treasuries on independent political expenditures in support of, or opposition to a candidate affecting U.S. politics. According to an analysis sponsored by Bloomberg Law, the Citizens United ruling has sparked a huge controversy about the role of corporate money in politics, about deference to legislative judgments and about the role of the Supreme Court in the U.S. democracy system.

Under the federal Bipartisan Campaign Reform Act of 2002, corporations and unions could make campaign expenditures through separate funds, namely "Political Action Committees (PACs). These PACs were limited in getting funds and were not allowed to use union or corporation money. However under the new law approved by the Supreme Court, the PACs could donate to candidates and could make independent expenditures to support candidates without limits, regulations and disclosure requirements. This law fundamentally changed the campaign financing landscape where corporations and unions are entitled to the protection of the First Amendment for political speech.

THE REACTION AND IMPLICATIONS — ARE WE GOING BACK TO THE ROBBER-BARON ERA OR GILDED AGE? OR BOTH?

In 1873, Mark Twain and Charles Dudley Warner published a novel entitled *The Gilded Age: A Tale of Today* where they analyzed the story of greed and political corruption in post-Civil War America, a time of rampant greed and speculative frenzy of the marketplace and corruption, pervading national politics. During those years, America's economy grew at an extraordinary rate, generating unprecedented levels of wealth.

Railroads and soon telephone lines, stretched across the country, creating new opportunities for entrepreneurs and cheaper goods for consumers. However a nation that had long viewed itself in idyllic terms, as a nation of small farmers and craftsman, confronted the emergency of a society increasingly divided between the haves and the have-nots – a society in which many poor workers struggled just to survive while an emerging industrial and financial aristocracy lived in palatial homes and indulged in opulent amusements. Some Americans celebrated the new wealth, others lamented, it, all could agree that profound changes were taking place in the country.

Times changed and in 1907 another greed surfaced from robber baron – era scandals forced Congress to ban corporate contributions to federal candidates and in 1947 the ban was formally applied to corporate expenditure including that of labor unions. To further enforce the law, in 1974 after the Watergate scandal Congress passed another law to limit individual contributions to federal candidates and political committees. In 1989, after the "Keating Five" scandal, John McCain became the lead advocate to establish a much tougher campaign finance reform in collaboration with Senator Feingold resulting in the passing of the law later called the "McCain-Feingold law". This law was planned to prohibit corporation and labor union funding for any broadcast ads that mentioned a candidate within thirty days of a primary or caucus or within sixty days of a general election. Furthermore it was to differentiate between the candidate vs. issue advertisement since the previous law permitted corporations and unions to directly advertise attacking candidates. Twenty years later in 2010, the U.S. Supreme Court gave corporations the permission to give unlimited amounts to other groups to spend as long as the expenditure was made independently from the supported candidate.

THAT WAS HOW THE SUPER PACS WERE BORN. A DISASTER FOR DEMOCRACY

According to Fred Wertheimer, "The Citizens United ruling that gave rise to Super PACs was one of the worst in Supreme Court history. Super PACs are federally registered political action committees that raise unlimited contributions from the super-rich, corporations, labor unions and other entities and spend these funds to make "independent expenditure in federal elections." He continued, "Super PACs are a game for millionaires and billionaires. They are a game for corporations and other wealthy interests while citizens are pushed to the sidelines to watch the corruption of our democracy. People who argued against the ruling warned it opened the floodgates allowing corporations to spend hundreds of millions of dollars to influence federal, state and local elections. Furthermore, the Supreme Court repealed its own ruling which limited the protection of the first Amendment to individuals. Some analysts went further, arguing that the court scrapped its own precedents and substituted another judgment against that of Congress about whether corporate funds harm or have a corrupting influence on elections or not. On the other hand, groups which support the decision argue that the influence of corporate funds has not had a harmful impact on voters and is offset somewhat by the expenditure of the Union funds. Others lauded the action and underlined the fact that the Supreme Court has made the application of First Amendment principles to political campaigns more rational and consistent and even argued that neither Congress nor the executive branch provided any hard evidence of actual corrupting influences from campaign expenditures. They also did not shy away from their remarks that corporations have an important role to play in political debate and public discourses.

AND WE WERE TOLD THAT THEY ARE INDEPENDENT FROM CANDIDATES—REALLY?
Questions:
- Taking the Supreme Court's view, how can one justify the independence of a senator, if a corporation spends $30 million to elect him or her, for surely there is a corrupting influence over the senator's position. What is the justification to not believe that Super PACs with their handful of very rich contributors have influence over the result of the election?
- What is the convincing argument that independent expenditure by corporations cannot have a corrupting influence on federal officeholders?

According to Open Secrets, as of March 8, 2013, over 1,318 groups were organized as Super PACs and have reported total receipts of

$838,082,215 and total independent expenditures of $ 631,470,703. The two conservative Super PACs that supported Romney for the 2012 presidential election (Restore Our Future with $142 million, and American Crossroads with $104 million) followed by three liberal PACs (Priorities USA Action with $65 million, Majority PAC with $38 million and House Majority PAC with $31 million) were the top in the list. On January 17, 2013 a joint study between Demos and the U.S. PIRG Education Fund published a research paper entitled *Billion-dollar democracy: the unprecedented role of money in the 2012 elections* on the influence of Super PACs in the 2012 presidential election and provided the following astonishing numbers:

- The top 32 Super PAC donors, giving an average of $9.9 million each, matched the $313.0 million that President Obama and Mitt Romney raised from all of their small donors combined – that is, at least 3.7 million people giving less than $200.

- Nearly 60% of Super PAC funding came from just 159 donors contributing at least $1 million. More than 93% of the money Super PACs raised came in contributions of at least $10,000 – from just 3,318 donors, or the equivalent of 0.0011% of the U.S. population.

- It would take 322,000 average-earning American families giving an equivalent share of their net worth to match Sheldon Abelson's' $91.8 million contribution (the couple who gave $10 million to the Super PAC supporting Newt Gingrich).

- Super PACs accounted for more than 60% of outside spending reported to the FEC

- For the 2012 cycle, Super PACs received more than 70% of their funds from individuals, and a significant percentage (12%) from for profit business.

THE RISE OF THE TEA PARTY — FED BY SUPER PAC MONEY

Even though the birth of the Tea Party movement started in early 2009 as a movement of anti-taxation, anti-regulation, anti-abortion, anti-anything that came from the White House, it later got support from the

Supreme Court's decision on the freedom of corporations to finance and support specific candidates by wealthy individuals like the Koch brothers (David and Charles) and interest groups like Americans for Prosperity and Freedom, to pump money into congressional races resulting in a clean sweep of Republicans in the House during the 2010 mid-term election, and positioned the party to come out a divided but strong contender for the general election. The discussion among political analysts on the relevance of the party was pointed out in the media and included whether the movement represented a new paradigm in American politics or was simply the latest and the noisiest manifestation of the long-term right-ward shift of the Republican party – a shift that marked the beginning of a political agenda masked by hidden objectives to further divide the country. Many believed that the other crucial factor for the emergence of the party movement at the grass roots level was the 2008 Democratic victory with the election of the president because he is not only the first African-American president, but also the first non-southern Democratic president since John F Kennedy, and also the most progressive Democratic president since Franklin D. Roosevelt.

APPOINTMENT OF THE FIRST LATINO JUDGE TO THE HIGHEST COURT OF THE LAND

After serving over 18 years as Associate Justice of the Supreme Court of the United States, Justice David Hackett Souter announced that he was retiring on May 1, 2009 providing President Obama an opportunity to nominate his replacement. The search for the new judge was intense and the White House came up with a short list of candidates which included Judge Sonia Sotomayor of the Second Circuit, Judge Diane Pamela Wood of the Seventh Circuit, Solicitor General Elena Kagan, Homeland Security Secretary Janet Napolitano, California Supreme Court Justice Carlos Moreno and Michigan Governor Jennifer Granholm. Four women (Sotomayor, Wood, Kagan and Napolitano) made the final list and were interviewed by the president and vice-president. On May 26, 2009 a few months after being sworn in as the first African-American president, Obama announced that he had decided to nominate the federal appeals judge Sonia Sotomayor to the Supreme Court to become the nation's first Hispanic and the Court's 111th justice. When announcing the nomination, the president commented, "When Sonia

Sotomayor ascends those marble steps to assume her seat on the highest court of the land, America will have taken another important step towards realizing the ideal that is etched above its entrance, 'Equal justice under the law'. Sotomayor was a graduate from Princeton University and Yale Law School and later became editor for the law review. Entering into her professional life, she served as a prosecutor and partner in a law firm. She was nominated in 1992 by President Bush, Sr to the U.S. District Court for the Southern District of New York and later confirmed by unanimous consent. In 1997, President Clinton nominated her to the U.S. Court of Appeals for the Second Circuit. However, in spite of her excellent record and a rating of "well-qualified" by the American Bar Association, her nomination was delayed by Senate Republicans for more than a year. In October 1998, Republican Sen. Alfonse D'Amato of New York re-initiated the confirmation process by supporting her nomination and she was confirmed with a 67-29 vote and with 25 Republicans' support. Her outstanding record indicated that from over 3,000 cases and 380 opinions, only three were reversed by the Supreme Court.

The confirmation process was intense, highlighting her career and remarks including her 2001 speech on diversity when she said, "I would hope that a wise Latina woman with richness of her experience would more often than not reach a better conclusion than a white male who hasn't lived that life." Some conservatives took the statement as evidence of bias or worse, with a few including Newt Gingrich labeling her remarks as "racist". Responding to the allegation at the confirmation hearing, Sotomayor replied that her remark was "a rhetorical flourish that fell flat" and she asserted that "I do believe that every person has an equal opportunity to be a good and wise judge, regardless of their background or life experience." On July 28 the Senate Judiciary Committee voted 13-6 to recommend her to the full Senate with only one Republican (Senator, Lindsay Graham) supporting her and on August 6, the full Senate voted 68-31 including nine Republicans in support to confirm the nomination. This event marked the inclusion of the first Latina Justice since the first public session of the court in 1790.

THE LIFE OF SONIA SOTOMAYOR: AN AMERICAN STORY

Born from two Puerto Rican immigrant parents Celina Baez and Juna Sotomayor, who came to the U.S. for a better life, Sonia is an example of how successful anybody can be if he or she gets the opportunity to pursue the American dream. She was raised with her brother by her mom in a South Bronx housing project, after being diagnosed with Type 1 diabetes at the age of eight and having lost her dad to a heart attack at the age of nine. Her mother struggled to make ends meet while determinedly pursuing her own education, being trained as a nurse practitioner. This allowed her to send her children to a Catholic school and Sonia experienced a fair share of ups and downs in her life. These events shaped her and were followed by a scholarship to Princeton, where she graduated with honors before being accepted to Yale Law School.

Sonia Sotomayor recognizes the fact that some of the decisions the government made including the 'Affirmative Action', impacted her. Jeffrey Toobin wrote in his book, "For all of her achievements, Sotomayor held no illusions about one of the reasons for her success. As she said in a speech after she became a judge, 'I am a product of affirmative action. I am the perfect affirmative action baby. My test scores were not comparable to that of my colleagues at Princeton or Yale, but not so far off the mark that I wasn't able to succeed at those institutions'".

Social Energy and Environmental Policies

"In a nod to a dramatic shift in public opinion, Barack Obama on Wednesday became the first sitting president to announce his support for same-sex marriage." *The Huffington Post*

THE OBAMA PRESIDENCY is also shaped by many social issues that are close to all Americans and sometimes were emotional and questionable. These issues are partly personal but bounded by the norm and culture and considered as a normal way of life. Some of them are identified 'normal' for humanity collectively, but personal in most cases. These social issues are equal pay, Don't ask Don't tell, Gay marriage, abortion, contraception, civil rights, separation of church and state and embryonic stem cell research. The debate over these issues and the decision made during his first term, had a significant effect on the way the country lives as well as on his 2012 re-election bid.

EQUAL PAY RIGHTS

Lilly Ledbetter, a former Goodyear Tire employee, filed a sex bias suit under Title VII of the Civil Rights Act of 1964 against Goodyear Tire and Rubber Company claiming that over a period of 19 years she was paid merit increases between 15 and 40 percent lower than similarly situated and in some cases lesser qualified men. The Eleventh Circuit dismissed her case and ruled in favor of Goodyear and the Supreme Court affirmed the Eleventh Circuit's decision with the justification that an employee must file charges with the Equal Employment Opportunity Commission (EEOC) within 180 days of a discriminatory pay decision. In 2009, the case was presented to Congress which found that the Supreme Court's ruling significantly impaired statutory protections against discrimination by unduly restricting the time period in which victims of discrimination could challenge and recover for discriminatory compensation decisions or other practices contrary to the intent of Congress. In January 2009, the Lilly Ledbetter Fair Pay Act of 2009 was passed and on January 29, 2009 it became the first bill that president Obama would sign into law.

Under this law, individuals subjected to compensation discrimination may file a charge within 180 or 300 days when a discriminatory compensation decision or other practice is adopted, or a person becomes subject to a discriminatory compensation decision or other practice, or a person is affected by the application of a discriminatory compensation decision or other practice, including each time wages, benefits, or other compensation is paid resulting in whole or in part from such a compensation decision or other practice. At the signing ceremony the president underlined the importance of equal pay saying, "it is fitting that with the very first bill I signed – the Lily Ledbetter Fair Pay Restoration Act – we are upholding one of this nation's first principles: that we are all created equal and each deserves a chance to pursue our own version of happiness."

Eight Republicans out of 219 voted in favor of the bill and notably, the 2008 Republican presidential candidate John McCain opposed while in 2012 Mitt Romney declined to take a public stand on it. Senator Marco Rubio, the Florida Republican supported Mitt Romney's position and argued that he supported the principle of equal pay for women but not the bill itself as it could be a boon for trial lawyers.

LESBIAN AND GAY RIGHTS

The history of reaction to homosexuality in the U.S. was both emotional and confrontational. In 1950 homosexuals were included in the list of anarchists, communists and other people deemed un-American and subversive who were considered to be security risks for the country. In the 1950s and 1960s the Federal Bureau of Investigation (FBI) and police departments kept lists of known homosexuals, their favored establishments, and friends and the U.S. Post Office kept track of addresses where materials pertaining to homosexuality were mailed. State and local governments followed suit. Bars catering to homosexuals were shut down and their customers were arrested and exposed in newspapers. Cities performed "sweeps" to rid neighborhoods, parks, bars and beaches of gays. They outlawed the wearing of opposite gender clothes, and universities expelled instructors suspected of being homosexual.

Thousands of gay men and women were publicly humiliated, physically harassed, fired, jailed or institutionalized in mental hospitals. Many lived double lives, keeping their private lives secret from their professional ones. According to Barry Adam's report, between 1947 and 1950, 1,700 federal job applications were denied, 4,380 people were discharged from the military and 420 were fired from their government jobs for being suspected homosexuals. In the early 1950s, in their Diagnostic and Statistical Manual, the American Psychiatric Association (APA) listed homosexuality as a sociopathic personality disturbance and subsequent studies justified the disorder as a pathological hidden fear of the opposite sex caused by traumatic parent-child relationships. APA later in 1973 removed that statement from their manual. A few organizations were formed to support those marginalized as homosexual and promote their cause to the society.

THE 1969 STONEWALL RIOT

The Stonewall Inn located at 51 and 53 Christopher Street in Greenwich Village, New York City was the birth place for the official homosexual movement that resisted and protested against police raids and arrests. On June 28, 1969 the Stonewall Inn was seized by the police and many people were arrested. Many homosexuals again gathered to protest the raid and the arrests. On the first anniversary of the Stonewall riot, the first Gay Pride march began in Central Park and later expanded throughout the country and the free world.

On June 29, 2009 on the 40th anniversary of the Stonewall Rebellion, president Obama and the First Lady hosted the LGBT Pride month reception at the White House for families, volunteers, community leaders, lawmakers and heads of LGBT organizations. At the program the president said,

> "Now this struggle, I don't need to tell you, is incredibly difficult, although I think it's important to consider the extraordinary progress that we have made. There are unjust laws to overturn and unfair practices to stop. And though we've made progress, there are still a few citizens, perhaps neighbors or even family members and loved ones, who still hold fast to worn

arguments and old attitudes, who fail to see your families are like their families, and who would deny you the rights that most Americans take for granted. And I know this is painful and I know it can be heartbreaking … It's the story of the Stonewall protest, which took place 40 years ago this week, when a group of citizens with few options and fewer supporters – decided they'd had enough and refused to accept a policy of wanton discrimination. And two men who were at those protests are here today. Imagine the journey that they've travelled…. As we've seen so many times in history, once that spirit takes hold there is little that can stand in its way. And the riots at Stonewall gave way to protest, and protests gave way to a movement and the movement gave way to a transformation that continues to this day. It continues when a partner fights for her right to sit at the hospital bedside of a woman she loves. It continues when a teenager is called a name for being different and says, 'So what if I am?' It continues in your work and in your activism, in your fight to freely live your lives to the fullest."

On June 17, 2009, the president issued a memorandum directing executive agencies to extend benefits to the domestic partners of federal employees within the authority of existing law. The law allows administration personnel to take leave to care for sick partners and requires the government to recognize their partners as household members when determining overseas housing allocations for State Department employees, among other things. In June, 2010, the president released a second memorandum that extended specific benefits to the same-sex partners of federal employees, including coverage of travel, relocation and subsistence payments. According to the Congressional Research Service's 2011 report, it is estimated that there are 34,000 federal employees in same-sex relationships including state-recognized marriages, civil unions, or domestic partnerships. This act was criticized by most prominent gay and lesbian political leaders as short of his campaign promise to repeal the Defense of Marriage Act while conservatives criticized the president's action as outrageous. The Defense of Marriage Act (DOMA) enacted September 21, 1996 defines marriage as the legal union of one man and one woman for federal and inter-state recognition. Both Houses passed the law by large majorities and was signed by President Bill Clinton. Part of the law underlines marriage stating:

> "In determining the meaning of any Act of Congress, or of any ruling, regulation, or interpretation of the various administrative bureaus and agencies of the United States, the word 'marriage' means only a legal union between one man and one woman as husband and wife, and the word 'spouse' refers only to a person of the opposite sex who is a husband or wife."

DON'T ASK DON'T TELL

Since 1950 when President Harry Truman signed the Uniform Code of Military Justices, which sets up discharge rules for homosexual service members, the issue has been long, emotional and sometimes confrontational. In 1982, president Regan signed a defense directive that underlined the fact that "homosexuality is incompatible with military services" and the directive was to discharge people who engaged in homosexual acts or stated that they were homosexual or bisexual. Ten years later in 1992 presidential candidate Bill Clinton promised to lift the ban and a year later he issued a defense directive that military applicants should not be asked about their sexual orientation, resulting in the directive being referred to as "Don't ask, don't tell". One year later, a federal court reinstated Col. Grethe Cammermeyer who was discharged due to her sexual orientation to the Washington State National Guard where she served openly until her retirement in 1997. Later the documentary film *Serving in Silence: The Colonel Margarethe Cammermeyer Story* was produced based on her life. In 2003 after leaving Office, President Bill Clinton called for an end to "Don't ask, don't tell". The Supreme Court's decision ruling unanimously that federal government could withhold funding to force universities to accept military recruiters in violation of university nondiscrimination policies, especially upholding "Don't ask, don't tell" was another milestone for this initiative. During the 2008 presidential election, the then senator

Obama promised to repeal the law. After taking office he worked with Senate and House members to craft a bill that will repeal the ban. In 2010 the House and Senate committee approved an amendment to the annual defense spending bill that would end the ban, but added a provision that no change would take place until the Pentagon conducted a study to reveal how the repeal would affect armed force's military readiness. In November 2010, a Pentagon report was released concluding that military service members regarded gays in the military as a low risk to armed force's abilities and effectiveness. A Senate Republicans' filibuster on the December 9th vote repealed the ban as part of the defense reauthorization bill. On Dec 15, 2010 the House approved a bill to repeal the "Don't ask, don't tell" directive and three days later the Senate voted 65-31 to repeal the law later signed by the president. At the signing ceremony the president said:

> "… I am proud to sign a law that will bring an end to "Don't ask, don't tell". It is a law – this law I'm about to sign will strengthen our national security and uphold the ideals that our fighting men and women risk their lives to defend. No longer will our country be denied the service of thousands of patriotic Americans who were forced to leave the military – regardless of their skills, no matter their bravery or their zeal, no matter their years of exemplary performance – because they happen to be gay. No longer will tens of thousands of Americans in uniform be asked to live a lie, or look over their shoulder, in order to serve the country that they love …. Now, many fought long and hard to reach this day. I want to thank the Democrats and Republicans who put conviction ahead of politics to get this done together… Today we're marking an historic milestone, but also the culmination of two of the most productive years in the history of Congress, in no small part because of their leadership. And we are very grateful to them."

GAY MARRIAGE

One of the events that energized both sides of the argument in the time leading to the 2012 election was the president's endorsement of gay marriage, a highly debated and contested issue in America. Huffington Post announced it saying, "In a nod to a dramatic shift in public opinion, Barack Obama on Wednesday became the first sitting president to announce his support for same-sex marriage." On May 9, 2012 in an interview with ABC News Network the president said,

> "… I had hesitated on gay marriage in part because I thought that civil unions would be sufficient. I was sensitive to the fact that – for a lot of people, you know the word marriage was something that invokes very powerful traditions, religious beliefs and so forth. But I have to tell you that, over the course of several years as I talked to friends and family and neighbors, when I think about members of my own staff who are in incredibly committed monogamous relationships, same-sex relationships, who are raising kids together, when I think about those soldiers or airmen or marines or sailors who are out there fighting on my behalf and yet feel constrained, even now that Don't ask, don't tell' is gone, because they are not able to commit themselves in a marriage – at a certain point I've just concluded that for me personally, it is important for me to go ahead and affirm that I think same sex couples should be able to get married."

The decision energized conservative Christian leaders and liberal bases to use the event as an organizing tool during the general election. The decision came after the landmark federal statute that establishes a legal process for ending the Don't ask, don't tell policy - "Don't ask, don't tell Repeal Act of 2010" was signed by the president on December 22, 2010. The question was how big was this as a factor in the election?

Gay marriage is legal or in the process of being approved by nine states – Connecticut, Iowa, Maine, Maryland, Massachusetts, New Hampshire, New York, Vermont, Washington, and the District of Columbia. Even though the appeal process is on-going, the federal courts in California have struck down the state's constitutional ban on same-sex marriage. In the 2012 election voters in Main, Maryland and Washington approved gay marriage. On the other hand, 31 states have amended their constitution to prohibit same-sex marriage. The Supreme Court is weighing in to decide California's Proposition 8, the constitutional ban on gay marriage that voters adopted in 2008 after the Supreme Court ruled that gay Californians could marry.

ABORTION

On his third day in office and the 36th anniversary of the Supreme Court decision that legalized abortion, the president issued a formal statement reaffirming his commitment to defending the court's ruling with his remark, "this decision not only protect women's health and reproductive freedom, but stands for a broader principle: That government should not intrude on our most private family matters." He also said that it was appropriate to place limits on late-term abortions if those restrictions included an exception for the woman's health. At his commencement address at the University of Notre Dame the president called for partisans on each side of the polarizing abortion debate to find other ways to respect one another's basic decency and he recommended working together to reduce the number of unwanted pregnancies. Part of his speech at the commencement includes:

> "Maybe we won't agree on abortion, but we can still agree that this heart-wrenching decision for any woman is not made casually, it has both moral and spiritual dimensions. So let us work together to reduce the number of women seeking abortions, let's reduce unintended pregnancies. Let's make adoption more available. Let's provide care and support for women who do carry their children to term. Let's honor the conscience of those who disagree with abortion and draft a sensible conscience clause, that makes sure that all of our health care policies are grounded not only in sound science, but also in clear ethics, as well as respect for the equality of women."

On the 39th anniversary of Roe v. Wade decision, the president underlined his view on abortion as follows:

"As we mark the 39th anniversary of Roe v. Wade, we must remember that this Supreme Court decision not only protects a woman's health and reproductive freedom, but also affirms a broader principle: that government should not intrude on private family matters. I remain committed to protecting a woman's right to choose and this fundamental constitutional right. While this's a sensitive and often divisive issue – no matter what our view, we must stay united in our determination to prevent relationships, and promote adoption. And as we remember this historic anniversary, we must also continue our efforts to ensure that our daughters have the same rights, freedoms, and opportunities as our sons to fulfill their dreams". January 22, 2012

CONTRACEPTION

In August 2011, the Department of Health and Human Services (HHS) issued an interim final rule that would require most health insurance plans to cover preventive services for women including recommended contraceptives services without charging a co-pay or co-insurance. The interim final rule requires private health plans to include coverage for all FDA- approved prescription contraceptives, female sterilization procedures and related "patient education and counseling for all women with reproductive capacity", under the "preventive service for women." The rule also allows certain non-profit religious employers that offer insurance to their employees, the choice of whether or not to cover contraceptive services. The department received several comments from concerned groups, especially from those that are religiously affiliated and as a result the Department published final rules on the coverage of contraceptive services by adopting the definition of "religious employer". It also issued a one year enforcement safe harbor for organizations with religions objections for contraceptive coverage. The new health care law requires employers and insurers to fully cover contraception and later carved out an exemption for religiously affiliated hospitals and universities that place the cost of birth-control coverage on the insurer rather than the employer.

EMBRYONIC STEM CELL RESEARCH
To fulfill his campaign promise to make scientific decision based on facts, rather than ideology, on March 9, 2009, the president lifted the Bush administration's limit on human embryonic stem cell research by signing Executive Order 13505, removing the barrier to responsible scientific research involving human stem cells and lifting the long standing ban on the federal funding of steam cell research. Many Republicans lawmakers opposed the move and some (Christopher Smith of New Jersey) even called the president "the abortion president."

The importance of Stem Cells: Stem cells according to the Quality Health's Medical Advisory Board are undifferentiated cells within the human body that have the potential to become many different cells and are categorized into two groups, adult and embryonic. The main purpose of the adult stem cells is to repair and maintain the tissue in which they are found. Adult stem cells can also renew themselves and differentiate in order to become a specialized cell in a certain kind of tissue or organ. Embryonic stem cells on the other hand are derived from embryonic stem cells and can form nerve, blood, muscle and many other cells types. The challenge for stem cells is that they need to be isolated by researchers in order to be manipulated for a specific purpose. The hope from scientists is that these stem cells could provide potential cures for many diseases, including the potential to develop treatments for degenerative heart disease and stroke and replacing the damaged nerves in the brain to improve Parkinson's disease.

ENERGY, CLIMATE CHANGE AND ENVIRONMENTAL POLICIES - *"the greenest president ever"*
The vision of building a clean energy economy that address the issue of climate change as well as protect the environment was the topic of discussion during the last four years. On March 30, 2011 releasing the White House *Blueprint for a Secure Energy Future*, the president underlined the importance of combining the effort to become energy independent while at the same time keeping the environment safe, as "we cannot keep going from shock to trance on the issue of energy security, rushing to propose action when gas prices rise, then hitting the snooze button when they fall again. The United States of America cannot afford

to bet our long-term prosperity and security on a resource that will eventually run out. Not anymore. Not when the cost to our economy, our country and our planet is so high. Not when your generation needs us to get this right. It is time to do whatever we can to secure our energy future."

ENERGY

In 2009, when the president took office, the country was importing 11 million barrels of oil daily and in 2012 America produced more oil than in the last seven years. The administration announced fuel efficiency standards for cars and trucks that will save consumers thousands of dollar and conserve 1.8 billion barrels of oil, and to accomplish this goal the following three strategies were designed:

Develop and Secure American's Energy Supplies: The country needs to deploy its assets, innovation and technology to develop more energy in the U.S. and become a leader in the global energy economy.

Provide consumers with choices to reduce costs and save energy: The unstable gasoline prices reinforce the need for innovation that will make it easier and more affordable for consumers to buy more advanced and fuel efficient vehicles, use alternative means of transportation, weatherizing their homes and workplaces, and eventually save money and protect the environment.

Innovate to a clean energy future: Leading the world in clean energy was one of the critical strategies used, in strengthening the U.S. economy. The solution for that according to the White House Report is by creating markets for innovative clean technologies that are ready to deploy, and by funding cutting-edge research to produce the next generation of technologies. As new, better and more efficient technologies hit the market, the Federal government needs to put words into action and lead by example.

Clean Energy: In the last four years the administration invested in more than 15,000 clean energy projects throughout the country supporting over 225, 000 jobs. By the end of 2012 electricity generated from renewable sources was planned to be doubled. The president proposed that by 2035 the U.S. will generate 80% of its electricity from different clean and renewable energy sources including wind, solar, biomass and hydropower, nuclear power, efficient natural gas and clean coal. According to Clean Journal, over a third of new electricity generators added since 2008 have been wind powered and in 2011 the U.S. produced more than twice as much solar power as it did in 2008. The production of renewable electricity generation was close to double in 2008 (from 72.6 Terawatt-hours in 2008 to 174 Terawatt-hours in 2012)

Leading by Example: The U.S. Federal Government owns and manages close to 500,000 buildings and operates more than 600,000 fleet vehicles. According to the report from the White House, the electricity used in these buildings, the fuel used in its cars and trucks, and the energy required in military operations make it the largest energy consumer in the U.S. economy. To lead by example the president signed an Executive Order that made it the responsibility of every Federal Agency to help move the nations towards a clean energy economy by leading by example to use clean energy.

DOMESTIC OIL AND NATURAL GAS PRODUCTION:

Gas Production: Since 2008 there has been steady increase of domestic gas production and in 2012, the country imported 2.6 million fewer barrels of oil and petroleum products compared to the 2008 numbers. In 2010, American oil production was at its highest level (5.51 millions of barrels per day) since 2003, and the U.S. natural gas production reached its highest level in more than 30 years. This increase is attributed to the increasing natural gas and oil production from shale formations using new technologies.

Public Land for oil and gas leasing: The government has offered millions of acres of public land Federal waters for oil and gas leasing. Since 2008, oil production from the Outer Continental Shelf increased more than a third – from 446 million barrels to over 600 million. Oil production from onshore public lands increased from 109 million barrels in 2009 to 114 million barrels in 2010.

Carbon Pollution: One of the most visible accomplishments of the Obama administration was the development of historic new fuel efficiency standards which nearly doubled the average fuel economy of cars and light trucks to 54.5 miles per gallon by 2025, as well as reduced greenhouse gas emissions by 6 billion metric tons. Furthermore Obama proposed the first carbon pollution standards for new coal and oil fired power plants.

Public Land Conservation: the president signed executive orders to protect the conservations of more than 1000 rivers plus 26 million acres of historically significant landscapes including thousands of miles of nature trails. This decision was considered to be one of the largest expansions of wilderness protections in many generations.

Part Three
After the Fact

ELECTION DAY – AMERICA GOES TO THE POLLS

After all has been said and done, the American people went to cast their votes on November 6, 2012 to elect their president. It was estimated that out of 222 million eligible voters, 130.3 million of them turned out to vote. The result showed that President Obama won the election with 332 Electoral College votes. It appeared that despite the strong political campaign against his accomplishments and record, the American people listened to his message and acknowledged the progress made in his first four years. The election results were testimony to the fact that voters believed in the major legislative accomplishments listed in part two of this book, and validated his record.

Chapter 11

The Morning After

– SHELL SHOCKED –

"We went into the evening confident we had a good path to victory. I don't think there was one person who saw this coming." *Romney's Senior Advisor Reported by Jan Crawford*

"Romney was stoic as he talked to the president", an aide said, but his wife Ann cried. "Running mate Paul Ryan seemed genuinely shocked", the advisor said. "Ryan's wife Janna also was shaken and cried softly … There's nothing worse than when you think you're going to win, and you don't. It was like a sucker punch." *Report fromJan Crawford. CBS News analysis. November 8, 2012*

"They thought intensity and enthusiasm were on their side this time – poll after poll showed Republicans were more motivated to vote than Democrats – and that would translate into votes for Romney."

WHAT WENT WRONG?

A FEW DAYS AFTER THE 2012 Election Day, Jan Crawford from CBS analyzed the reaction of the Romney Campaign to the result, and summarized the cause as three key miscalculations made by his team mostly based on historical trends. These assumptions were:

Misread turnout. The campaign had expected the turnout to be between 2004 and 2008 levels with a +2 or +3 Democratic electorate. The result however showed that it was +7 as it was in 2008. The other assumption made was that the president's base would not get out and Romney's would – the opposite result occurred. More African- Americans voted in Ohio, Virginia, North Carolina and Florida than in 2008. Fewer

Republicans did and as a result Romney got just over 2 million fewer votes than John McCain.

The Independent factor: State polls showed Romney winning big among Independents. Historically, according to Crawford's analysis, any candidate polling that well among the Independents wins. But as it turned out, many of them were former Republicans who now self-identified as Independents. The State polls weren't oversampling Democrats and under sampling Republicans – there just weren't as many Republicans this time because they were calling themselves something else.

Undecided Voters: The perception was that they always break for the challenger, since people know the incumbent and would have decided already if they were backing him. Romney was counting on that trend to continue. Instead, exit polls show that president Obama won among people who made up their minds on Election Day and in the few days just before the election. Many believed that Romney, after running for six years, was in the same position as the incumbent.

ADDITIONAL ASSUMPTIONS LED THE ROMNEY CAMPAIGN TO BELIEVE THEY HAD IT

Many assumptions were used to predict the outcome of the election and most of these turned out to be wrong. Some of them are:

The Incumbent rule: if an incumbent cannot rise above 47 percent or thereabouts in head to head polling, he is unlikely to win.

The minority (non-white) share of the electorate will not be changed – In this election the non- white vote rose from 26% to 28% making the assumption a false one.

Generation Gap – Voters over 65 years old were more enthusiastic about voting than the younger generation. In this election, the numbers of seniors who voted were slightly lower than in 2008, whereas those of young voters were marginally up.

Inaccurate campaign Internal poll: According to the report from The New Republic, the Romney internal polling data from seven States showed that on average, President Obama ahead by a few points (+1) whereas the actual result showed Obama ahead by +5.7 points with a bias of (+4.7 points). This meant that the president won all seven States by an average margin of 5.7 percentage points. In summary, the polls obtained from the Republican internal polling team were biased in Romney's favor, by five percentage points. The following table shows the detailed information:

State	Romney Campaign Poll	Actual Results	Bias
Colorado	Romney +2.5	Obama +5.4	Romney +7.9
Iowa	Tie	Obama +5.8	Romney +5.8
Minnesota	Obama +4.0	Obama +7.7	Romney +3.7
New Hampshire	Romney +3.5	Obama +5.6	Romney +9.1
Ohio	Obama +2.0	Obama +3.0	Romney +1.0
Pennsylvania	Obama +3.0	Obama +5.4	Romney + 2.4
Wisconsin	Obama +4.0	Obama +6.8	Romney +2.8
Average	**Obama +1.0**	**Obama +5.7**	**Romney +4.7**

Table 10: Romney Campaign Poll vs. Election Results: Source: Five Thirty Eight Blog

OVER CONFIDENT POLLSTERS AND NETWORK NEWS – MISLEADING THE MEDIA

Public opinion polls have been a key source in determining the possible outcome of any event including elections, consumer confidence, job approval as well as sports predictions. Data from polling is used to forecast election outcomes, understand voters or public option behavior and plan campaign strategy. Since the early 1930s, where scientific polling started to be used to forecast election outcomes, tools, techniques and technology have evolved. Over the period of 80 years since polling began, there has been a significant evolution in the methods used for election survey. From telephone and live interviews on behalf of media organizations or political candidates to Internet research where instant results of the survey are posted in blog and web sites, the complexity as well as the accuracy of predictions has become questionable. According to Panagopolous' 2009 analysis in the 2008 election, there were an estimated 975 presidential related sets of questions, and well over a million interviews, conducted between Labor Day and Election Day. The 2012 election poll coverage was much higher than the previous one.

After the election, Fordham's *Center for Electoral Politics and Democracy* conducted a study comparing 2012 pre-election polling against the results on Election Day and published the ranking of 28 pollsters, using a measure of predictive accuracy to permit examination of the data for both accuracy and bias. The result showed that 26 out of 28 polls overestimated Romney support, while two overestimated Obama's win. The outliers of the study were Gallup and YouGov which showed significant partisan (pro-Republican) bias. The analysis also showed that the top news and polling organizations including CNN, FOX, and Rasmussen ranked on the lower bottom of the rated 28 - CNN/ORC (15th), Politico/GWU/Battleground (15th), Fox News (15th); Rasmussen (24th), Gallup (24th), NPR (26th), National Journal (27th) and AP/GfK (28th out of 28). The top ranking pollsters were PPP (1st), Daily Kos/SEIU/PPP (2nd), YouGov (3rd), Ipsos/Reuters (4th), Purple Strategies (5th), NBC/WSJ (6th), CBS/NYT (7th) and Pew Research (13th).

GALLUP WAS OFF THE MARK: - CONSTANT BIAS FOR THE ROMNEY CAMPAIGN AND THE GOP

Of all the major polling organizations, Gallup was the one that was clearly wrong giving Romney and his supporters, false hope. Gallup's final poll of had a 1 percentage point lead to Mitt Romney over the president and in the months leading to election the pollster gave a 7 point lead to Romney. Several analyses were done on the polling strategy used and some of them are listed below:

Fewer young voters were polled: The Gallup final poll included only 13% of the 18 to 29 year old voters as opposed to the 19% recorded at the exit polls. This six point discrepancy made a big difference as 23% of young voters chose Obama.

Overestimating the White voter's number: Gallup's likely sample had white voters at 78% of the electorate. This is exactly the same estimate as the one used for the 2008 election and the actual result showed that the number had decreased by a couple points. The ABC/Washington Post poll showed a drop of 3 – 3.5% from 2008 on this group. According to Harry J. Enten of Guardian analysis, had Gallup shown a decrease as the

ABC/Washington Post poll did, Obama would have led in their final poll by 2 points instead of trailing by 1 point. Enten continued: "why did Gallup have too many whites? It seems the most likely answer at this point is that Gallup's likely voter screen cuts off too many minority registered voters. Remember that likely voters are those registered voters who a pollster thinks are ones that will come out and vote. Gallup's final registered voter poll had Obama defeating Romney by 3 points – near perfect."

Acknowledging the mistakes, the Gallup Editor in Chief Frank Newport noted that the organization was reviewing its methodology, saying that, "we don't have a definitive answer." The question raised by many was: was Gallup's struggle this year the result of sampling bias – through its random-digit – dialing interviews? Did Gallup simply talk to too many Romney supporters? Was it likely that voter screening filtered out Obama supporters who would go on to cast ballots for the president? Or was it some combination of the two?

RASMUSSEN REPORT: TIED 24TH WITH GALLUP OUT OF 28 POLLSTERS.
Scott Rasmussen, tried to explain why the respected research group he founded failed to predict the election outcome without getting into his sampling and analysis methodology error, saying,

> "In general the projections were pretty good. The two differences I noted were share of white vote falling to 72 percent. That's what the Obama campaign, to their credit, said all along. We showed it just over 73 percent. Also, youth turnout was higher and senior turnout lower than expected. That's a pretty big deal given the size of the generation gap. I think it showed clearly that the Obama team had a great game plan for identifying their vote and getting it to the polls. The problem with these polls – which are automated, as opposed to using live callers – was that they missed the correct model of the electorate. The reality is that there were eight toss-up States. Some people projected Romney would do a couple of points better than the polls and sweep those States. Instead, it was Obama who did a bit better and swept them. I look at the

campaign as about fundamentals. Obama job approval on Election Day was 50 percent. That meant there was a good chance he would get 50 percent of the vote. Also, 36 percent said their finances were in good shape. Up from 35 percent the day Obama took office. In other words, the fundamentals were just good enough for the president to keep his job."

Remarks by some pollsters leading to the Election Day were also misleading and gave false hope to Romney supporters. Some of these remarks included:

- *"Romney has pretty much nailed down Florida."* - Bard Coker – Pollster at Mason-Dixon polling and Research
- *"I think in places like North Carolina, Virginia and Florida, we've already painted those red, we're not polling any of those States again."* David Paleologos – Pollster from Suffolk University on the Fox O'Reilly TV show on Oct 9
- *In Minnesota, Romney has a good chance to pull off one of the biggest upsets of the election cycle in this State. Minnesota is very much a battleground State due to the low minority population of the State and President Obama's problems with white voters."* - Glen Bolger, pollster at public Opinion Strategies

THE ECSTASY AND THE AGONY: REACTION TO THE RESULT. EMOTIONS AT WORK

"Congrats to @ KarlRove on blowing $400 million this cycle. Every race @CrossroadsGPS ran ads in , the Republicans lost. What a waste of money … " *Donald Trump*

In this election we have seen a lot of activities from both sides of the political spectrum, with donors pumping money into the various super packs. After the election, noteworthy reactions were observed from various individuals including wealthy donors and radio hosts. One of the visible reactions was toward Karl Rove's Super PAC the American Cross Road. Considering Rove's political strategy achievements in the past helping the Republicans, the result of the 2012 election was a big miss.

1.29% RETURN ON INVESTMENT – AMERICAN CROSS ROAD SUPER PAC

A study by the Sunlight Foundation showed that the return on the $104 million spent by the American Crossroads Super PAC led by Carl Rove was only 1.29%. The Super PAC spent $85 million to defeat the president and $6.5 million to support Mitt Romney. The PAC also spent millions more opposing many Democratic Senate candidates including Bill Nelson in Florida, Jon Tester in Montana, Joe Donnely in Indiana, Tammy Baldwin in Wisconsin and Tim Kaine in Virginia, all of whom won seats. The other Super PAC Crossroads GPS saw a 14% return on its investment out of the $70 million spent on the election supporting Republican candidates. The U.S. Chamber of Commerce was no better than the others with a 6.9% return on its $33 million spent whilst the National Rifle Association got 0.81% on the $12 million spent. Some of the reactions to the election were posted in most news media and a few are mentioned below.

Sean Hannity:

> "America has shown bad judgment. Americans, you get the government you deserve. And it pains me to say this, but America right now deserves Barack Obama. You deserve what you voted for. Four years ago, the public could be excused for voting for Obama because, frankly, he was a blank canvas … now he is a known entity. And just barely over 50 percent looked at his pathetic record and decided they wanted more of the same."

Donald Trump:

> "We can't let this happen. We should march on Washington and stop this travesty. Our nation is totally divided. Election Day … Lets fight like hell and stop this great and disgusting injustice! The world is laughing at us ….This election is a total sham and a travesty. We are not a democracy! …Congrats to @ KarlRove on blowing $400 million this cycle. Every race @CrossroadsGPS ran ads in, the Republicans lost. What a waste of money … Our country is now in serious and unprecedented trouble ... like never before."

Robert Sewell, MD:

"Notice to all patients, prepare for LONG LINES & government denial of care. That's what you have voted for today. Hope you love Obamacare."

Jack Welch:

Before the election: "Unbelievable jobs numbers ... these Chicago guys will do anything ... can't debate so change numbers." After the election: "Congratulations to Pres Obama and his team on their terrific victory."

WHAT DO OBAMA SUPPORTERS SAY WHY THEY WANT TO VOTE FOR HIM?
The official Obama web page listed the following 25 reasons from 25 people throughout the country who are voting for the president.

- "The Affordable Care Act is saving my daughter's life." *Stacey, Arizona*
- "Obama is for the vets. He helped us wind down in Iraq. He's improved mental health policy with VA benefits." *Joel, Minnesota.*
- "Obama stuck his neck out for us. The auto industry. He wasn't going to let it just die, and I'm driving in the morning because of that, because of him." *Brian, Ohio*
- "Osama bin Laden is dead, and General Motors is alive." *Joe Biden, Delaware*
- "Supreme Court, Supreme Court Supreme Court." *Andrew, California*
- "Arithmetic." *Bill Clinton, New York*
- "He cares for the 100%." *Shana, Texas*
- "When Obama came into office, he successfully renewed our country's place in the community of nations, making cooperation in tackling the world's challenges possible." *Wills, North Carolina*
- "The actions he has taken with respect to protecting us from terrorism have been very, very solid." *Colin Powell, Virginia*

- "I was really very grateful to him for standing up for those kids who are having a really rough time out there because of their orientation." *Jan Lynch, California*
- "For me, President Obama is our best choice because he has a vision of the United States as a place where we are in this together." *Bruce Springsteen, New Jersey*
- "He has a real plan for rescuing the economy that passes the 'math' test." *Teresa, Virginia*
- "Having someone in office who understands how powerful our voice can be is very important." *Jay Z, New York*
- "I am voting for Barack Obama and Joe Biden because I can trust them to care for the middle class and restore the American dream." *Steven Florida*
- "The first measure he signed into law after becoming president was the Lilly Ledbetter Fair Pay Act – so a female high school counselor or physical education teacher can fight for equal pay for equal work." *Connie Britton, California*
- "I believe in the America he wants for my grandchildren." *Nancy, Michigan*
- "We need four more years of repair, of helping the middle class achieve a sustainable economy." *James Taylor, North Carolina*
- "I've watched him fight for our country, stand by the middle class, the working class, the military, the education of our children, universal health care, women, the environment, and matters of national and domestic security." *Susan, Virginia*
- "The gifted 12-year-old I taught, whose parents were deported and left her here with her grandmother, will be allowed to stay and finish her education. She's been in the U.S. since age one." *Jamie, North Carolina*;
- "I want our president to place scientific evidence and risk management above electoral politics." *Michael Bloomberg, New York*
- "I have four children who are under 26 and able to stay on my health care plan. That's been huge." *Amy, Pennsylvania*

- "He's fighting to defend and better Social Security and Medicare – because millions of Latino seniors rely on them." *Cristina Saralegui, Florida*
- "Thanks to the President's efforts to keep student loan rates low, I can expect to save nearly $1,000 as I work to repay my student loans. And I don't have too many of those, thanks to the Federal Pell Grant program." *Sam, Minnesota*
- "It's been wonderful to have President Obama as a champion for access to health care for all women in this country." *Cecile Richards, New York*

12 Chapter

Is it Time for a Third Party?

- "Our world has become a multi-channel, multiplex, multi-site, multi-task universe. In fact, we no longer live in a two-anything world – except in our politics, with its two-party system. The greatest weakness of this ossified way of governing is its exclusion of millions of Americans from the democratic process. But the disenfranchised – or the merely disgusted – may finally be tired of waving the white flag.... Either the existing two parties will expand to include them, with new ideas, fresh thinking or reordered priorities, or an outsider will step in to fill the ball." *Arianna Haffington,*
- "The two parties remind me of those old French Foreign Legion Movies. You see this fort, and it looks fine from the outside. But when you go through the gate, almost everyone inside is dead." *Ann Lewis, former political director of the Democratic National Committee*
- In a 1992 Wall Street Journal/NBC News poll, most respondents said, 41%-55% that they want a third major political party.
- If Independent (swing) voters have determined the outcome of every Presidential election since World War II, why doesn't the country have a strong third party to ease the gridlock between the two party systems?

WHY DID THE FOUNDING FATHERS OPPOSE THE CREATION OF ANY PARTY?

B EING THE FIRST AND only president of the United States who's not a member of a political party, George Washington warned against the creation of what he called a "faction with an artificial and extraordinary force, to put in the place of the delegated will of the nation, the will of a party." In his letter to Thomas Jefferson, Washington underlined the danger of having parity in the political system as "I was no party man myself, and the first wish of my heart was, if parties did exist, to reconcile them." Many of the Founding Fathers including James Madison showed a negative view toward political parties. In his Federalist *Paper #10* Madison made his case against any system as he believed those "factions" (his interpretation for parties) might be able to seize control of the government. Aligning with the thinking of his fellow Founding Fathers, George Washington included people with diverse political philosophies and policies to his administration. When drafting the Constitution of the United States, the Founding Fathers made no provision in the governmental structure for the functioning of political parties, partly because they believed that they were a source of corruption and an impediment to the freedom of people to judge issues on their merits.

In his farewell address to the American people, George Washington spoke about the issues of having parties in the government and political system:

> "There is an opinion that parties in free countries are useful checks upon the administration of the government and serve to keep alive the spirit of liberty. This within certain limits is probably true, and in governments of a monarchical cast, patriotism may look with indulgence, if not with favor, upon the spirit of party. But in those of the popular character, in governments purely elective, it is a spirit not to be encouraged. From their natural tendency, it is certain there will always be enough of that spirit for every salutary purpose. And there being constant danger or excess, the effort ought to be by force of public opinion, to mitigate and assuage it. A fire not to be quenched, it demands a uniform vigilance to prevent its

bursting into a flame, lest, instead of warming, it should consume."

Over six major eras of political parties were recorded in the U.S. political party system, with 1796 to 1828 being marked as the time when the first political parties, the "Federalist" and "Democratic–Republican" were formed. Despite the desire to stay away from creating a party system, an informal party (faction) was established by Alexander Hamilton and John Adams later called the Federalist Party. The Federalists got support from merchants, manufacturers and residents of New England. At the same time, Thomas Jefferson and James Madison created another faction called Democratic–Republican Party (or anti-Federalist party), which advocated a limited federal government, less government involvement in economic affairs and a pro-French foreign policy. *They* attracted the support of farmers, artisans and southerners. Even though the Federalists won their cause for the Constitution, the efforts by the Democratic–Republican Party influenced the populace, weakening the Federalist Party, and eventually leading to its demise.

Between 1828 and 1860, the Democratic–Republican Party consolidated its power and in 1829, after Andrew Jackson was elected as president, the party's name was changed to the Democratic Party. Its fundamental principles were, to include the ordinary citizen, support small business, farmers, pioneers and slave owners. It was during this era that the American election and political landscape was designed as the party established the current convention system, took the power of choosing the party's candidate from the party leaders to party representatives from the States as well as strengthen voting rights. Opposing slavery and supporting tariff and federal involvement in the economy, the Whig Party was established. By the end of 1852, due to opposing views between members on the issue of slavery, the party crumbled, leading the group that opposed slavery to create a new party – the Republican Party.

From 1860 to 1932, the Republican Party dominated the political landscape of the country especially after the election of Abraham Lincoln in 1860. The same issue of slavery that divided the Whig Party now divided the country leading to the Civil War. This era is also considered as the time where the core principles of the two opposing parties were shaped. Elected officials became political pawns in the hands of party leaders who controlled government policies. Politicians became savvy and corruption began to rise. From 1932 – 1968 the Democratic Party dominated the political show after the election of Franklin Roosevelt as the New Deal President ending Republican control. During this era, the role of government expanded to deal with the Great Depression by providing aid to the millions of people out of work reinforcing the long held belief that Democrats believe in big government while Republicans support limited government involvement. Since the early 1970s, the country is considered by some as "divided government" where control of the government has shifted back and forth between the two parties without one or the other gaining extended control.

WHY ONLY TWO PARTIES?

Although the freedom to establish a new political party exists and attempts were made to create a few, no strong third party has been able to gain the support of the majority to survive. However, many argue that this trend may change as the two existing parties take extreme positions on certain social and political issues leaving millions of Americans exempt from political participation. In the last several presidential and State elections the two parties struggled to convince these independent voters and they are considered to be the balancing power for every election. A fight to win the largest voting bloc in the country – the Independents, which in some accounts constitute up to 40 percent of the vote, was the key strategy in the 2012 presidential election. Swing voters have determined the outcome of every presidential election since World War II, and the strategy to capture this group has become a challenge as they are seen as disengaged from the existing political system due to partisanship, the increasing influence of special interest and super PACs, failure of the two parties to solve the real problems of the American people including the shrinking manufacturing jobs, deteriorating infrastructure, troubled education system, mounting federal debt, the existing tax code and financial system that favors only the few at the top, the digital and financial divide between the ever shrinking middle class and the top, the fiscal cliff, the all-time low approval rate of the legislative branch of the government, the extreme positions the parties take on key social issues including abortion, same sex marriage, immigration, health care and others.

THE NEED FOR A THIRD POLITICAL PARTY

In his article *What this Country Needs: A New Political Party*, John Kimberling argues that neither the Republicans nor the Democrats seem able or willing to deal with the existing serious problems the country is facing today, and that what this country needs is "a new political party, a third party that will bring new, creative ideas and take imaginative and sensible action to solve those problems." Part of his analysis states:

"Congress is dysfunctional. The government is paralyzed. Millions of people are out of work, and the national debt keeps increasing. The Republicans openly declare that nothing will be done in 2012 before the election. They seem more interested in defeating Obama's re-election bid than helping the country. The Democrats take no aggressive action to help things. Since the midterm election in 2010, in which the Republicans gained control of the House of Representatives, nothing has been accomplished by Congress. Extreme partisanship has prevented any significant progress toward solving jobs, tax reform, immigration reform, and Social Security or Medicare reforms. Public opinion polls indicate less than 15% of the American people approve of the job Congress is doing. According to a poll several years ago, 40 percent of the American people think a third major political party is needed. The need has never been greater than now."

TWO POLARIZED PARTIES – NEGATIVE EFFECT ON HEALTHY POLITICAL PARTICIPATION

"For the second year in a row, but only the third time in the 30 years that the *National Journal* has published these ratings, no Senate Democrat compiled a voting record to the right of any Republican, and no Senate Republican came down on the left of any Democrat … the 435 members of the House are as polarized as their Senate colleagues. Only six Republicans compiled a slightly more "liberal" voting record than the most conservative Democrat." *National Journal.*

Linda Killian in her book *The Swing Vote*, analyzed a number of reasons for the hyper-partisanship and polarization in Congress which have resulted in more voters identifying themselves as Independent. Some of the reasons are the growing influence of special interest lobbyists, the small number of truly competitive congressional districts, which means that to get elected, most members of the House have to worry about keeping only their base supporters happy and not those voters in the middle, the financial pressure to raise huge sums of campaign cash, which is a big reason to be beholden to party leaders and core supporters as well as to special interest campaign donors, State election laws that prevent Independents from voting in most primary elections, an ever more partisan, opinion-driven and shrill media which rewards the most outrageous and partisan players with airtime and positive coverage while often ignoring those who are working in a bipartisan way to solve problems.

NEEDS LITTLE EFFORT TO CONVINCE THE VOTER - THE ROSS PEROT EFFECT

In 1992, 19 percent of the American population voted for an Independent Party candidate Ross Perot, who had no prior political experience, no grassroots organization, no "high caliber" consultants and strategists advising him, never been elected to public office and yet was able to get attention from many who believed in the need for a balancing party. No third party candidate has ever won the presidency of the United States and Perot was the second candidate next to Theodore Roosevelt who, in 1912 ran as the candidate of the Bull Moose Party, a progressive party and came second to Woodrow Wilson. In June 1992, Perot led the national public opinion polls with support from 39% of the voters compared to 31 percent for Bush, and 25 percent for Clinton.

THE MAJORITY OF THE COUNTRY WATCHES THE DRAMA IN ONLY A FEW SWING STATES:

The 2012 presidential campaigns targeted only 10 States (Colorado, Florida, Iowa, Nevada, New Hampshire, North Carolina, Pennsylvania,

Ohio, Virginia and Wisconsin), bypassing the remaining 40 States. Here are some interesting numbers from Nonprofit Vote:

- Nearly six times as much money was spent in Florida alone, than was spent in the 40 non-swing States and DC.
- 99% of campaign stops by the presidential or vice-presidential candidates were in these States.
- Average turnout in these 10 States was 65.2%, 7.2 points more than the non-battleground States which trailed with 58%.
- 96% of the $896 million spent on TV ads between April 11th and November 6th, 2012 were in these battleground States. This number showed more money was spent in each battleground State than a combination of the 40 other States.

With a population of 300 million, politics could be messy ... However, in most presidential elections, only a few States (swing States), play a role in electing the president that will represent the country. While the campaigning is extensive in those States, the rest of the country – divided into red and blue – ends up watching the candidates crisscrossing the swing States from a distance.

LOW VOTER TURNOUT – LESS INTEREST TO VOTE IN RED OR BLUE STATES

The national voter turnout was negatively affected by low turnout in the large States including California, New York and Texas which constitute a quarter of the country's eligible voters. In 2012, these three States ranked 41st, 44th, and 48th from the 50 States. This is because the President of the United States is selected by the Electoral College vote, not by the popular vote, and the majority of the States' electors are given to the winner with the highest vote, therefore causing all resources to be directed to a few battleground states. This approach has affected the political activities and energy of voters in over 40 States resulting in low turnout in those areas.

Governing Gridlock and the Role
of the Federal Government

"When two Elephants fight it is the grass that Suffers."
Anonymous

GOVERNMENT ORGANIZATIONS OPERATE in fluid, highly politicized and unpredictable environments as well as being intensely scrutinized by the media and forced to adhere to a number of rigid rules, policies and constraints. They are subjected to the changing views and needs of elected officials and politicians. Even though these organizations function under four different environments (political, economic, social and technological), under the current political structure, the political environment tends to dominate and shape the direction the agencies go,. Being the largest segment of the government responsible for the security of the country and day to day activities of its citizens, the executive branch of the government led by the President of the United States employs over 4 million Americans (including the Armed forces). The branch has fifteen executive departments, CIA and EPA, as well as more than 50 independent federal commissions with leaders all appointed by the president. 15% of the nearly two million civilian federal workforce lives in the Washington DC Metropolitan area, while 85% lives in other parts of the country.

THE POLITICAL ENVIRONMENT IN GOVERNMENT

Public sector entities, according to Cohen and Brand's analysis, are by nature political entities that are easily disrupted by power struggles. Conflict often occurs between agency senior management committed to the mission of the organization and politicians, who for one reason or another, may feel it is politically expedient to undercut the organization making it difficult to function effectively. In some cases conflict between the legislators and the elected chief executive can place the agency in difficult position to perform its function. The ideology of public services as defined by Gerald Caiden in his article *Ethics in the public sector* shows that government is an instrument for carrying out the will of the people, as defined by their elected representatives and public officials who are elected, appointed, or hired to serve the interest of the public. This ideology is now far from being implemented as politicians use their power and interest to influence the function of the government.

The size and role of the federal government was the center of discussion throughout the campaign and the federal work force was taken hostage by political maneuvering, to convince voters that government is big, bulky and did not help. In reality the million people who chose to serve their country in the public sector often with low payment, perform their jobs with dignity to ensure that the business of the government is open, that nearly 80 million checks are distributed to millions of private companies, citizens and States (nearly 20 percent of every State's budget comes from the federal government) every month, that the security of citizens is protected, that our water is clean, our air is safe to both breathe and fly in, our food is inspected, our drugs pass the trial period before coming to the marketplace, our environment is safe, our saving and investment is protected, that we get information on the weather so that we are well prepared and informed of the path of hurricanes and tornadoes, that our kids get the proper education, our colleges fulfill the best standards, our creativity and intellectual rights are protected, our elderly are getting paid and their health is protected, our veterans who served the country get treatment, our fish, wildlife and environment is protected, our nuclear facilities and critical infrastructure are secured, that we are able to purchase our fist dream home using federal loan and insurance, that the law of the land is enforced, our workplace safety is ensured and no one is being discriminated against because of race, sex or sexual orientation, that citizens get support and assistance traveling abroad and that our roads, bridges and other infrastructure are built to last.

Most politicians/people agree on the role the government plays, but the difference comes in the extent to which the government should extend its influence. These views range from little support for societal members to advocating a more expanding role to protect citizens from various problems. The question is, what's the right balance of the government in society? In 1776, the Scottish economist and moral philosopher Adam Smith wrote the famous book entitled, *The Wealth of Nations: An inquiry into the nature and Cause of the Wealth of Nations*, where he argued that the government's role should be limited to only three areas – national defense, overseeing the justice process and providing services that are not covered by the private sector. His explanation went as follows:

"According to the system of natural liberty, the sovereign has only three duties to attend to; three duties of great importance, indeed, but plain and intelligible to common understanding: first the duty of protecting the society from the violence and invasion of other independent societies; secondly, the duty of protecting as far as possible, every member of society from the injustice or oppression of every other member of it, or the duty of establishing and exact administration of justices; and thirdly, the duty of creating and maintaining certain public works and certain public institutions, which can never be of interest to any individual, or small number of individuals, to erect and maintain because the profit could never repay the expense to any individual or small number of individuals, thought it may frequently do much more than repay it to a great society."

Until the late 19th century, the government role in the U.S. was limited to only the three tasks Smith outlined, but as government taxation and spending have increased, the role began to change and as a result, the share of national spending by the government doubled in 2005 from that of 1962. Research done by Lipford and Slice indicates that since the early sixties, federal spending on income redistribution – composed of spending on labor and social services, health, Medicare, income security and Social Security – has escalated and resulted in social spending as a percentage of total spending, rising from 23.4 percent in 1962 to approximately 60 percent by the late twentieth and early twenty-first centuries. The trend is also true for State and local government expenditure.

In this presidential election, the role of government was the center point for the first debate where the President acknowledged that it is not the solution for all problems but he underlined its role in promoting economic growth and providing assurance to fairness for various groups of society. On the other hand, Romney argued that even though the role of government was acceptable to the society within certain limits, it should not be the primary objective to impose threats to the American entrepreneurial spirit. In this and previous elections the federal workforce got caught between the Republicans' and Democrats' fight on the size and role of the government and dodged a bullet. For example, the Democratic President and the Republican-controlled House disagreed over the role of government and its spending trend in Medicare, education, environment and public health, leading the government to put non-essential government workers on furlough and suspend non-essential services between late 1995 and early 1996 for 28 days. This resulted in 800,000 workers being sent home in the first shutdown and 284,000 in the second. In 2010, the president announced a two-year pay freeze, later extending it by another three months to all federal civilian workers, in an effort to save $2 billion for fiscal year 2011 and $60 billon over the next few years. If the task of the federal government touches almost everything we do in life, why is there a discussion to cut or reduce its size? According to the Bipartisan Policy Center, the federal government sends out 80 million checks a month totaling many million dollars to various sections of the society including Medicare, Social Security, food stamps, disability, defense personnel, veterans, federal salaries, federal retirees, tax refunds, non-defense contracts, defense invoices and others.

THE GRIDLOCK IN WASHINGTON - WHY DID THE 112TH CONGRESS HAVE THE LOWEST APPROVAL RATE IN HISTORY?

Two scholars (Mary L. Rucker and Theresa Myadze) from Wright State University published a paper entitled, *Obama, the Obstructionist 112th U.S. Congress and Tea Party Adamantine: A Political Spectacle* on the U.S. democracy and two main functions of ideology – representation of sectional interest and ideological hegemony, which analyzed how the Republican-controlled Congress' main objective was to say NO to any of the president's proposals. They summarized how the gridlock between the executive and legislative branches of the government affects progress saying

"Many politicians benefit from the way this centuries-old infrastructure operates because it benefits their interests, which is one reason the 112th Congress obstructs Obama's presidential agenda. The power elites "resist change that could reduce their power, status and financial resources and the strategies they use to maintain the cooperation of conservative-minded American citizens which furthers their interests."

14 Chapter

The New American Mosaic and
Challenges to Political Participation

"I can remember a Republican Party that was not backward-looking. I can remember a Republican Party excited by science and its possibilities. I can remember a Republican Party that regarded those Americans who thought differently not as aliens and enemies, but as fellow citizens who had not yet been convinced of the merit of our ideas." *David Frum*

- "What Republicans need to learn is: How do we speak to all Americans? You know, not just the people who look like us and act like us, but how to do we speak to all Americans?" Answer to a question by John Boehner
- In 1980 nearly 81% of voters were non-Hispanic whites. In 2012, the number went down to 72%.
- In the 2012 presidential election 28% of voters were African-American, Latino, Asian-American and other "minority", and this increased by 2% from 2008. Only 58% of white young voters ages 18 - 29 cast their votes, a noticeable demographic change in the racial and ethnic composition.
- Young voters, ages 18,- 29, surprised observers by increasing their share of national voter turnout from 18% to 19%.
- The percent of eligible young Latinos and black people grew to 42% in 2012 making up 24% share of the vote.

THE U.S. IS ON COURSE to reach the year 2043 (according to the latest census projections), with no clear racial or ethnic majority. The United States Census Bureau published its analysis of the change in demographic composition of the U.S. population from 1960 through 2010. In this fifty year analysis, the foreign-born population has undergone significant changes in size, origins and geographic distribution. In 1960, one in 20 residents were foreign-born mostly from European countries, and fifty years later in 2010 the number changed to one in eight residents with the majority of them coming from Latin America and Asia. The detailed source showed that in 2010, 53% of foreign-born voters came from Latin America, 28% from Asia, 12% from Europe and 5% from other areas. Mexico was the number one source (11.7%) followed by China (2.2), India and the Philippines (1.8% each) when an analyis by countries was done.

2060 – U.S. THE PLURALITY NATION

Based on the 2010 census report, the 2060 U.S. population will be considerably older, more racially and ethnically diverse, and will grow much more slowly than previous projections. The analysis also showed that:

- The non-Hispanic white population is projected to peak in 2024, at 199.6 million up from 197.0 million in 2012. Unlike other races or ethnic groups, according to the report, this group however is projected to slowly decrease, falling by nearly 20.6 million from 2024 to 2060.
- The Hispanic population would more than double, from 53.3 million in 2012 to 128.8 million in 2060. Nearly one in three U.S. residents would be Hispanic, up from about one in six today.
- The black population is expected to increase from 41.2 million to 61.8 million over the same period and its share would rise slightly, from 13.1 percent in 2012 to 14.7 in 2060.
- The Asian population is projected to more than double from 15.9 million in 2012 to 34.4 million in 2060.
- In 2043, the U.S. is projected to become a majority-minority nation while the non-Hispanic white population remains the largest single group, but no group would have a the majority. This number is expected to increase from 37% in 2012 to 57% in 2060.

THE LATINO FACTOR:

In the 2012 elections, Latino voters played a significant role in key swing States to tip the election results. As the population grows rapidly, its political influence will continue to be an interesting discussion for the coming elections. The Center for American Progress analysis using the 2010 census report shows that over the next four years, the number of eligible Latino voters nationwide is projected to increase by over 4 million people – close to a 17 percent jump. The report also revealed that this increase will be seen most clearly in the swing States where they will outpace other groups. In 2012 the estimated numbers of eligible Latino voters were 23.7 million and this number will be up by two million for the 2014 mid-term elections and further increase ion by 2016. The following table is created from data published by the center analyzing the expected increase in proportions of the Latino voters in 12 States by 2014 and 2016, resulting from fast-paced growth in this group coupled with slow or negative growth among non-Hispanic whites in these States.

States	Eligible Voters 2012	Eligible Voters 2014	Eligible Voters 2016
Alabama	71,600 (2%))	111,400 (3.01%)	173,200 (4.52)
Arizona	919,700 (21.97%)	1,005,200 (23.35%)	1,098,600 (24.76%)
California	6,483,400 (28.07%)	7,128,800 (29.86%)	7,838,400 (31.68)
Colorado	514,300 (14.35%)	558,400 (15.06%)	606,400 (15.79%)
Florida	2,305,200 (17.00%)	2,588,100 (18.49%)	2,905,800 (19.94%)
Georgia	289,200 (4.25%)	372,300 (5.33%)	479,200 (6.68%)
Iowa	59,700 (2.66%)	70,400 (3.1%)	82,900 (3.61%)
New Mexico	575,400 (43.71%)	607,800 (44.57%)	642,100 (45.43%)
Nevada	296,200 (16.88%)	343,500 (18.56%)	398,400 (20.32%)
North	241,200 (3.49%)	326,600 (4.53%)	442,100 (5.87%)

States	Eligible Voters 2012	Eligible Voters 2014	Eligible Voters 2016
Carolina			
Texas	4,568,000 (28%)	5,000,300 (29.3%)	5,473,500 (30.62%)
Virginia	259,800 (4.49%)	317,300 (5.33%)	387,500 (6.31%)

Table 11: Percentage of statewide net increase in all eligible Latino voters: Source Center for American Progress (Progress 2050)

NEW VOTERS — LATINOS WILL OUTNUMBER WHITE PEOPLE IN FLORIDA, ARIZONA, AND TEXAS

As shown in the table above, in 2016 over 600,000 new Hispanic voters will be eligible to vote in Florida compared to only 125,000 new white voters. In Arizona, close to 175,000 Latinos will be eligible to vote compared to only 10,000 new white voters. The biggest surprise is in Texas where close to 900,000 new Latino voters are expected to enter the voting block compared to only 185,000. These numbers poses a question of whether Democrats would get a chance to change Texas and Arizona to Blue.

REACTION TO THE CHANGE IN DEMOGRAPHY

"We're going the way of the dinosaurs, and quick. The meteor's already hit, and we're just trying to wonder what the blast zone will look like."*David Johnson, top GOP strategist in Florida (reported by Washington Post)*

Stunned by the results of the election, Republican officials did not waste time beginning an exhaustive review to try to figure out what went wrong and build a 'lessons learned' database to fix the problem. This data collection process included a series of voter-based polls and focus groups, meeting with constituency group leaders and various discussions with the party volunteers, donors and staff members. The party also began what a Washington Post reporter referred to as what "promised to be an extended period of internal strife over how a party that skews toward older white men can compete in an increasingly diverse nation." He continued, "President Obama's decisive victory over Mitt Romney served as a clinic in the 21st century politics, reflecting expanded power for black and Hispanic voters, persistent strength among women, a dominant showing among young voters and even a rise in support among Asians."

The debate within the party took a different twist as some of the party members blamed the losses on the creation and rise of the Tea Party movement, which put extreme pressure on GOP candidates to shift toward the right in order to reflect the brand of conservatism that helped them, only win the base and the primaries but lose voters in the general election. Others blamed GOP leaders and the candidates' who took the center ground.

THE REPUBLICAN PARTY DILEMMA AND ITS SELF-CRITIC

Super-glued to the Past: As shown in the Republican National Convention in Tampa, Florida, it was obvious that the homogeneity of the party consisting overwhelmingly of elderly and white voters raised questions on the future of the demography of the party. As the American population continues to become more diverse and the proportion of the electorate becomes less white, less rural and less evangelical, it seems that the crisis the party faced in 2012 would also continue beyond. On the other hand, the Democratic National Convention showed true diversity. The election results also affirmed that non-white voters have become a key part of the society. Close to 90% of African-Americans, over two thirds of the Latinos, more young voters, gays and single women overwhelmingly went to the Obama camp. Some within the Republican Party still say that there is no need to appeal to the minority but to stay 'true to who we are and what we believe in'. Michael Grunwald of Time wrote an article days after the election entitled, *Why the GOP will double down on a losing strategy* arguing the concept of 'what we believe':

> "It is the 'what we believe' part that could cause Republicans more problems down the road. In the Obama era, the GOP has coalesced around an agenda that in some way simply denies reality, rejecting the science of climate change, insisting that government (except the Pentagon) is incapable of creating jobs and denouncing debt while proposing debt-exploding tax cuts.

Some of its fire breathers argued last year that shutting down the federal government and even defaulting on its obligations could be good for the economy. More recently, its leaders suppressed a Congressional Research Service report questioning supply-side dogma …"

The moderate wing is getting smaller in the Senate and almost eliminated in the House: The retirement of Olympia Snowe and the defeat of Scott Brown left Susan Collins as the only moderate Republican in the Senate. In the House the base shifted toward the right and it is difficult to find one Republican in the center.

Defeat can be habit-forming: Niall Ferguson, the Scottish historian and professor of History at Harvard, senior fellow at the Hoover Institute and Republican supporter wrote an article entitled *The losing Habit: How long will the GOP stay in denial?* He argues that to break the losing habit, Republicans must resist the temptation to make excuses. He continued, "we should dismiss the following thought from our mind: It was Hurricane Sandy's fault; it was Chris Christie's fault; the mainstream media gave Obama a pass on Benghazi; a Mormon can never be president; a private-equity guy can never be president; the Tea Party went too far; the Dems' ground game was better in Ohio. Forget all that. These are just ways of denying the deeper cause of Mitt Romney's defeat. Until we face up to these, we will keep on losing. Indeed, I predict now that we will lose in 2016, even when faced with a less ruthlessly effective campaigner than President Obama. Ferguson pointed out the following key lessons learned for the GOP:

- Improve the data driven marketing strategy for the campaign – The Democrats understand the new world of Internet – data-driven marketing better than the Republicans do.
- Demographic 101 – Ferguson argued that demographic trends doom any Republican campaign that appeals more to white males than to any other voter group. As a result Hispanics voted Democratic in even larger numbers than four years ago and the Hispanic share of the population is set to rise from 16 percent in 2010 to nearly 30 percent by 2050.

- Running on the economy doesn't work if people remember your own party's role in screwing it up and think improvement is in sight.
- The more entitlement you create the more votes you get – taking experience from the European Social Democrats, the Democratic Party is benefiting from those entitlement benefits. Given the choice between higher taxes on the 1 percent and cuts in entitlement for the 47 percent, voters had a clear choice.

Another Republican, David Frum asked, "if we [Republicans] know that extremism is dangerous, why do we see so much of it? Victorious presidential candidates have always spoken to the entire country and promised to represent all Americans." He reminded his fellow GOP of the Ronald Reagan Republican nomination acceptance speech in the 1980's, when he said, "I ask you to trust that American spirit which knows no ethnic, religious, social, political, regional or economic boundaries: the spirit that burned with zeal in the hearts of millions of immigrants from every corner of the earth who came here in search of freedom. … The tragedy of the modern Republican Party is that it remembers Ronald Reagan's lyrics – the specific policies he recommended for the problem of his time – but has lost his music." Frum provided his solution for the party to move forward as follows:

- "For the Republican, the road to renewal begins with this formula: 21st century conservatism must become economically inclusive, environmentally responsible, culturally modern, and intellectually credible."

BOBBY JINDAL'S WINNING FORMULA FOR THE GOP IN 2016 AND BEYOND

Governor Bobby Jindal wrote a note on CNN.com a few days after the election, providing his analysis for moving forward to help the party win again. He took a holistic approach to solving the problems the party currently have and provided valuable advice. His argument was that despite losing an election, conservative ideals still hold true. On the question of where the party will abandon its core principles as a necessary prerequisite for winning future elections, he responded, "America already has one liberal party and there is no need for another one," and outlined seven lessons the party should learn to move forward:

- Stop looking backward. We have to boldly show what the future can look like with the free market policies that we believe in. Conservative ideals are aspirational and our country is aspirational.

- Compete for every single vote. The 47% and the 53%. And any other combination of numbers that adds up to 100 percent. President Barack Obama and the Democrats can continue trying to divide America into groups of warring communities with competing interests, but we will have none of it. We are going after every vote as we try to unite all Americans.

- Reject identity politics – The old notion that ours should be a color-blind society is the right one and we should pursue that with vigor. Identity politics is corrosive to the great American melting pot and we reject it. WE will treat all people as individuals rather than as members of special groups.

- Stop being the stupid party- it's time for a new Republican party that talks like adults. It's time for us to articulate our plans and visions for America in real terms. We had a number of Republicans damage the brand this year with offensive and bizarre comments. Enough of that.

- Stop insulting the intelligence of voters. WE need to trust the smarts of the American people. We have to stop dumbing down our ideas and stop reducing everything to mindless slogans and tag lines for 30-second ads. We must be willing to provide details in describing our views.

- Quit "big." We are not the party of big business, big banks, big Wall Street bailouts, big corporate loopholes or big anything. We must not be the party that simply protects the well-off so they can keep their toys. We have to be the party that shows all Americans how they can thrive. We are the party whose ideas will help the middle class and help more folks join the middle class. We are a Populist Party and need to make that clear.

- Focus on people, not government. We must stop competing with Democrats for the job of "Government Manager", and come up with ideas that can unleash the dynamic abilities of the American people. We need to lead the way with politics that can create prosperity. We believe in organic solutions. Not big government solutions. We need a bottom-up government that fits the digital age. Right now we have an outdated centralized government trying to manage a decentralized economy."

The demographic composition, educational level, awareness of the population on current issues, the technology through which people receive news and the speed with which news travels, should give a signal to both parties to play it safe. This election has taught us many things including the power of information, the power of being marginalized, the power of organization, the power of grassroots mobilization, the power of technology in data management and analysis, the power of inclusiveness, the power of openness, the power of fairness and truth, the power of believing in oneself to make change in the system, the power of the single vote, the power of democracy, the power of listening and empathy and above all the power of doing what is right. Hopefully the two parties will remember what happened in the 2008, 2010 and 2012 elections and prepare well for "the next elections."

ACKNOWLEDGMENTS

———

A FEW DAYS AFTER the election, I got an email from my college friend, Ermias who was following the campaign from 5,000 miles away. His email ended with the comment, "Like the 2008 election I hope we will read another *How this Happened* analysis for this election." Then came a number of texts and emails from friends asking me more questions regarding what had happened. Even though I was involved in the campaign I did not have all the information, nor was I in a position to provide expert analysis for this huge and complicated election. But I told myself, I can read and collect and compile the data in order to put together a document which could provide most of the facts in one place. This is the book you have asked me to deliver and I would like to thank all my friends, family members and colleagues for believing that I could produce, if not a perfect analysis, something you can use now or refer back to, years from now so as to remember how it happened. From providing the title of the book, *"perfecting the science of presidential campaigning,"* to reluctantly accepting this project among the many I already have (raising three kids, fulltime work, teaching MBA courses, volunteering at the church and community and running a marathon), Beza, my wife and friend was instrumental in the completion of this document. She was also my first line editor, giving me her "don't exaggerate and check the facts" yellow marks in almost every chapter. She put her own Ph.D research work aside to fully support this project and enable me to complete the work. For that Beza, I'm both intellectually and personally indebted to you.

My children Dagmawi, Berketeab and Redet were with me, giving me their encouragement along the process. Even though it is now difficult for them to understand the content of the book, they took it seriously and supported me from day one. Once in a while, my daughter who is nine years old, comments on my accent, "Daddy how can you write a book if you do not know how to speak English. I'll teach you American-English," and I would answer "Redet, I will take the offer seriously and thank you for that, but remember it is creating the idea, gathering data and going through the ups and downs of writing a book that matters, for the rest I have your mother and good editors to guide me on my way." Dagem, Chuchu and Fiker, you inspired me with your innocent and humble comments and taught me that every day is the best day for learning and that I do not have to travel far to get what I need. I'm blessed to see you every day.

I would be remiss not to mention the following friends who helped shape the book. Mulushewa Mulat, Dr. Darrell Burrell, Dr. Walter McCollum, Dr. Balemwal Atnafu ,and Dr. Assefa, Wondimu who read the manuscript and provided their feedback, Dr. Seble Mengesha who was canvasing and making phone calls with me, sending me material on the election and following up on the status of the work every time we met, Dr. Rahel Bekele and Getaneh Abinet who developed the web page for the book, Habtamu Tadesse and Berhanu Zergaw who developed the marketing materials. Your input and critic has made the book look better and more organized.

Many thanks to my editor Mel Dawson who gave me full professional services as well as her English argument in every chapter, "didn't I tell you that there is no comma before the 'and'", and Mahedere Atnafu for her meticulous proof-reading skills.

Finally to my Dad who will be 90 in a few months and my mom who survived a terrible car accident, your daily prayers follow me wherever I go and always give me energy to work harder. I thank you for giving me all you have. Heartfelt thanks go to my brothers and sisters for your continuous encouragement and support – it means a lot.

BIBLIOGRAPHY

PROLOGUE

1. The 2012 Presidential Election – Referendum of Choice. Retrieved on November 21, 2012 from http://www.lakeresearch.com/

2. National Survey of 1,000 likely voters conducted on September 6, 2012 by Rasmussen Reports on the choice between referendum on the Presidents performance or candidates. Retrieved on November 21, 2012 from http://thehill.com/images/stories/news/2012/09_september/crosstabs_91012.pdf

3. Marshall Ganz (2010). Leading Change: Leadership, organization, and social movements. Handbook of Leadership Theory and Practice. *A Harvard Business School Centennial Colloquium*

4. Abramowitz, A. (2011). Partisan Polarization and the Rise of the Tea Party Movement. APSA 2011 Annual Meeting Paper

5. Congress Approval Rating Hits All-Time Low in Gallup Poll. Retrieved on November 23, 2012 from http://www.huffingtonpost.com/2012/08/14/congress-approval-rating-all-time-low-gallup-poll_n_1777207.html

6. 2010 Census Redistricting Data (Public Law 94-171) Summary File. Retrieved on November 25, 2012 from https://www.census.gov/prod/cen2010/doc/pl94-171.pdf

7. 2012 Elections – Reapportionment and Redistricting. Retrieved on November 20, 2012 from http://www.electionprojection.com/2012elections/redistricting12.php

8. *Schneider. N. (2011). From Occupy Wall Street to Occupy Everywhere. Nation, 293, (18), 13-17.*

9. Stephen, K. (2012). The Sixties Redivivus: the "Occupy Wall Street" Protest. *Catholic Social Science Review, 17, 365-367.*

10. Scherer, M. (2012). Elections will never be the same. *Time International, 180(9), 22-24.*

11. Congressman Tim Ryan (2013). *A Mindful Nation: How a Simple Practice can help us Reduce Stress, Improve Performance and Recapture the American Spirit.* Hay House

CHAPTER 1: ORGANIZATIONAL DEVELOPMENT AND LEADERSHIP AT BEST

1. Green, Joshua (2012). Corporations Want Obama's Winning Formula. *Bloomberg BusinessWeek, (4306), 37-39.*

2. An Introduction to Triangulation. UNAIDS Monitoring and Evaluation Division

3. The Road to Victory: Multiple Pathway to 270 Electoral Votes in 2012. Obama for America (OFA)

4. Inside the Secret world of quants and data crunchers who helped Obama Win. (2012). Time Commemorative Election Special edition.

5. Harness the Power of Big Data: The IBM Big Data Platform. McGrawHill (2013).

6. Ryan, Lizza (2012), the Final Push, New Yorker, 88(34).

7. Obama for America 2012 Campaign Organization. Retrieved on December 8, 2012 from http://www.p2012.org/candidates/obamaorg.html

8. Independent reliable news and perspective on presidential campaigns. Retrieved on December 16, from http://www.p2012.org/

9. Why a Principle Created His Own Currency. Retrieved on December 18, 2012 from http://www.npr.org/blogs/money/135511603/radio

10. National voter turnout in federal elections: 1960-2010. Retrieved on December 18, 2012 from http://www.infoplease.com/ipa/A0781453.html.

11. Schein, E. H. (2010). *Organizational culture and leadership* (4th ed.). San Francisco, CA: Jossey-Bass.

12. Work Culture. Retrieved on December 22, 2012 from http://www.scribd.com/doc/7711281/6-Work-Culture

CHAPTER 2 — THE GROUND GAME

1. Republican Party Mocks Obama Campaign Fashion Show as "Ritzy." Retrieved on January 2, 2013 from http://www.styleite.com/media/rnc-obama-fashion-show-ad/

2. Joshua Green (2012). Obama's CEO: Jim Messina Has a President to Sell. Retrieved on January 2, 2013 from

http://www.businessweek.com/articles/2012-06-14/obamas-ceo-jim-messina-has-a-president-to-sell

3. Clarke Camper (2012). Wall Street and Silicon Valley Influence Campaigning. Retrieved on January 2, 2013 from http://exchanges.nyx.com/clarke-camper/wall-street-and-silicon-valley-influence-campaigning?page=1

4. Obama, Sarah Jessica Parker & Mariah Carey: How the President Stays Cozy with the stars. Retrieved on January 2, 2013 from http://www.huffingtonpost.com/2012/06/14/obama-sarah-jessica-parker-mariah-carey-fundraisers_n_1596020.html

5. George Clooney Obama Fundraiser Nets $15 Million. Retrieved on January 2, 2013 from http://www.huffingtonpost.com/2012/05/11/george-clooney-obama_n_1508850.html

6. Los Angeles event brings in nearly $15 million for Obama campaign. Retrieved on January 2, 2013 from http://articles.latimes.com/2012/may/10/nation/la-na-0511-obama-clooney-20120511

7. 2012 Election fundraising data. Retrieved on January 2, 2013 from http://www.opensecrets.org/pres12/index.php?ql3

8. Meet Obama's Digital Gurus. Retrieved on January 5, 2013 from http://www.motherjones.com/politics/2012/10/obama-campaign-tech-staff

9. Project Dreamcatcher. How cutting-edge text analytics can help the Obama campaign determine voters' hopes and fears. Retrieved on January 5, 2013 from

http://www.slate.com/articles/news_and_politics/victory_
lab/2012/01/project_dreamcatcher_how_cutting_edge_te
xt_analytics_can_help_the_obama_campaign_determine_
voters_hopes_and_fears_.html

10. Obama's White Whale: How the campaign's top-secret
project Narwhal could change this race and many to
come. Retrieved on January 5, 2013 from
http://www.slate.com/articles/news_and_politics/victory_
lab/2012/02/project_narwhal_how_a_top_secret_obama_
campaign_program_could_change_the_2012_race_.singl
e.html

11. How Romney's ORCA was defeated by Obama's
Narwhal & Dreamcatcher. Retrieved on January 5, 2013
from
http://www.dailykos.com/story/2012/11/10/1160145/-
How-Romney-s-ORCA-was-defeated-by-Obama-s-
Narwhal-Dreamcatcher

12. Andrew Romano (2012). Yes We can (Can't We?). While
the GOP Votes, team Obama is crafting a juggernaut.
Andrew Romano talks to top advisers about their 2012
strategy including David Axelrod, who admits that he
shares some of the blame for the president's dismal
approval rating. Retrieved on January 6, 2013 from
http://www.thedailybeast.com/newsweek/2012/01/01/ins
ide-president-obama-s-reelection-machine.html

CHAPTER 3 – THE DONE OF DATA MANAGEMENT
1. NPR- All things Considered November 7, 2012. We
profile the years "it" prognosticator, Nate Silver, the
baseball guru turned Electoral College whiz. Retrieved on
November 14, 2012 from
http://www.npr.org/2012/11/07/164631093/-statistician-
nate-silver-scores-big-on-election-night

2. Bayes' Theorem definition. Retrieved on November 27, 2012 from http://plato.stanford.edu/entries/bayes-theorem/

3. Sasha Issenberg (2012). The Victory Lab. Crown Publishers

4. Panagopoulos Costas (2011). Thank you for Voting: Gratitude Expression and Voter Mobilization. Journal of Politics, 73 (3), 707-717.

5. "General indifference." Charles E. Merriam and Harold F. Gosnell, Non-Voting: Cause and Methods of control. (Chicago: University of Chicago Press, 1924)

6. Gosnell, Harold F. (1940). The Polls and Other Mechanisms of Democracy. The Public Opinion Quarterly. 4 (2), 224-228.

7. Gosnell, Harold F. Does Campaigning Make a Difference?. The Public Opinion Quarterly, 14(3), 413-418.

8. Gosnell, Harold F. (1942). A Critique of Polling Methods. The Public Opinion Quartely, 6(3), 378-390.

9. Gosnell, H F. (1939). The Study of Voting Behavior by Correlational Techniques. American Sociological Review, 4(6), 809-815.

10. Microtargeting : How campaigns know you better than yourself. Retrieved on January 6, 13 from http://www.cnn.com/2012/11/05/politics/voters-microtargeting/index.html

11. Content Analytics: Research tools for unstructured content and rich media. Retrieved on January 6, 2013

from http://www.aiim.org/Research-and-
Publications/Research/Industry-Watch/content-analytics

12. How President Obama's campaign used big data to rally
individual voters. Retrieved on January 7, 2013 from
http://www.technologyreview.com/featuredstory/508836/
how-obama-used-big-data-to-rally-voters-part-1/

13. Understand the Math Behind it All: Bayesian Statistics.
Retrieved on January 7, 2013 from
http://blogs.adobe.com/digitalmarketing/personalization/
conversion-optimization/understand-the-math-behind-it-
all-bayesian-statistics/

14. Analysis: Obama's ad team used cable TV to outplay
Romney. Retrieved on January 9, 2013 from
http://www.reuters.com/article/2013/01/05/us-usa-
politics-cabletv-idUSBRE90406820130105

15. Romney spent more on TV ads but got much less.
Washington Post. Retrieved on January 9, 2013 from
http://articles.washingtonpost.com/2012-12-
11/politics/35767760_1_romney-campaign-officials-
obama-campaign-ad-strategy

16. Secret the Obama Victory? Rerun Watchers, for One
Thing. Jim Rutenberg, The New York Times. Retrieved
on January 9, 2013 from
http://www.nytimes.com/2012/11/13/us/politics/obama-
data-system-targeted-tv-viewers-for-support.html?_r=0

17. Obama for America asked GMMB to serve as a lead
strategic advertising firm to tell Barack Obama's story,
communicate his vision and help make the potential for
transformational change a reality. For 20 months, we
helped in directing strategy, developing and placing

advertising and executing campaign events around the
country. Retrieved on January 9, 2013 from
http://www.gmmb.com/work/view/president-barack-
obama/

18. Exclusive: Obama's 2012 Digital Fundraising
Outperformed 2008. Michael Scherer. Time. Retrieved
on January 10, 2013 from
http://swampland.time.com/2012/11/15/exclusive-
obamas-2012-digital-fundraising-outperformed-2008/

19. Fundraising: The Science Behind Those Obama
Campaign E-mails. Joshua Green. Bloomberg
BusinessWeek. Retrieved on January 11, 2013 from
http://www.businessweek.com/articles/2012-11-29/the-
science-behind-those-obama-campaign-e-mails

20. Obama's Billion-Dollar Bet. Bloomberg BusinessWeek.
Retrieved on January 11, 2013 from
http://www.businessweek.com/articles/2012-11-
02/obamas-billion-dollar-bet#r=lr-fst

21. The 2012 Money Race: Compare the Candidates. The
New York Times. Reprieved on January 11, 2013 from
http://elections.nytimes.com/2012/campaign-finance

22. Obama's Re-Election Path May be Written in Will St.
Clair's Code. Julianna Goldman, Bloomberg. Retrieved
on January 11, 2013 from
http://www.bloomberg.com/news/2011-12-14/obama-s-
re-election-path-may-be-written-in-will-st-clair-s-
code.html

23. Obama's victory starts with strong ground game, ends
with perfect storm. Scott Wilson and Philip Rucker, The
Washington Post. Retrieved on January 16, 2013 from

http://www.independent.co.uk/news/world/americas/us-elections/obamas-victory-starts-with-strong-ground-game-ends-with-perfect-storm-8293314.html

24. Ground Game: Obama Opens Up Big Lead in State Headquarters. As of mid-October, the Obama campaign has 755 offices nationwide for its get-out-the-vote effort – nearly three times as many as the Romney campaign. The Daily Beast. Retrieved on January 16, 2013 from http://www.thedailybeast.com/articles/2012/10/19/ground-game-obama-opens-up-big-lead-in-state-headquarters.html

25. In Swing states, the Obama camp has opened twice as many offices, but the RNC might help Romney compete on Election Day. John Avlon and Michael Keller. The Daily Beast. Retrieved on January 16, 2013 from http://www.thedailybeast.com/articles/2012/10/19/ground-game-obama-campaign-opens-up-a-big-lead-in-field-offices.html

26. Ohio Working Class May Offer Key to Obama's Reelection. Jeff Zeleny and Dalia Sussman. The New York Times. Retrieved on January 17, 2013 from http://www.nytimes.com/2012/10/31/us/politics/ohio-working-class-may-be-key-to-obama-re-election.html?pagewanted=all

27. Ohio Election 2012: Obama, Mitt Romney Focus on Key States in Final Lap. The Huffington post. Retrieved on January 17, 2013 from http://www.huffingtonpost.com/2012/11/05/ohio-election-2012_n_2075881.html

28. Presidential Ad War Tops 1M Airings. 2012 Shatters 2004 and 2008 Records for Total Ads Aired. Wesleyan Media Project political Advertising Analysis. Retrieved on

January 17, 2013 from
http://mediaproject.wesleyan.edu/2012/11/02/presidentia
l-ad-war-tops-1m-airings/

29. Thank you, Mr. President: You Held Back the Worst.
Deepak Chopra. Retrieved on January 20, 13 from
http://www.huffingtonpost.com/deepak-chopra/thank-
you-mr-president-you-held-back-the-
worst_b_2077413.html

30. Strategy update: What We're Building This Summer.
Video Message from Mitch Stewart, the battleground
state director. Retrieved on January 29, 2013 from
http://www.youtube.com/watch?v=QCa2OI2Qioc

31. Introducing Grassroots Planning Sessions. Obama for
America. Retrieved on January 29, 2013 from
http://www.barackobama.com/news/entry/introducing-
grassroots-planning-sessions/

32. In Presidential campaign ads, political science meets
excess. AlinaSelyukh. Reuters. Retrieved on January 20,
2013 from
http://www.reuters.com/article/2012/11/01/us-usa-
campaign-ads-idUSBRE8A006M20121101

33. Ohio Sees Enough Campaign Ads to Air Nonstop for 80
Days. Julie Bykowicz. Bloomberg. Retrieved on January
25, 2013 from http://www.bloomberg.com/news/2012-
10-26/ohio-sees-enough-campaign-ads-to-air-nonstop-
for-80-days.html

34. Obama is the first Facebook President – What Now?
Deepak Chopra. Retrieved on January 20, 13 from
http://www.huffingtonpost.com/deepak-chopra/obama-

is-the-first-facebook-president-what-now_b_2389434.html

35. Danah Zohar & Ian Marshall (2000). Spiritual
Intelligence the ultimate intelligence. Bloomsbury
Publishing. New York

36. Paths to 270 Electoral Votes - Jim Messina – Obama for
America. Retrieved on January 27, 2013 from
http://www.youtube.com/watch?NR=1&v=_7Y-
Q9ZY5Ao&feature=endscreen

37. One Million Person-to-Person Conversations – Obama
For America. Video message from Jim Messina. Retrieved
on January 29, 2013 from
http://www.youtube.com/watch?v=SiEXniU40g0

38. Time, The Year in Review, 2012.

39. Peter Senge (1994) The fifth Discipline Field book:
Strategies and tools for building a learning organization.

40. Barak Obama, Fashion Magnate. Retrieved on January 2,
2013 from http://www.businessweek.com/articles/2012-
11-21/barack-obama-fashion-magnate

41. Obama is selling yoga pants and soy candles. Retrieved on
January from http://radio.foxnews.com/toddstarnes/top-
stories/obama-is-selling-yoga-pants-and-soy-candles.html

42. Romney Economics: It didn't work in Massachusetts, and
it won't work now. Retrieved on January 29, 2013 from
http://www.barackobama.com/romney/economics/

43. Donald P. Green. Alan S. Gerber (2008). Get Out the
Vote: How to Increase Voter Turnout. Brookings
Institution Press.

44. Borrow Money From you Parents. Retrieved on January 26, 2013 from http://www.youtube.com/watch?v=CIa4VdtKlO0

45. TV Land: The home of original sitcoms and classic TV shows. Retrieved on December 25, 2012 from http://www.tvland.com/

CHAPTER 4 — THE ECONOMY - STIMULUS PACKAGE
1. Barack Obama and Keynesian Economics will prevail. Retrieved on January 12, 2013 from http://www.policymic.com/articles/12587/barack-obama-and-keynesian-economics-will-prevail

2. John. M., Keynes (1935). The General Theory of Employment, Interest, and Money.

3. Presidential debate 101: Did Obama really double the deficit? Retrieved on February 12, 2013 from http://www.csmonitor.com/USA/DC-Decoder/Decoder-Wire/2012/1005/Presidential-debate-101-Did-Obama-really-double-the-deficit

4. Congress moves on Stimulus Bill and Bailout Money. January 15, 2009. The New York Times. Retrieved on December 23,2012 from http://www.nytimes.com/2009/01/16/business/economy/16webstimulus.html?scp=1&sq=house%20%24825%20stimulus%20plan&st=cse

5. The debt to the penny and who holds it. The Bureau of the Public Debt. Retrieved on February 27, 2013 from http://www.treasurydirect.gov/NP/BPDLogin?application=np

6. How did Economist get it so wrong? Paul Krugman, September, 2, 2009 The New York Times. Retrieved on January 12, 2013 from http://www.nytimes.com/2009/09/06/magazine/06Econo mic-t.html?pagewanted=all

7. Chicago school of economics as a neoclassical school of thought with the academic community of economists, with a strong focus around the faculty of University of Chicago. Retrieved on February 27, 2013 from http://en.wikipedia.org/wiki/Keynesian_economics

8. Keynesian Economics is the view that in the short run, especially during recessions, productive activity is strongly influenced by aggregate demand. Retrieved on December 30, 2012 from http://en.wikipedia.org/wiki/Keynesian_economics

9. The Demand Doctor: What would John Maynard Keynes tell us to do now – and should we listen? John Cassidy. The New Yorker. Retrieved December 14, 2012 from http://www.newyorker.com/reporting/2011/10/10/11101 0fa_fact_cassidy

10. The recovery Act. The place to follow American's recovery. Retrieved on December 16, 2012 from http://www.whitehouse.gov/recovery/about/

11. Obama seeks wide support in Congress for Stimulus. Jeff Zeleny and David M. Herszenhorn. The New York Times. January 5, 2009. Retrieved on December 22, 2012 from http://www.nytimes.com/2009/01/06/us/politics/06stimu lus.html?scp=7&sq=stimulus%20plan%20obama%20jan uary&st=cse&_r=0

12. Economic stimulus – Jobs Bills. The New York Times. March 15, 2012. Retrieved on February 23, 2013 from http://topics.nytimes.com/top/reference/timestopics/subjects/u/united_states_economy/economic_stimulus/index.html?scp=1-spot&sq=stimulus&st=cse

13. Tracking the Money. Recovery.gov is the U.S. government official website that provides easy access to data related to Recovery Act spending and allows for the reporting of potential fraud, waste, and abuse. Retrieved on February 28, 2013 from http://www.recovery.gov/About/Pages/The_Act.aspx

14. Did the stimulus work? A review of the nine bet studies on the subject. Dylan Matthews. Washington Post. August 8, 2011. Retrieved on January 10, 2013 from http://www.washingtonpost.com/blogs/wonkblog/post/did-the-stimulus-work-a-review-of-the-nine-best-studies-on-the-subject/2011/08/16/gIQAThbibJ_blog.html

15. 35 Straight months of growth. Private Sector Job Creation (December 2007 to Present). Obama for America. Retrieved on February 28, 2013 from http://www.barackobama.com/economy?source=footer-nav

16. James Feyrer, Bruce Sacerdote. February 2011. Did the Stimulus Stimulate? Real Time Estimates of the Effects of the American Recovery and Reinvestment Act. The National Bureau of Economic Research Working Paper No. 16759. Retrieved on January 10, 2012 from http://www.nber.org/papers/w16759.pdf

17. Reich. G, C, Feiveson. L. Liscow.Z, William Gui. Woolston. (2001). Does State Fiscal Relief During Recessions Increase Employment? Evidence from the American Recovery and Reinvestment Act.

18. Daniel J. Wilson. Federal Reserve Bank of San Francisco (2011). Fiscal Spending Jobs Multipliers: Evidence from the 2009 American Recovery and Reinvestment Act. Retrieved on January 12, 2013 from http://www.frbsf.org/publications/economics/papers/2010/wp10-17bk.pdf

19. Estimated Impact of the American Recovery and Reinvestment Act on Employment and Economic Output from January 2011 through March 2011. Congressional Budget Office. Washington DC. Retrieved on January 12, 2013 from http://www.cbo.gov/sites/default/files/cbofiles/ftpdocs/121xx/doc12185/05-25-arra.pdf

20. The Economic Impact of the American Recovery and Reinvestment Act of 2009. Executive Office of the President Council of Economic Advisers. Fifth Quarterly Report. November 18, 2010. Retrieved on January12,2013 from http://www.whitehouse.gov/sites/default/files/cea_5th_arra_report.pdf

21. Hyunseung Oh, Richardo Reis. The National Bureau of Economic Research. Targeted Transfer and the Fiscal Response to the Great Recession. NBER Working Paper No. 16775. Retrieved on January 12, 2013 from http://www.nber.org/papers/w16775.pdf

22. Timothy Conley & Bill Dupor (2011). The American Recovery and Reinvestment Act: Public Sector Jobs Saved, Private Sector Jobs Forestalled. Retrieved on January 12, 2013 from http://web.econ.ohio-state.edu/dupor/arra10_may11.pdf

23. John B. Taylor. University of Stanford. An Empirical Analysis of the Revived of Fiscal Activism in the 2000s. Retrieved on January 12, 2013 from http://www.stanford.edu/~johntayl/JEL_taylor%20revised.pdf

24. Why Obama's Economic Stimulus Worked. Chad Stone. Retrieved on January 30, 2013 from http://www.usnews.com/opinion/blogs/economic-intelligence/2012/06/20/why-the-economic-stimulus-worked

25. Economic Stimulus. Survey of 40 economists from the top U.S. universities on the impact of the stimulus on the economy. University of Chicago School of Booth. Retrieved on January 23, 2013 from http://www.igmchicago.org/igm-economic-experts-panel/poll-results?SurveyID=SV_cw5O9LNJL1oz4Xi

26. With all due respect, Mr. President, that is not true. CATO Institute's respond to the January 9, 2009 statement of the president elect Barack Obama "There is not disagreement that we need action by our government, a recovery plan that will help to jump start the economy." Retrieved on January 10, 2013 from http://www.cato.org/doc-download/sites/cato.org/files/documents/cato_stimulus.pdf

27. Letter to Congress: Economists Across the Spectrum Endorse Stimulus Package. Center for American Progress Action Fund. January 27, 2009 . Retrieved on December 28, 2012 from http://www.americanprogressaction.org/issues/economy/news/2009/01/27/5490/letter-to-congress-economists-across-the-spectrum-endorse-stimulus-package/

28. Nobel Laureate Paul Krugman: Too Little Stimulus in Stimulus Plan. Paul Krugman, the 2008 Nobel Prize in Economics. Retrieved on December 17, 2012 from http://knowledge.wharton.upenn.edu/article.cfm?articleid =2167

CHAPTER 5 – THE AUTO BAILOUT

1. The Unpopular, Successful Auto Bailout. Retrieved on December 31, 2012 from http://prospect.org/article/unpopular-successful-auto-bailout

2. Let Detroit Go Bankrupt. Mitt Romney, Published November 18, 2008, The New York Times. The Opinion Pages. Retrieved on December 23, 2012 from http://www.nytimes.com/2008/11/19/opinion/19romney .html?_r=0

3. Boehner Statement on Auto Bailout Proposal from House &Senate Democrats. Retrieved on December 26, 2012 from http://www.speaker.gov/press-release/boehner-statement-auto-bailout-proposal-house-senate-democrats

4. Senate GOP looks to halt auto bailout. S.A. Miller – The Washington Post. Retrieved on January 12, 2013 from http://www.washingtontimes.com/news/2008/dec/11/senate-gop-looks-halt-auto-bailout/?page=all

5. Senate GOP puts break on bailout – The Washington Times. Retrieved on February 18, 2013 from http://www.campbell.house.gov/index.php?option=com_content&view=article&id=1406

6. Romney accuses Obama for trying to "fool" voters. Nicole Busch, September 23, 2012. Retrieved on December 20, 2012 from

http://politics.blogs.foxnews.com/2012/09/23/romney-accuses-obama-trying-fool-voters

7. U.S.: Loss on auto bailout down 16%. Surge in GM stock helps cut estimate by $4 B to $20.3B. Retrieved on January 23, 2013 from http://www.detroitnews.com/article/20130212/AUTO01/302120334

8. Troubled Asset Relief Program (TARP): Implementation and Status. Congressional Research Services, October 19, 2012

9. Agnieszka Gryska (2012). Impact of restructuring on the U.S. Automotive Industry: Case Study of General Motors. Unpublished Thesis paper. Virginia International University, School of Business

10. U.S Bureau of Labor Statistics Automotive Industry: Employment, Earnings, and Hours. Retrieved on February 20, 2013 from http://www.bls.gov/iag/tgs/iagauto.htm#iag31cessaemp.f.P

11. Contribution of the Automotive Industry to the Economy of all five states and the United states. Center for Automotive Research, 2010.

12. Steven Klepper (2001).The Evolution of the U.S. Automobile Industry and Detroit as its Capital. Carnegie Mellon University.

13. Zupan, Mark (2008). University of Rochester Roundtable on Bankruptcy and Bailouts: The case of the U.S. Auto Industry. Journal of Applied Finance, 18 (2).

14. Canis, B. & Yacobucci, B. D. (2010). "*The U.S. Motor Vehicle Industry: Confronting a New Dynamic in the Global Economy*" (2010).Federal Publications, Congressional Research Services, Paper 722

15. Cooney, S. & Yacobucci, B. D. (2005). *U.S. Automotive Industry: Policy Overview and Recent History*. Federal Publications, Congressional Research Services.

16. Cooney, S, et.al. (2009). U.S. Motor Vehicle Industry: Federal Financial Assistance and Restructuring. Congressional Research Service

17. Chrysler Restructuring Plan for Long-Term Viability. Executive Summary. Chrysler. February 17, 2009. Retrieved on January 16, 2013 from http://www.media.chrysler.com/dcxms/assets/attachments /Chrysler_Restructuring_Plan_Summary.pdf

18. Ford Motor Company Business Plan. Submitted to the Senate Banking Committee. December 2, 2009.

19. White House. Press Briefing, December 12, 2008, Press Secretary Dana Perino on Presidential Action to Aid the Auto Industry.

20. White House. Office of the Press Secretary. "President Bush Discusses Administration's Plan to Assist Automakers", December 19, 2008.

21. The presidency of Barack Obama. The New York Times. February 21, 2013. Retrieved on February, 22, 2013 from http://topics.nytimes.com/top/reference/timestopics/peop le/o/barack_obama/presidency/index.html

22. Study: U.S. Aid to Auto Industry saved 1 million jobs. Retrieved on February, 20, 2013. From http://www.thedetroitbureau.com/2010/11/study-u-s-aid-to-auto-industry-saved-1-million-jobs/

23. Auto Bailout Now Backed, Stimulus Divisive. Mixed Views of Regulation, Support for keystone Pipeline. Retrieved on December 12, 2012 from http://www.thedetroitbureau.com/2010/11/study-u-s-aid-to-auto-industry-saved-1-million-jobs/

24. Steven Rattner (2010) Overhaul: An Insider's Account of the Obama Administration's Emergency Rescue of the Auto Industry. Houghton Mifflin Harcourt

25. The big 2/3 Auto Bailout and Its Aftermath: Measuring the Effects on the Past, Present & Future of the Big Three. Retrieved on January 16, 2013 from http://dritoday.org/feature.aspx?id=429

26. Obama Touts Auto Bailout In Weekly Address" "I Bet on American Workers." Retrieved on December 29, 2012 from http://www.realclearpolitics.com/video/2012/10/13/obama_touts_auto_bailout_in_weekly_address_i_bet_on_american_workers.html

27. Obama Leverages Auto Bailout for Crucial Midwest Wins. Jeff Green and Mark Niquette. Bloomberg. Retrieved on January 6, 2013 from http://www.bloomberg.com/news/2012-11-07/obama-leverages-auto-bailout-for-crucial-midwest-wins.html\

28. Obama's Announcement on the Auto Industry. Remarks by the president . Retrieved on December 27, 2012 from

http://www.nytimes.com/2009/03/30/us/politics/30obam
a-text.html?pagewanted=all&_r=0

CHAPTER 6 — FINANCIAL REGULATIONS

1. Dilbar Khakimova (2012). the impact of "Ponzi Scheme" on the Economy: A Case study of Bernard Madoff. Unpublished Master Thesis, Virginia International University, School of Business

2. Ten Myths about Subprime Mortgages. Yuliya Denyanyk. Senior Research Economist Federal Reserve Bank of Cleveland. Retrieved on January 25, 2013 from http://www.clevelandfed.org/research/commentary/2009/0509.cfm

3. Financial Crisis and Bank Failures: A Review of Prediction Methods. Yuliya Demyanyk and Lftekhar Hasan. Working Paper 0904R. Federal Reserve Bank of Cleveland. (2009)

4. Jobs & the Economy: Putting America Back to Work. Wall Street Reform: The Dodd – Frank Act. Retrieved on January 15, 2013 from http://www.whitehouse.gov/economy/middle-class/dodd-frank-wall-street-reform

5. Bureau of Economic Analysis, Interactive Access to Industry Economic Accounts Data. Retrieved on February 13, 2013 from http://www.bea.gov/iTable/iTable.cfm?ReqID=5&step=1#reqid=5&step=4&isuri=1&402=15&403=1

6. Congress passes financial reform bill. Washington Post. Retrieved on January 2, 2013 from

http://www.washingtonpost.com/wp-dyn/content/article/2010/07/15/AR2010071500464.html

7. Transcript of the remarks by the President at Signing of Dodd-Frank Wall Street Reform and Consumer Protection Act. Retrieved on January 5, 2013 from http://www.whitehouse.gov/the-press-office/remarks-president-signing-dodd-frank-wall-street-reform-and-consumer-protection-act

8. Reinventing financial regulation. The landmark legislation approved by Congress represents the most profound restructuring of financial regulation since the Great Depression. Here are some of the highlights of the bill, which was born out of the wreckage of the financial crisis and the problem it is designed to address. Brady Dennis and Alberto Cuadra. Washington Post Retrieved on December 30, 2012 from http://www.washingtonpost.com/wp-srv/special/nation/financial-regulation-graphic/?sid=ST2010071504699

9. Financial reform bill passes House, 237-192. Los Angeles Times July 01, 2010. Retrieved on February 13, 2013 from http://articles.latimes.com/2010/jul/01/business/la-fi-financial-reform-20100701

10. Financial Crisis of 2007 -2008. Retrieved on January 3, 2012 from http://en.wikipedia.org/wiki/Financial_crisis_of_2007%E2%80%932008

11. Wall Street and the Financial Crisis: Anatomy of Financial Collapse. United States Permanent Subcommittee on Investigations, Committee on

Homeland Security and Government Affairs. Majority
and Minority Staff Report. April 13, 2011

12. Final Rule: Alternative Net Capital Requirements for
Broker-Dealers That are Part of Consolidated Supervised
Entities. Securities and Exchange Commission. Retrieved
on February 14, 2013 from
http://www.sec.gov/rules/final/34-49830.htm

13. Goldstein V. Securities and Exchange Commission.
Toddy Zaun. Retrieved on December 31, 2012 from
http://www.nyls.edu/user_files/1/3/4/17/49/NLRvol52-
106.pdf.

14. Description: Expanding Guidance for Subprime Lending
Programs. Office of the Comptroller of the Currency.
U.S. Department of the Treasury. Retrieved on February
14, 2013 from http://www.occ.gov/news-
issuances/bulletins/2001/bulletin-2001-6.htm

15. Nonprime Mortgage: Analysis of Loan Performance,
Factors Associated with Defaults, and Data Sources,
Government Accountability Offices (GAO). Report No.
GAO-10-805. Retrieved on January 15, 2013 from
http://gao.gov/products/GAO-10-805

16. Definition of Hybrid ARM. Retrieved on February 15,
2013 from
http://www.investopedia.com/terms/h/hybridarm.asp#axz
z2KvOlNLgZ

17. Characteristics and Performance of Nonprime Mortgages.
GAO, Report No. GAO – 09-848R. Retrieved on
January 12, 2013 from
http://www.gao.gov/new.items/d09848r.pdf

18. Leon Courville. Financial Crisis: a perfect storm or regulatory failure. Retrieved on February 16, 2013 from http://www.hec.ca/iea/seminaires/120508_leon_courville.pdf

19. Viral V. Acharya, Cooley, M. and Ingo Walter (2011). Market Failures and Regulatory Failures: Lessons from Past and Present Financial Crises. ADBI working Paper Series.

20. Bruner, Robert, and Sean D. Carr (2007). The Panic of 1907: Lessons Learned from the Market's Perfect Storm. New York, NY: John Wiley.

21. Office of Thrift Supervision. Retrieved on February 16, 2013 from http://en.wikipedia.org/wiki/Office_of_Thrift_Supervision

22. Investment banking. Retrieved on December 29, 2012 from http://en.wikipedia.org/wiki/Investment_banking

23. Investment Banking Overview. Retrieved on December 30, 2012 from http://www.jhu.edu/careers/NewMattinProject/careers/banking.html

24. Alan D. Morrison and William J. Wilhelm (2007). Investment Banking: Past, Present, and Future. Journal of Applied Corporate Finance, 19, (1)

25. Top 10 Investment Banks. Retrieved on February 17, 2013 from http://finance.mapsofworld.com/investment/banks/top-10-bank.html

26. List of banks acquired or bankrupted during the 2007-2012 global financial crisis. Retrieved on January 12, 2012 from http://en.wikipedia.org/wiki/List_of_banks_acquired_or_bankrupted_during_the_2007%E2%80%932012_global_financial_crisis

27. Jonas Prager (2012) The financial crisis of 2007/08: misaligned incentives,bank mismanagement and troubling policy implications. Austrian Colloquium.

28. The Financial Crisis Inquiry Report. Final Report of the National Commission on the Causes of the Financial and Economic Crisis in the United States. Financial Crisis Inquiry Commission.

29. Lawrence G. McDonald and Patrick Robinson (2009). A Colossal Failure of Common Sense: The Inside Story of the Collapse of Lehman Brothers.

30. Jared Dillian (2011). Street Freak: Money and Madness at Lehman Brothers. A memoir of Money and Madness.

31. Joseph Cassano, Ex-AIG Exec is unapologetic, Blames Auditors for Losses. Huffington Post. Retrieved on January 12, 2013 from Joseph Cassano

32. Perkins J. E. (2005). Ponzi: The man and his legendary scheme. Business History Review, 79(1), 141-142.

33. Lewis S. L. (2010). Madoff's victims and their day in court. *Society,* *47*(5), 439-450.

34. Lewis S. L. (2011). How Madoff did it: Victims' accounts. *Society,* *48*(1), 70-76.

35. Hurt C. (2009), "Evil Has a New Name (And A New Narrative): Bernard Madoff", Michigan State Law Review

36. Transcript of candidate Obama's speech on "Renewing the American Economy" on March 2008 at the Cooper Union. Retrieved on December 29, 2012. From http://www.nytimes.com/2008/03/27/us/politics/27text-obama.html?pagewanted=all&_r=0

37. Morrison & Foerster. The Dood-Frank Act: A cheat Sheet. Retrieved on February 10, 2013 from http://www.mofo.com/files/Uploads/Images/SummaryDo ddFrankAct.pdf

38. Josh Wolfson, Corinne Crawford, Barry N. Cooper and Wilbert Donnay, October 2010, "A Regulatory Overhaul for Wall Street and Banks"

39. Goldman Turns Table on Obama Campaign: Article by Liz Rappaport and Brody Mullins. The Wall Street Journal, October 10, 2012. Retrieved on November 16, 2012 from http://online.wsj.com/article/SB10000872396390444752 504578024661927487192.html

CHAPTER 7 – HEALTH CARE

1. Timeline: President Obama's first term, 2009-2012. A look back through president Barack Obama's first term as he seeks re-reelection. Retrieved on January 30, 2013 from http://www.newsday.com/timeline-president-obama-s-first-term-2009-2012-1.3435163

2. Children's Pre-Existing Conditions. Under the Affordable Care Act, health plans cannot limit or deny benefits or deny coverage for a child younger than age 19 simply because the child as a "pre-existing condition" – that is a

health problem that developed before the child applied to join the plan. Retrieved on December 28, 2012 from http://www.healthcare.gov/law/features/rights/childrens-pre-existing-conditions/

3. On Behalf of My Mother. This morning the President made it official: things are going to change quite a bit between Americans and their health insurance companies. The White House signing ceremony of the Affordable Health Care Act. March 23, 2010. Retrieved on January 30, 2013 from http://www.whitehouse.gov/blog/2010/03/23/behalf-my-mother

4. A more secure future. What the new health care law means for you and your family? Retrieved on December 19, 2012 from http://www.whitehouse.gov/healthreform

5. What is changing and when. Health care implementation timeline. Retrieved on December 30, 2012 from http://www.healthcare.gov/law/timeline/

6. Take health care into your own hands. Retrieved on December 6, 2012 from http://www.healthcare.gov/law/features/rights/preventive-care/index.html

7. Supreme court of the United States Decision on Patient Protection and Affordable Care Act. Retrieved on January 1, 2013 from http://www.supremecourt.gov/opinions/11pdf/11-393c3a2.pdf

8. The 100 Year – old debate: How Far Has Health Care Come? The idea of universal healthcare insurance isn't the brainchild of the Obama or Clinton administrations. It

started in 1912. NRP report. Retrieved on January 24, 2013 from
http://www.npr.org/templates/story/story.php?storyId=11 1089777

9. Theodore Roosevelt's speech before the convention of the National Progressive Party in Chicago, August, 1912. Retrieved on December 31, 2012 from
http://www.ssa.gov/history/trspeech.html
10. Medicare &Medicaid Fraud Reporting Center. Retrieved on December 30, 2012 from
http://medicarefraudcenter.org/medicare-fraud-news.html

11. Health care timeline from NRP. Retrieved on January 1, 2012. From
http://www.pbs.org/healthcarecrisis/history.htm

12. Lobbyists swarm capitol to influence health reform. Tally of 4525 Means Eight Lobbyists for Each Member of Congress. Retrieved on December 25, 2012 from
http://www.publicintegrity.org/2010/02/24/2725/lobbyis ts-swarm-capitol-influence-health-reform

13. Morris, L. (2009) Combating fraud in health care: An essential component of any cost containment strategy. *Health Affairs,* 28(5), 1351-6

14. Health Reform 3.0: what's in the health care reform bill's final draft? Timothy Noah. Retrieved on December 30, 2012 from
http://www.slate.com/articles/news_and_politics/prescrip tions/2010/03/health_reform_30.html

15. U.S. Department of Justice Federal bureau of Investigation (FBI) financial Crimes Section, Criminal Investigative Division Financial Crimes Report to the

Public. Retrieved on January 26, 2013 from
http://www.fbi.gov/stats-services/publications/financial-
crimes-report-2010-2011/financial-crimes-report-2010-
2011.pdf

16. Malcolm K. Sparrow. Corruption in health care systems:
The U.S. experience. Retrieved on December 29, 2012
from
http://www.bu.edu/actforhealth/actforhealth04/Part1_1_
causesofcorruption.pdf

17. Government agencies blew $125 billion on improper
payments. Retrieved on January 31, 2013 from
http://www.publicintegrity.org/2011/04/15/4167/govern
ment-agencies-blew-125-billion-improper-payments

18. Emergency Medical Treatment & Labor Act (EMTA) of
1986. Centers for Medicare & Medicaid Services.
Retrieved on December 22, 2012 from
http://www.cms.gov/Regulations-and-
Guidance/Legislation/EMTALA/index.html

19. GAO Testimony before the Subcommittee on
Government Organization, Efficiency, and Financial
Management, Committee on Oversight and Government
Reform, House of Representatives. Improper Payments:
Recent Effect to Address Improper Payments and
Remaining Challenges. Retrieved on December 19, 2012
from http://www.gao.gov/new.items/d11575t.pdf

20. AMA: Once Again Fewer Doctors Choose AMA.
Retrieved on February 2, 2013 from
http://www.medpagetoday.com/MeetingCoverage/AMA/
27147

21. American Association for Labor Legislation, 1905-1943.
ProQuest Publication (http://www.proquest.com/en-

US/catalogs/collections/detail/American-Association-for-Labor-Legislation-38.shtml)

22. Approved, March 23, 2010. President Barack Obama's signature on the health insurance reform bill at the White House, March 23, 2010. By Chuck Kennedy, the White House. Retrieved on December 26, 2012 from http://content.usatoday.com/communities/theoval/post/2 010/03/obamas-many-pens-stamp-health-care-law/1

23. Health Insurance Exchange. Retrieved on December 31, 2012 from http://en.wikipedia.org/wiki/Health_insurance_exchange

24. Us health care costs: the crushing burden. Engineering the system of healthcare delivery. Edited by W.B Rouse and D.A. Cortese. IOS Press, 2010. Dio: 10.3233/978 -1 – 60750 – 533 – 4 – 87.

25. Health care in the United States. Retrieved on December 26, 2012 from http://en.wikipedia.org/wiki/Health_care_in_the_United _States

26. National Health Expenditure Data – Centers for Medicare & Medicaid Services. Retrieved on January 1, 2013 from https://www.cms.gov/Research-Statistics-Data-and-Systems/Statistics-Trends-and-Reports/NationalHealthExpendData/NationalHealthAcc ountsHistorical.html

27. David U. Himmelstein, Deborah Thorne, Elizabeth Warrenand Steffie Woolhandler. Medical Bankruptcy in the United States, 2007: Result of a National Study. *The American Journal of Medicine.* Retrieved on Jan 21, 2013 from http://www.washingtonpost.com/wp-

srv/politics/documents/american_journal_of_medicine_0
9.pdf

28. President Obama's Accomplishments – March 2012.
Retrieved on February 5, 2013 from
http://www.aflcio.org/content/download/14741/177141/
Obama+Accomplishments+DJ+w+DS.pdf

29. Supreme Court decision hands Romney election. Chief
Justices John Roberts has just handed you the presidency
of the United States. Retrieved on November 7, 2012
fromhttp://blog.syracuse.com/opinion/2012/07/supreme
_court_decision_hands_r.html

30. John Boehner. 'Obamacare is the law of the land'.
Retrieved on January 29, 2013 from
http://nbcpolitics.nbcnews.com/_news/2012/11/08/1502
9606-boehner-obamacare-is-the-law-of-the-land?lite

31. Clients lobbying on Patient Protection and Affordable
Care Act (HR. 3590). Retrieved on January 2, 2013 from
https://www.opensecrets.org/lobby/billsum.php?id=1107
38

32. Health Care Overhaul Proposals. The Wall Street
Journal. Retrieved on December 19, 2012 from
http://online.wsj.com/public/resources/documents/st_hea
lthcareproposals_20090912.html

33. Mourning in America – Here's Those Layoffs We Voted
For Last Night. Rusty Weiss. Retrieved on January 19,
2013 from
http://www.freedomworks.org/blog/grusbf5/good-
morning-america-heres-those-layoffs-you-voted

34. Pre-Existing Condition Insurance Plan. The Official U.S. Government Site for PCIP. Retrieved on February 10, 2013 from https://www.pcip.gov/About_PCIP.html

35. Expanding Medicaid to low income adults leads to improved health, fewer deaths. Harvard School of Public Health. Retrieved on February 10, 2013 from http://www.hsph.harvard.edu/news/press-releases/medicaid-expansion-lower-mortality/

36. Affordable Care Act fills in current gaps in coverage for the poorest Americans. Retrieved on December 31, 2012 from http://www.medicaid.gov/AffordableCareAct/Provisions/Eligibility.html

CHAPTER 8 — NATIONAL SECURITY

1. The American Invasion of Iraq: Causes and Consequences. Raymond Hinnebush. Retrieved on February 23, 2013 from http://sam.gov.tr/wp-content/uploads/2012/01/Raymond-Hinnebusch.pdf

2. The public record of violent civilian deaths following the 2003 invasion of Iraq. Retrieved on January 12, 2013 from http://www.iraqbodycount.org/

3. Casualties in Iraq. The human cost of Occupation. Retrieved on December 23, 2012 from http://antiwar.com/casualties/

4. American Military Death since May 1st 2003. Retrieved on December 12, 2012 from http://antiwar.com/casualties/list.php

5. DoD report on U.S. Causality Status. Retrieved on March 1, 2013 from http://www.defense.gov/news/casualty.pdf

6. Cost of war to the United States Since 2001. Retrieved on March 1, 2013 from http://costofwar.com/

7. National Priorities project. Bringing the Federal Budget Home. Retrieved on January 30,2013 from http://nationalpriorities.org/

8. Obama's October 2002 Speech: Against Going to War with Iraq. Retrieved on December 14, 2012 from https://www.commondreams.org/archive/2008/02/28/73 43

9. The Architects of war: where are they now? Faiz Shakir. Retrieved on January 22, 2013 from http://thinkprogress.org/report/the-architects-where-are-they-now/?mobile=nc

10. Project for the New American Century. The power behind the Bush throne. Information Clearing House. Retrieved on December 15,2012 from http://www.informationclearinghouse.info/article6413.htm

11. Neoconservative Think Tank Influence on U.S. Policies. Project for the New American Century (PNAC). January 26, 1998: The Think Tank urges U.S. to Attack Iraq. Retrieved on December 16, 2012 from http://www.historycommons.org/timeline.jsp?neoconinfl uence_neoconservative_think_tanks=neoconinfluence_pn ac&timeline=neoconinfluence

12. Statement of Principles from Project for the New American Century. Retrieved on December 19, 2012 from http://www.newamericancentury.org/statementofprincipl es.htm

13. Henry R. Luce. The American Century first published in 1941. We American are unhappy. We are not happy about America. We are not happy about ourselves in relation to America. We are nervous - or gloomy – or apathetic. Retrieved on December 19, 2012 from http://www.informationclearinghouse.info/article6139.htm

14. Obama Favoring Mid-2010 Pullout in Iraq, Aids Say. New York Times February 24, 2009. Retrieved on March 1, 2013 from http://www.nytimes.com/2009/02/25/washington/25troops.html?_r=1&

15. Report Warned Bush Team about Intelligence Doubts. The New York Times. November 6, 2005. Retrieved on March 1, 2013 from http://www.nytimes.com/2005/11/06/politics/06intel.ready.html?ei=5090&en=a943ec3b39b0a896&ex=1288933200&partner=rssuserland&emc=rss&pagewanted=print

16. Hours after 9/11 attacks, Rumsfeld allegedly said, "My interest is to hit Saddam." Raw Story. Wednesday May, 2007. Retrieved on March 3, 2013 from http://rawstory.com/news/2007/Hours_after_911_attacks_Rumsfeld_allegedly_0502.html

17. A transcript of George Bush's war ultimatum speech from the Cross Hall in the White House. The guardian. Retrieved on March 1, 3013 from http://www.guardian.co.uk/world/2003/mar/18/usa.iraq

18. Threats and Responses: The White House; Bush orders stat of war on Iraq; missiles apparently miss Hussein. Retrieved on March 3, 2013 from http://www.nytimes.com/2003/03/20/world/threats-

responses-white-house-bush-orders-start-war-iraq-missiles-apparently.html?pagewanted=all&src=pm

19. Withdrawal of U.S. Troops from Iraq. The withdrawal of American military forces from Iraq was started in June 2009 and was completed by December 2011, bringing an end to the Iraq War. Retrieved on March 3, 2013 from http://en.wikipedia.org/wiki/Withdrawal_of_U.S._troops_from_Iraq.

20. Obama Announces Complete Withdrawal from Iraq. Antonio Cano, El Pais, Spain. Translated by Jonathan DeYoung. October 21, 2011. Retrieved on March 2, 2013 from http://watchingamerica.com/News/127362/obama-announces-complete-withdrawal-from-iraq/

21. U.S. war in Afghanistan. NBCNews.com. Retrieved on March 4, 2013 from http://www.nbcnews.com/id/33210358/ns/world_news-south_and_central_asia/

22. Council on Foreign Relations. U.S. War in Afghanistan interactive timeline from 1999 to 2012. Retrieved on March 4, 2013 from http://www.cfr.org/afghanistan/us-war-afghanistan/p20018?gclid=CLuWyfel47UCFUZV4AodA24Acg

23. Al-Qaeda and Taliban Sanctions Committee Resolution 1267. Security Council Committee Pursuant to resolutions 1267 (1999) and 1989 (2011) concerning Al-Qaida and associated individuals and entities. United Nations. Retrieved on December 22, 2012 from http://www.un.org/sc/committees/1267/

24. Editor's Notebook: Afghan War Now Country's Longest. ABC News. Retrieved on January 11, 2013 from http://abcnews.go.com/Politics/afghan-war-now-longest-war-us-history/story?id=10849303

25. Joint Resolution to authorize the use of United States Armed Forces against those responsible for the recent attacks launched against the United States. Retrieved on February 12, 2013 from http://www.gpo.gov/fdsys/pkg/PLAW-107publ40/html/PLAW-107publ40.htm

26. Afghanistan: Post-Taliban Governance, Security, and U.S. Policy. Kenneth Katzman, Specialist in Middle Eastern Affairs, February 8, 2013. Congressional Research Services. Retrieved on March 3, 2013 fromhttp://www.fas.org/sgp/crs/row/RL30588.pdf

27. Afghanistan, Iraq: Two Wars Collide. Barton Gellman and Dafna Linzer. Washington Post Staff Writers. Friday October 22, 2004. In the second half of March 2002, as the Bush administration mapped its next steps against al Qaeda, Deputy CIA Director John E. McLaughlin brought an unexpected message to the White House Situation Room. According to two people with firsthand knowledge, he told senior members of the president's national security team that the CIA was scaling back operation in Afghanistan. Retrieved on March 2, 2013 from http://www.washingtonpost.com/wp-dyn/articles/A52673-2004Oct21.html

28. Afghanistan Profile. Landlocked and mountainous, Afghanistan has suffered from such chronic instability and conflict during its modern history that its economy and infrastructure are in ruins, and many of its people are refugees. BBC News. Retrieved on March 5, 2013 from

http://www.bbc.co.uk/news/world-south-asia-
12011352Afghanistan war timeline. Retrieved on January
12, 2013 from http://www.cfr.org/afghanistan/us-war-
afghanistan/p20018?gclid=CLuWyfel47UCFUZV4AodA
24Acg

29. Editor's Notebook: Afghan War Now Country's Longest.
Thomas Nagorski, ABC News Managing Editor,
International. June 7, 2010. Retrieved on January 23,
2013 from http://abcnews.go.com/Politics/afghan-war-
now-longest-war-us-history/story?id=10849303

30. Putting Stamp on Afghan War, Obama Will Send 17,000
Troops. The New York Times. February 17, 2009.
Retrieved on February 22, 2013 from
http://www.nytimes.com/2009/02/18/washington/18web
-troops.html?_r=1&

31. Obama's Wise approach toward Afghanistan. Christopher
A. Preble and Malou Innocent. Cato Institute. Retrieved
on December 28, 2012 from
http://www.cato.org/publications/commentary/obamas-
wise-approach-toward-afghanistan

32. Memorandum to the President. Chaos in Kabul. Vanda
Felbab-Brown. Retrieved on December 10. 2012 from
http://www.brookings.edu/research/papers/2013/01/chao
s-in-kabul?cid=gADs_BBBS_Search-BBBS-BS-
US_Kabul-
Afghanistan_20025885035&gclid=CLCs2ZjM5rUCFYd
lOgodSX8APg

33. Obama Will Speed Pullout from war in Afghanistan. Jun
22, 2011. Retrieved on January 5, 2013 from
http://www.nytimes.com/2011/06/23/world/asia/23prexy
.html?hp=&pagewanted=print

34. The war in Afghanistan: Overview. Retrieved on December 23, 2012 from http://topics.nytimes.com/top/news/international/countri esandterritories/afghanistan/index.html

35. Obama Signs Pact in Kabul, Turning Page in Afghan War. New York Times. May 1, 2012. Retrieved on January 17, 2013 from http://www.nytimes.com/2012/05/02/world/asia/obama-lands-in-kabul-on-unannounced-visit.html?ref=global-home

36. Timeline: The Intelligence hunt leading to Bin Laden. May 6, 2011. Retrieved on January 12, 2013 from http://www.bbc.co.uk/news/world-south-asia-13279283

37. The Hunt. A different sort of search requires a new set of tactics. Peter Finn, Ina Shapira and Marc Fisher, May 6, 2011. The Washington Post. Retrieved on January 10, 2013 from http://www.washingtonpost.com/wp-srv/projects/osama-hunt/

38. Osama Bin Laden Dead: Obama Speech Video and Transcript. http://www.youtube.com/embed/ZNYmK19-d0U Retrieved on March 3, 2013 from http://www.huffingtonpost.com/2011/05/02/osama-bin-laden-dead-obama-speech-video-transcript_n_856122.html

39. Osama bin Laden killed. World Reaction to Osama Bin Laden's Death. May 2, 2011. Retrieved on December 15, 2013 from http://www.npr.org/2011/05/02/135919728/world-reaction-to-osama-bin-ladens-death

40. After Osama bin laden death, Obama visits Ground Zero. Reuters. May 6, 2011. Retrieved on January 12, 2013 from http://in.reuters.com/article/2011/05/05/idINIndia-56806020110505

CHAPTER 9 – THE OBAMA PRESIDENCY AND THE ROBERTS COURT

1. Summary of Citizens United V. Federal Election Commission. Retrieved on December 21, 2012 from http://www.cga.ct.gov/2010/rpt/2010-R-0124.htm

2. Citizens United v. Federal Election Commission. Reversed in part, affirmed in part, and remanded. Supreme Courte of the United States. Retrieved on January 12, 2013 from http://www.law.cornell.edu/supct/html/08-205.ZS.html

3. Scotus for law students: A campaign finance face-off. Retrieved on January 10. 2013 from http://www.scotusblog.com/?p=144987

4. It's Obama vs. the Supreme Court, Round 2, over campaign financing ruling. Washington Post Staff Writer. March 11, 2010. Retrieved on December 22, 2012 from http://www.washingtonpost.com/wp-dyn/content/article/2010/03/09/AR2010030903040.html

5. Alito v. Obama. Reaction split on Obama's remark, Alito's response at State of the Union. Robert Barnes. Washington Post Staff Writer. January 29, 2010. Retrieved on December 9, 2012 from http://www.washingtonpost.com/wp-dyn/content/article/2010/01/28/AR2010012802893.html

6. Super PACs a disaster for democracy. Fred Wertheimer. February 15, 2012. Retrieved on January 12, 2012 from http://www.cnn.com/2012/02/15/opinion/wertheimer-super-pacs

7. America's Headed Back to the Robber-Baron Era. 8 ways that we are recreating the Gilded Age", a period when corporations ruled this nation, buying politicians, using violence against unions and engaging in open corruption. Retrieved on January 20, 2013 from http://jcwinnie.biz/wordpress/?p=10861

8. Mark Twain and Charles Dudley Warner. (1873). The Glided Age: A Tale of Today.

9. The Gilded Age Summary and Analysis. Retrieved on January 4, 2013 from http://www.shmoop.com/gilded-age/summary.html

10. Auctioning Democracy: The Rise of Super PACS and the 2012 Election. Adam Lioz and Blair Bowie. A Joint Project by Demos and USPiRG. Retrieved on January 11, 2013 from http://www.demos.org/publication/auctioning-democracy-rise-super-pacs-and-2012-election

11. Billion – Dollar Democracy: The Unprecedented Role of Money in the 2012 Elections. The first presidential election since Citizens United Lived up to its hype, with unprecedented outside spending from new sources marking headlines. Adam Lioz and Blair Bowie. January 17, 2013. Retrieved on March 7, 2013 from http://www.demos.org/publication/auctioning-democracy-rise-super-pacs-and-2012-election

12. Super PACs. Are a new kind of political action committee and may rise unlimited sums of money from corporations, unions, associations and individuals, then spend unlimited sums to overtly advocate for or against political candidates. The number of Super PACs and their 2012 contribution. Open Secrete. Retrieved on March 8,

2013 from
http://www.opensecrets.org/pacs/superpacs.php

13. First Hispanic Justice Confirmed to U.S. Supreme Court.
Robyn Kurland and Corrine Yu. Retrieved on January 23,
2013 from http://www.civilrights.org/monitor/winter-
2010/first-hispanic-justice-2009.html

14. Civil Rights Monitor. Winter 2010. Retrieved on
December 13, 2012 from
http://www.civilrights.org/monitor/winter-2010/first-
hispanic-justice-2009.html

15. Barack Obama's speech before Planned Parenthood
Action Fund. July 17, 2007. Retrieved on December 24,
2012 from
https://sites.google.com/site/lauraetch/barackobamabefore
plannedparenthoodaction

16. Barack Obama Supreme Court Candidates. Retrieved on
December 17,
2012 from
http://en.wikipedia.org/wiki/Barack_Obama_Supreme_C
ourt_candidates

17. Bush, V. (2012). The oath: The Obama White House
and the Supreme Court. *The Booklist, 109*(2), 7-7.
Retrieved from
http://search.proquest.com/docview/1082427527?accoun
tid=40833

18. David Hackett Souter is a former Associate Justice of the
Supreme Court of the United States. Retrieved on
January 12, 2012 from
http://en.wikipedia.org/wiki/David_Souter

19. Barack Obama Supreme Court Candidates. Retrieved on December 19, 2012 from http://en.wikipedia.org/wiki/Barack_Obama_Supreme_C ourt_candidates

20. Liberty Central. America's Public Square. We listen. We Inspire. We Activate… to secure the blessing of liberty. Retrieved on January 26, 2013 from http://www.libertycentral.org/about/.

21. Scherer, Michael, Backer, Kim, Elliott, Justin (2012). Dark Money. Time, Vol. 1809, Issue 20.

22. Gosnell, H. F. (1936). Factorial Analysis of the Relation of the Press to Voting In Chicago. Journal of Social Psychology, 7(4), 375-385.

23. McChestney, Robert W. (2012). The Assault of the SuperPacs. Nation, 294(6), 11-17.

CHAPTER 10 - SOCIAL, ENERGY, AND ENVIRONMENTAL POLICIES

1. Barack Obama Social Policy. Retrieved on December 15, 2012 from http://en.wikipedia.org/wiki/Barack_Obama_social_policy

2. The Obama Abortion Agenda: Reviewing the last four years. Steven Ertelt. LifeNews.com. Retrieved on January 23, 2013 from http://www.lifenews.com/2012/10/15/the-obama-abortion-agenda-reviewing-the-last-four-years/

3. Obama's position on Social Issues. National Journal Staff. November 7, 2012. Retrieved on January 12, 2013 from http://www.nationaljournal.com/pictures-video/obama-s-positions-on-social-issues-20120713

316 | DEREJE B. TESSEMA

4. Transcript of Obama's commencement address at Norte Dame. May 17, 2009. Retrieved on January 12, 2013 from http://www.nytimes.com/2009/05/17/us/politics/17text-obama.html?pagewanted=all&_r=0

5. United States: HHS/CCIIO Revised Temporary Enforcement Safe Harbor on Contraceptive Coverage Offered by Religiously Affiliated Tax-Exempt Entities. Retrieved on February 12, 2013 from http://www.mondaq.com/unitedstates/x/194084/Healthc are/HHSCCIIO+Revises+Temporary+Enforcement+Safe +Harbor+On+Contraceptive+Coverage+Offered+By+Reli giously+Affiliated+TaxExempt+Entities

6. A statement by U.S. Department of Health and Human Services Secretary Kathleen Sebelius. January 20, 2012. Retrieved on December 23, 2012 from http://www.hhs.gov/news/press/2012pres/01/20120120a. html

7. 2012 Presidential Candidate and issues. Retrieved on January 13, 2012 from http://2012.presidential-candidates.org/Obama/Abortion.php

8. Obama signs DADT repeal before big, emotional crowd. William Branigin, Debbi Wilgoren and Perry Bacon. December 22, 2010. Retrieved on January 18, 2013 from http://www.washingtonpost.com/wp-dyn/content/article/2010/12/22/AR2010122201888.html

9. A history of 'don't ask, don't tell'. After 17 years, the controversial policy has been repealed. Here is how it happened. Washington Post. Retrieved on December from http://www.washingtonpost.com/wp-srv/special/politics/dont-ask-dont-tell-timeline/

10. Remarks by the President and Vice President at Signing of the Don't Ask, Don't Tell Repeal Act of 2010. December 22, 2010, the White House. Retrieved on January 12, 2013 from http://www.whitehouse.gov/the-press-office/2010/12/22/remarks-president-and-vice-president-signing-dont-ask-dont-tell-repeal-a

11. Wendy R. Ginsberg (2011). Federal Employee Benefit and Same-Sex Partnerships: Analyst in Government Organization and Management. Congressional Research Service.

12. The Defense of Marriage Act. Retrieved on January 23, 2013 from http://www.gpo.gov/fdsys/pkg/BILLS-104hr3396enr/pdf/BILLS-104hr3396enr.pdf

13. Remarks by the President at LGBT Pride Month Reception. The White House Office of the Press Secretary. June 29, 2009. Retrieved on March 12, 2013 from http://www.whitehouse.gov/the_press_office/Remarks-by-the-President-at-LGBT-Pride-Month-Reception/

14. Summary of the Lilly Ledbetter Fair Pay Act of 2009. Senator Barbara A. Mikulski, January 8, 2009.

15. Stonewall Riots. Retrieved on December 15, 2012 from http://en.wikipedia.org/wiki/Stonewall_riots#cite_ref-9

16. Summary of the Lilly Ledbetter Fair Pay Act of 2009. State Personnel System, Division of Human Resource Management, State of Florida.

17. Remarks of President Obama on the Lilly Ledbetter Fair Pay Restoration Act bill signing. The White House, Office of the Press Secretary. January 29, 2009. Retrieved

on March 21, 2013 from
http://www.whitehouse.gov/the-press-office/remarks-
president-barack-obama-lilly-ledbetter-fair-pay-
restoration-act-bill-signin

18. How Many Republicans voted for the Lilly Ledbetter Act?
Retrieved on December 13, 2012 from
http://www.motherjones.com/kevin-drum/2012/10/how-
many-republicans-voted-lilly-ledbetter-act

19. Obama Lifts Bush's Strict Limits on Stem Cell Research.
The New York Times. March 9, 2009. Retrieved on
December 22, 2012 from
http://www.nytimes.com/2009/03/10/us/politics/10stem.
html?_r=0

20. The importance of Stem Cell Research. Quality Health's
Medical Advisory Board. Retrieved on March 21, 2013
from http://www.qualityhealth.com/health-lifestyle-
articles/importance-stem-cell-research

21. Obama's Four- Year Energy, Environmental Record Seen
as a Mixed Bag. Michael Lewis. September 26th 2012.
Retrieved on January 19, 2013 from
http://news.thomasnet.com/green_clean/2012/09/26/as-
the-election-nears-a-look-at-president-obamas-
environmental-and-energy-record-and-what-a-second-
term-would-bring/

22. Energy, Climate Change and Our Environment. The
president has taken unprecedented action to build the
foundation for a clean energy economy, tackle the issue of
climate change, and protect our environment. Retrieved
on April 15, 2013 from
http://www.whitehouse.gov/energy.

23. Mark Sherman, Gay Marriage before Supreme Court?
Case Weighed. Retrieved on December 1, 2012 from

http://news.msn.com/politics/gay-marriage-before-supreme-court-cases-weighed

24. Blueprint for a Secure Energy Future. The White House. March 30, 2011. Retrieved on April 12, 2013 from http://www.whitehouse.gov/sites/default/files/blueprint_secure_energy_future.pdf

25. Goodman. Alana (2012). The War Obama Wanted: How Democrats got the better of Republicans on contraception's vs. religions liberty. *Commentary, 133 (5), 31-35.*

CHAPTER 11 - THE MORNING AFTER

1. Republican National Committee to look into what went wrong. Philip Elliott. Retrieved on December 12, 2012 from http://www.huffingtonpost.com/2012/12/10/election-2012-republicans_n_2272865.html

2. Gallup's 2012 election polling debacle: What went wrong? Retrieved on December 23, 2012 from http://www.guardian.co.uk/commentisfree/2012/nov/23/gallup-2012-election-polling-debacle

3. Gallup blew its presidential polls, but why? The polling giant and other experts delve into how to fix a persistent bias toward Romney and the GOP. Retrieved on January 12, 2013 from http://www.nationaljournal.com/politics/gallup-blew-its-presidential-polls-but-why--20121118

4. America Goes to the Poll 2012. A Report on voter turnout in the 2012 election. Nonprofit VOTE.

5. Scott Rasmussen Tries To Explain Why His 2012 Polling Was So Bad. Doug Mataconis. Retrieved on March 23,

2013 from http://www.outsidethebeltway.com/scott-rasmussen-tries-to-explain-why-his-2012-polling-was-so-bad/

6. Fordham Study: Public Policy Polling Deemed Most Accurate National Pollster In 2012. Retrieved on January 12, 2013 from http://livewire.talkingpointsmemo.com/entry/fordham-study-public-policy-polling-deemed-most-accurate

7. Scott Rasmussen Tries To Explain Why His 2012 Polling Was So Bad. Doug Mataconis. Outside the Beltway. Retrieved on February 12, 2013 from http://www.outsidethebeltway.com/scott-rasmussen-tries-to-explain-why-his-2012-polling-was-so-bad/

8. Doug Mataconis (2012). The Romney Campaign Was Full of Poll Denialists. Outside the Beltway. Retrieved on January 2, 2013 from http://www.outsidethebeltway.com/the-romney-campaign-was-full-of-poll-denialists/

9. Jan Crawford (2012). CBS News. Adviser: Romney "shell shocked" by loss. Retrieved on December 12, 2012 from http://www.cbsnews.com/8301-250_162-57547239/adviser-romney-shellshocked-by-loss/?tag=page

10. 25 reasons from 25 people who are voting Obama: Retrieved on January 12, 2013 from http://www.barackobama.com/news?source=primary-nav-see-more

11. Sean Hannity on his syndicated radio on Wednesday afternoon rallied his conservative audience..http://www.mediaite.com/online/sean-hannity-warns-america-you-get-the-government-you-deserve-with-barack-obama-good-luck-with-that/

12. Martin, Elizabeth Traugott, Michael and Kennedy Courtney (2005). A Review of Proposal for a New Measure of Poll Accuracy. Public Opinion Quarterly.

13. Sunshine Hillygus. D. (2011). The Evolution of Election Polling in the United States. Public Opinion Quarterly. 75 (5), 962-981.

14. Panagopolous, Costas (2009). "Polls and Elections: Pre-Election Accuracy in the 2008 General Elections." Presidential Studies Quarterly 39, 896-907.

15. Big GOP donors see small return on investment. CBS News November 8, 2012. Retrieved on April 18, 2013 from http://www.cbsnews.com/8301-250_162-57547103/big-gop-donors-see-small-return-on-investment/

16. Follow the Unlimited Money. Sunlight Foundation Reporting Group. Retrieved on April 18, 2013 from http://reporting.sunlightfoundation.com/outside-spending-2012/super-pacs/

17. The Ecstasy, the Agony: Reactions to Election 2012. Amanda Erickson; November 7, 2013. Retrieved on March 12, 2013 from http://www.theatlanticcities.com/politics/2012/11/ecstasy-agony-reactions-election-2012/3835/

CHAPTER 12 – IS THIS TIME FOR A THIRD PARTY?

1. Gosnell, Harold. F. (1925). The American Party System: Past and Present. Journal of Social Forces, 3 (4), 782-785.
2. Independents voters of America. Retrieved on April 1, 2013 from http://independentvotersofamerica.org/

3. American National Election Studies. Retrieved on April 2, 2013 from http://www.electionstudies.org/

4. Barone, M. (2012). Grand Old Parties. American Spectator, 45(9), 14-18.

5. Kloppenberg, J, T. (2012). Two Cities, Two Americas. Commonwealth, 139(18), 14-19

6. Merrill, Michael (1990). Why there will be a U.S. labor party by the year 200?. Social Policy (2)4.

7. Grunwald, Michael, Alarkon, Walter (2012). The party of NO. Time Inc., Vo. 180, issue 10.

8. Graham, Jesse and Estes, Sarah (2012). *Political Instincts.* New Scientist Archive, 216(2889, 40-43.

9. Post, Charles (2012). Why the Tea Party? New Politics (14)53, 75-82

10. Barrett, P. M. (2012). He's Back, Big Time. Bloomberg BusinessWeek, Issue 4290, 48-53.

11. Rucker, M and Myadze, Theresa (2012). Obama, the Obstructionist 112th U.S. congress and Tea Party Adamantine: A Political Spectacle. International Journal of Business & Social Science, 3(3), 108-115.

12. Obamacare 2013: Obama's Legacy Tide to Health Care Reform That Bears His Name. Jeffrey Young Retrieving on January 20, 2013 from http://www.huffingtonpost.com/2013/01/19/obamacare-

13. HUFFINGTON, A. (1999, Jul 03). The third-wheel parties of a two-party system. *New York Post.* Retrieved from

http://search.proquest.com/docview/333864852?accounti d=35812

14. Sanders Bernard (1989). This country needs a third party. The New York Times.

15. Washington's Farewell address (1766). The Avalon Project; Yale Law School Lillian Goldman Law Library. Retrieved on April 18, 2013 from http://avalon.law.yale.edu/18th_century/washing.asp

16. Divided We Stand. Our polarized Congress is starting to look more and more a parliament at odds with the nation's constitutional system. John Aloysius Farrell. March1, 2012. Retrieved on March 14, 2013 from http://www.nationaljournal.com/magazine/divided-we-stand-20120223

CHAPTER 13 – GOVERNING GRIDLOCK

1. Jody W. Lipford and Jerry Slice (2007). Adam Smith's Roles for Government and Contemporary U.S. Government Roles: Is the Welfare State Crowding Out Government's Basic Functions? The independent Review, v. XI,

2. OpenSecrets.org: 2012 Presidential Race Campaign Contribution summary. Retrieved on November 17, 2012 from http://www.opensecrets.org/pres12/index.php?ql3#out

3. Three branches of government. Retrieved on January 16, 2013 from http://www.factmonster.com/ipka/A0774837.html

4. Dred Scott v. Sandford case. Retrieved on December 23, 2012 from http://en.wikipedia.org/wiki/Dred_Scott_v._Sandford

5. Steven Cohen and Ronald Brand (1993). Total Quality Management in Government. A Practical Guide for the Real World.

6. Caiden, G.E. Ethics in the Public Service. *"Public Personnel Management,"* 1981, 10, 146 - 152

CHAPTER 14 – THE MOSAIC OF AMERICAN PEOPLE AND POLITICAL CHALLENGES

1. Latino Voters in the 2012 Election. Pew Research Center - Pew Hispanic Center. November 7, 2012

2. Infographics: The Growth of the Latino Electorate in Key States. A Center for American Progress and Progress 2050 Graphic. Patrick Oakford and Vanessa Cardenas. February 28, 2013. Retrieved on April 13, 2013 from http://www.americanprogress.org/issues/race/news/2013/02/28/54251/infographic-the-growth-of-the-latino-electorate-in-key-states-2/

3. America's Foreign Born in the Last 50 years. United States Census Bureau. Retrieved on March 12, 2013 from http://www.census.gov/how/infographics/foreign_born.html

4. Toward 2050 in Texas. A Roundtable Report on Houston's Experience as One of the Most Diverse Metros in the Nation. Julie Ajinkya. March 2013. Retrieved on April 13, 2013 fromhttp://www.americanprogress.org/issues/race/report/2013/03/13/56087/toward-2050-in-texas/

5. US Demographic Outlook 2005-2050. Infrastructure Implications of a Larger, More Concentrated, More Diverse Population. Master Project Team Meeting, June 29, 2009. Georgia Tech. Retrieved on January 12, 2013

from http://rftgf.org/PP/pdf-
thipp/THI_US_Demographic_Outlook.pdf

6. U.S Census Bureau Projections Show a Slower Growing,
   Older, More Diverse Nation a Half Century from Now.
   Retrieved on March 16, 2013 from
   http://www.census.gov/newsroom/releases/archives/popul
   ation/cb12-243.html

7. Republican Party begins election review to find out what
   went wrong. Washington Post, November 8, 2012.
   Retrieved on March 18, 2013 from
   http://articles.washingtonpost.com/2012-11-
   08/politics/35503128_1_illegal-immigrants-republican-
   party-election-results

8. Republicans face murky political future in increasingly
   diverse U.S. Retrieved on March 23, 2013 from
   http://www.washingtonpost.com/politics/decision2012/re
   publicans-face-murky-political-future-in-increasingly-
   diverse-us/2012/11/07/3b71e4f2-28e7-11e2-96b6-
   8e6a7524553f_story.html

9. Conservative Reaction to Election '12, Part II: More, Not
   Less, Ideology, Please. Ed Kilgore. Washington Monthly.
   November 8, 2012. Retrieved on April 20, 2013 from
   http://www.washingtonmonthly.com/political-animal-
   a/2012_11/conservative_reaction_to_elect_1041059.php

10. Weigel, D. (2012, The tea party: Picking the candidates
    and writing the agenda. *The Washington Monthly, 44*, 12-
    14. Retrieved from
    http://search.proquest.com/docview/917532262?accounti
    d=40833

11. David Frum. White person's party. Old person's party.
    Whatever happened to the Grand Ol' Party? How the

Republicans got stuck in the past. Newsweek, November 19, 2012.

12. Niall Ferguson (2012). The losing Habit: How long will the GOP stay in denial? Newsweek. November 19, 2012

13. How Republicans can win future elections. Bobby Jindal. November 15, 2012. Retrieved on March 19, 2013 from http://www.cnn.com/2012/11/15/opinion/jindal-gop-election